$6.00

THE TEACH YOURSELF BOOKS

MALAY

Uniform with this volume and in the same series

TEACH YOURSELF
MALAY

M. B. LEWIS

THE ENGLISH UNIVERSITIES PRESS LTD
ST. PAUL'S HOUSE WARWICK LANE
LONDON EC4

First printed   . . . 1947
Second edition   . . . 1968

Second Edition
Copyright © 1968
The English Universities Press Ltd

SBN 340 05804 8

*Printed in Great Britain for the English Universities Press Limited
by C. Tinling & Co. Ltd., Liverpool, London and Prescot.*

TABLE OF CONTENTS

PART II

PART III

APPENDIX

PREFACE

I have many debts to acknowledge :

To Sir Richard Winstedt, K.B.E., C.M.G., D.Litt. (Oxon.), F.B.A., formerly Reader in Malay, University of London, whose *Malay Grammar* is the ground work of the practical course offered to the student in this book. I have to thank Sir Richard, too, for helpful criticism of subject matter.

To my former colleague Mr. J. E. Kempe, B.A. (Oxon.) and to the late Mr. A. J. Sturrock, M.A. (Edin.) for contributions to the versions given in the Key to Part II. I have to thank Mr. Kempe also for much-appreciated encouragement during the writing of the book.

To the following for contributions to the conversations and to the versions given in the Keys :—

> Che'Abdullah bin Mohamed, M.A., LL.B. (Cantab.), Barrister-at-Law.
> Che'Ismail bin Mohamed Ali, M.A. LL.B. (Cantab.), Barrister-at-Law.
> Che' Tom binti Dato' Sětia Abdul Razak.
> Che' Salma binti Ismail.

Lastly, to a succession of Students who have helped to hammer the book into shape while it has been on the anvil.

Mr. C. C. Brown, Lecturer in Malay, School of Oriental and African Studies, University of London, has kindly read the proofs. I am grateful to Mr. Brown, also, for many helpful discussions on debatable points.

London 1946   M. B. L.

BOOKS RECOMMENDED FOR STUDY

Culture and History

A History of Malaya, F. J. Moorhead. 2 vols. 1957/1963. Longmans.

A History of Malaya by J. Kennedy. Macmillan.

The Malays: A Cultural History, Sir Richard Winstedt. Routledge and Kegan Paul, London 1961 (revised edition)

Malaya, J. M. Gullick. Ernest Benn, London 1963.

Malaysia edited by Wang Gangwu. Pall Mall Press, London 1964.

Papers on Malay Subjects edited by R. J. Wilkinson. Some republished by Malayan Branch, Royal Asiatic Society.

Land, People and Economy of Malaya by Oi Jin-Bee.

Grammar

Malay Grammar, Sir Richard Winstedt. Clarendon Press, Oxford 1927 (2nd edition).

Sentence Analysis in Modern Malay. M. Blanche Lewis. Cambridge University Press 1968.

Dictionaries

A Malay-English Dictionary, R. J. Wilkinson. Mitylene 1932. Reprinted London 1959.

An Unabridged Malay-English Dictionary, Sir Richard Winstedt. Kelly and Walsh, Singapore 1954.

An Unabridged English-Malay Dictionary, Sir Richard Winstedt. Marican and Sons, Singapore 1958.

Kamus Indonésia-Inggeris (Indonesian-English Dictionary) S. Wojowasito, W. J. S. Poerwadarminta and S. A. M. Gaastra, 3rd edition. Versluys, Djakarta 1959

Texts

Prosa Melayu Baharu (An Anthology of Modern Malay and Indonesian Prose), C. Skinner. Longmans, Green & Co. Ltd., 1959.

Hikayat Abdullah edited by A. H. Hill. Malaya Publishing House, Singapore 1955.

Pelayaran Abdullah edited by Kassim Ahmad. Oxford University Press, Kuala Lumpur 1960.

Pantun Melayu, Malay Literature Series, Malaya Publishing House 1955.

INTRODUCTION

Malay is an easy language. Bafflingly easy. At the end of ten weeks you feel that you know all that there is to be known. At the end of ten years, you know that you never will.

There are no declensions, no conjugations, almost no fixed grammatical rules, to be learned by heart at the outset. People will tell you that it is possible to 'pick up' Malay in a couple of months. So it is, if you are going to be content with the 'bazaar' Malay of the sea-ports. But if you are interested in language and wish really to know and understand the Malays, you will find that the initial confidence which such a method gives will prove illusory and will be succeeded by a feeling of frustration.

The ideal method of learning Malay—or any other living language—is to combine book work with practical work. You will understand much more of what you hear around you if you know, from book-work, what to listen for; and your book-work will mean more to you when you are able to check your theoretical knowledge by listening to the spoken word. But many students begin their study of Malay before they reach Malaya. It is for such students that this book has been written. It offers them practice in the application of the theory of the language set forth in Winstedt's *Malay Grammar* (Oxford University Press).

HOW TO USE THE BOOK.

This is a " self-service " book. Take from it what you want. Skip what you find too difficult. You will probably come back to it later.

Grammatical terms.

Malay is a flexible language. It cannot be brought into alignment with English or other European languages because its idiom is different. But it is not possible to discuss the structure of a language without using familiar grammatical terms even though it has to be made clear, from time to time, that those terms are being used with a slightly changed meaning.

A glossary of the grammatical terms used in the book has been included at the suggestion of a number of students. You will find it an easily accessible form of revision if you have not recently had occasion to use these terms.

Vocabularies.

Up to Chapter XI a vocabulary of the new words used has been placed at the beginning of each chapter. Read it through once or twice, partly as a pronunciation exercise, and partly so that when you come to the examples, your attention may be given to the idiom which they illustrate rather than to the new words they contain. But do not blunt your interest by attempting to learn each vocabulary by heart as you come to it. The words will constantly recur in sentences, and they are all included in the alphabetical vocabulary at the end.

Footnotes.

The footnotes have been used mainly to clarify finer points of language which interest some students but are not essential to the main exposition. Ignore those footnotes which shed no light for you.

Conversations and Proverbs.

The conversations have not been kept within the bounds of the chapter vocabularies. New words found in them should be looked up in the alphabetical vocabulary at the end of the book.

Nor has any attempt been made to restrict the idiom to that which has already been dealt with in the chapters. The translations are free; do not try to fit them to the Malay sentences, word for word. Take them on trust for the time being. Difficult points are dealt with in the Notes, and as you go further in the book you will find most of the idioms explained.

MALAY IDIOM.

It is from the conversations that you will learn Malay Idiom. After you have worked through the chapters on prefixes and suffixes (Chapters XII-XIV) you will find abundant additional material in the plays (Texts A and B) in *Sentence Analysis in Modern Malay*; see book-list p. x.

The following are the chief points to be noticed:

1. Economy of words.

The Malays have a proverb: " Pole downstream and the crocodiles will laugh at you." They never waste effort, or words. Here is the proverb in Malay:

Bĕrgalah hilir, tĕrtawa buaya.

Literally: Pole downstream, laugh crocodiles.

That is the way they talk. Subordinate clauses are seldom used in conversation.

Here are two examples of the short balanced statements which replace the English complex sentence:

If you can't find it, bring another one.
Ta' jumpa, bawa lain.
Literally : Not find, bring another.

When you have finished your work, you can go.
Habis kĕrja, balek-lah.
Literally : Work completed, return.

2. Balance.

The examples given above have illustrated this principle. Be on the look-out for comment upon it in the notes.

In the proverbs and the conversations you will find words (*pun, pula, juga, -lah*) which are frequently not rendered in the translation. Sometimes they cannot be translated. These, for want of a better term, are known as ' balance words.' They are dealt with in Chapter XVI, but you will have begun to feel their significance long before you reach that point.

3. Vocabulary.

(a) Precision.

Malays are seldom slip-shod in their use of words. Within its limitations Malay has a rich and sensitive vocabulary. When you come across groups of words which are apparently synonyms, learn the difference between them and use them discriminatingly. Here is one example :

pĕchah	.	.	. broken, shattered (e.g. of a cup)
patah	.	.	. broken, snapped off (e.g. of a pole)
putus	.	.	. broken, severed (e.g. of a rope)
rosak	.	.	. broken, spoilt, out of order, (e.g. of a watch'

(b) Sound Imitation (onomatopoeia).

In English we are used to such obvious sound imitations as " bang," " hiss," " rap." Malay is rich in words of this sort (e.g. *kĕtok* – to rap, knock ; *sĕpui-sĕpui* – blowing softly, of a breeze), but it has in addition many words which show a more subtle use of the device.

This is a point which you cannot properly appreciate until you have studied the rules of pronunciation, but the following example will give you an idea of the possibilities. (The " ĕ " is pronounced like the " a " in " above.")

dĕrek	used of, e.g., the snapping of dry twigs
dĕring	,,	,,	,,	jingling of a sword
dĕram	,,	,,	,,	roll of drums
dĕrap	,,	,,	,,	rain on a roof
dĕrang	,,	,,	,,	clanging of a gong
dĕrau	,,	,,	,,	rushing water
dĕrun	,,	,,	,,	falling water
kĕrosek	,,	,,	,,	scraping fish scales
kĕrosok	,,	,,	,,	treading on dry leaves
mĕnggĕ'ĕpek	,,	,,	,,	light flapping of a flag
mĕnggĕlĕpak	,,	,,	,,	heavier flapping of a sail

4. Fluidity of Syntax.

Malay words change their function according to context. Be prepared for this, and do not attempt to force the language into a set mould. It will escape.

PART I

PRONUNCIATION, GRAMMAR
AND EXERCISES

CHAPTER I

I. Scripts

II. Pronunciation

SCRIPTS

Par. 1.

Malay may be written in two ways

(a) In the Malay Script (sometimes called *Jawi*).

This script is an adaptation of the Arabic alphabet. The method of writing and spelling in this script is set forth in *A Handbook of Malay Script*, M. B. Lewis, Macmillan 1954.

(b) In the Romanised Script.

With the exception of a small number of Arabic sounds, which the Malays themselves commonly simplify (see paragraph 19), the Roman alphabet renders adequatley the sounds of the Malay language.

The system of spelling used in this book is that authorized for Government publications in the Malay Peninsula, with the exception that excerpts from books are given in the spelling of the editions from which they are taken. The Indonesian system of romanisation differs from the English system in the representation of a small number of sounds. A sample of Indonesian romanisation is given in paragraph 203.

II. PRONUNCIATION

Par. 2.

Malay   is   a   softly   spoken   language.   In   rapid

conversation the frequent elisions and the rhythmic modulations give it a blurred, indistinct effect. Make an effort, therefore, from the beginning, to avoid a clear-cut staccato pronunciation which is foreign to the language. Try to speak it gently and rhythmically. There is no strongly marked stress.

If you are among Malays, listen and imitate. If you are not, the following paragraphs will give you some guidance.

Pronunciation varies greatly according to locality, and the suggestions given below deal only with broad differences between Malay and English sounds.

It will pay you to spend a little time in the study of pronunciation before you begin your study of the language. The better your accent, the more easy will you find it to understand what Malays say to you.

MALAY VOWELS.

Note.—An open syllable is one which ends in a vowel, e.g., *buka* has two open syllables, *bu + ka*.
A closed syllable is one which ends in a consonant, e.g., *bimbit* has two closed syllables, *bim + bit*.

Par. 3.

The vowels " a ", " e " and " i " in Malay have their French or Italian sounds, not their English sounds, i.e., *roughly*, " a " and " e " as in " café ", and " i " as in " machine ".

Par. 4. The Malay vowel " A ".

This sound is not the " a " of " cat ", nor is it the " a " of " cart."

In an open syllable, which is not final, it comes somewhere between these two sounds, but never reaches either extreme.

Final " a," in the north of the Malay Peninsula, is shorter than the stressed open " a." It is pronounced like the last syllable of " Eva " or of " beaver," e.g.

> **kita** (*we*) rhymes with " Rita ".

In the south it is a sound made with more rounded lips, coming somewhere between the " ur " of English " curve," and the " eu " of French " feu."

In a closed syllable " a " is shortened. (But see par. 16c). Before a final " ng ", it is almost like the " u " in English " cut," e.g.

> **lang** (*eagle*) is nearer to English " lung " than to " lang ".

Before any consonant which closes a stressed final syllable, the " a " tends towards this short " u " sound, e.g.

> the second syllable of **pahám** (*understand*) is nearer to " hum " than to " ham " (see par. 15b for stress), the second syllable of **tahán** (*restrain*) is nearer to " hun " than to " han ", the second syllable of **tĕbál** (*thick*) rhymes with " lull " rather than with " pal ", and the second syllable of **sĕkám** (*rice-chaff*) rhymes with " rum ", rather than with " ram ".

When the closed syllable is not stressed the " a " has not this short " u " sound, e.g.

> in **lalat** (*a fly*) the two vowels are almost the same and the stress is usually even.

WARNING: The " a " of a final closed syllable *never* becomes the indeterminate sound that is heard in the unaccented last syllable of the English words " capstan " and " floral ".

Par. 5. The Malay vowel " e ".

(a) The Indeterminate " ě ".

The symbol ě represents the indeterminate sound which fills a very slight pause between two consonants. It is like the " e " in " broken " or the " a " in " around ", e.g.

    bětúl (*correct*) **těbál** (*thick*).

A note on Stress.

Most Malay words are two-syllabled words, and if there is any stress at all it falls on the first of the two syllables, if that syllable ends in a vowel other than " ě ", e.g.

    pátah (*snapped*) : **lálat** (*a fly*).

In disyllables such as **bětúl** and **těbál**, where the first syllable ends in " ě ", the stress, if there is any, falls on the second syllable.

When the first syllable is closed the stress is always even, e.g.

    bimbang (*anxious*) ; **rantai** (*chain*).

In a word of more than two syllables, if the penultimate (i.e. last but one) syllable ends in " ě " the stress goes back to the antepenultimate (i.e. last but two), e.g.

    jěntěra (*wheel—of a machine*).

Otherwise, the stress on a three-syllabled word is on the penultimate, e.g.

    binátang (*animal*); **jěndéla** (*window*); **mahkámah** (*court of justice*).

Stress marks are inserted in this chapter only. Remember that the stress is very light. It is never wrong to pronounce a two-syllabled word with evenly balanced syllables, but it *is* wrong to stress the second syllable, when the first syllable is an open syllable containing any other vowel than " ĕ." e.g. if **bárat** (*west*) is pronounced with the stress on the second syllable it becomes **bĕrát** (*heavy*). Unmarked words are to be pronounced with even stress.

(b) The full " e," or the continental " e ".

In paragraph 3 it was stated that the Malay " e " corresponds roughly to the " é " in " café ". That is to say, it is *not* the same sound as the English " a " in " cake ".

The English vowel is a diphthong, a *double* sound. The Malay vowel is a pure vowel, a *single* sound.

When you say the English word " cake " you make two vowel sounds between the two consonants : " ké + eek ". In Malay there is no second vowel sound.

> **beta** (*I*) does *not* rhyme with " gaiter ".

In an open accented syllable the Malay " e " may be anything from French " é " to French " è " (as in French " élève ") e.g.

> **pélat** (*provincial accent*) **pérak** (*silver*).

At its shortest, it approximates to the English vowel in " red."
The " full e " is of much less common occurrence than the " indeterminate ĕ."

Par. 6. The Malay vowel " i ".

In a stressed open syllable, it is pronounced like the " ee " in " seek," e.g.

> **bílek** (*room*) **tídor** (*sleep*).

In a closed syllable unstressed, it may be almost, but never quite, as short as the " i " of " bit ", e.g.

kúlit (*skin*).

In a closed syllable which is stressed it is longer, e.g.

bĕlít (*coil round*).

Par. 7. The Malay vowel " o ".

English " o " is a double sound, Malay " o " is a single sound.

In the southern English pronunciation of the word " coke " there are two vowel sounds between the two consonants : " ko + ook ".

In Malay there is no second vowel sound, e.g.

rokok (*cigarette*) does *not* rhyme with " cocoa,"

In an open accented syllable the Malay " o " is like the French " eau," e.g.

kólam (*pond*) **tólak** (*push away*).

Even in a closed syllable, e.g. the second syllable of **pohon** (*tree*), it is not as short as in the English word " hot." The lips are more rounded for the Malay sound, and pushed well forward.

Before " ng " the Malay " o " is almost like a French nasalized " o." The Malay name **'Long** (*short for* **Súlong**—*eldest*) is nearer to the first syllable of French " longtemps " than it is to the English word " long."

Par. 8. The Malay vowel " u ".

In an open stressed syllable, it is pronounced like the " oo " in " loot," e.g.

kúda (*horse*) **túlang** (*bone*).

In a closed syllable it may be anything from the " oo "
of " boot " to the " oo " of " foot," e.g.

pátut (*seemly*) **bágus** (*fine*).

It is never like the " u " in " cut." That sound is
represented by " a "   (See par. 4.).
It is never like the " u " in " mute". That sound is
represented by " iu " or " yu," e.g.

siul (*whistle*) **ayun** (*rocking*).

Note : The vowels " o " and " e " are sometimes interchangeable with the vowels " u " and " i."
The   change   represents   a   local   variation   of
pronunciation, e.g.

Southern pronunciation : **bogel** (*stripped*—e.g. of
a bare tree, or a fowl without feathers).
Northern pronunciation : **bugil**.

Par. 9.   The diphthong " ai ".

As a final open syllable the Malay diphthong is sounded
like the English diphthong in " fine ".

pantai (*shore*) **balai** (*an open hall*).

But when the letters " ai " are in a closed syllable they
are pronounced with a slight hiatus between them e.g.

lain (*other*) **kait** (*a barb*).

" ay " = ai (as in " fine ") + consonantal i, e.g.
bayan (*parrot*) **kayu** (*wood*).

Par. 10.   The Diphthong " au ".

As a final open syllable the Malay diphthong is
sounded like the English diphthong in " town ".

pulau (*island*) **bangau** (*stork*).

But when the letters " au " occur in the middle of a word they are pronounced with a slight hiatus between them, e.g.

> **laut** (*sea*) **laung** (*call out loudly*)—both disyllables.

Note : This hiatus occurs also between " a " and " e ", e.g.

daérah (*district*)—a trisyllable.

MALAY CONSONANTS.

Par. 11.

Most of the Malay consonants have roughly the same values as the corresponding English consonants. It is only points of marked difference that are noted below.

The letters c (except in " ch "), q, v and x are not used.

Par. 12.   " b ", " p ", " t ", " d ".

When these letters are final letters they are not "exploded," as they are in English.

The Malay word **sĕbab** (*because*) leaves the speaker with closed lips.

The English word " slab " leaves the speaker with lips which have opened with a slight explosion of sound.

The Malay word **Mat** leaves the speaker with closed teeth ; for the English word " cut " the teeth are opened with a slight explosion of sound.

There is no liaison between such a final consonant and a following vowel. In English, the " t " in such a phrase as " at all " tends to be carried on to the second word. In Malay the **t** in the phrase **kulit ubi** (*potato skins*) is scarcely heard at all, but it cuts off the preceding vowel with a jerk. (See par. 13 and contrast par. 15d.)

Par. 13.   " k ".

As a final letter, " k " is checked in the same way as the four consonants given above. The check takes place not at the front of the mouth but in the throat, by a catching of the breath, called a glottal check. This has the effect of abruptly closing the preceding vowel. It is not the quality of the vowel that it changes, but its duration in time.

In the word **rókok** (*cigarette*) the two vowels are almost the same in quality, but the second one is cut off short, with a jerk, in the same way as the vowel of " get " is jerked back when " get it " is pronounced, in illiterate fashion, " ge' it." It is short in time, not " short " in quality as is the " o " in English " hot ". In Peninsular Malay this glottal check for a final " k " is universal. Make an effort to conquer it ; it is not merely a silent k. It is better to pronounce it, as a " k," than to ignore it.

The glottal check is sometimes indicated by an apostrophe, e.g.

> **pókok** (*tree*) or **póko'**
> **dátok** (*chieftain*) or **dáto'**

Par. 14. " ch " and " j ".

" Ch " is pronounced almost like the " ch " in " chess " but with the tip of the tongue further forward, just above the teeth, almost as if it were pronounced " t+yes," i.e. without pushing the lips forward. Never as in " chute," or as in " chasm," e.g.

> **chinchin** (*a finger-ring*).
> **chári** (*seek*)

" J " is pronounced almost like the " j " in " jam," but with unrounded lips and the tip of the tongue forward, almost as if it were pronounced " d+yam." Never as in French " je," e.g.

> **jam** (*hour, watch*).
> **jári** (*finger*).

Par. 15. " h ".

(a) At the beginning of a word " h " is usually

pronounced lightly, and frequently omitted, e.g.

> **hĕrti** or **ĕrti** (*understand*)
> **híjau** or **íjau** (*green*)
> **hútan** or **útan** (*jungle*).

In some words, however, it represents an Arabic " h " and in such words it is never omitted, e.g.

> **hákim** (*judge*)
> **húkum** (*decree*)

(b) Between two like vowels " h " is clearly sounded, e.g.

> **dahán** (*bough*)
> **tahán** (*restrain*)
> **Paháng** (*name of a State*)
> **Johór**   ,,   ,,   ,,
> **bohóng** (*untruth*)
> **leher** (*neck*)

In such words the stress often falls on the second syllable, and the vowel of the first syllable then loses its distinct quality.

(c) Between two unlike vowels " h " is lightly sounded e.g.

> **lihat** (*see*).

or not sounded at all, e.g.

> **jahit** (*sew*)
> **sahut** (*answer*)

(d) At the end of a word " h " is *sounded* as a light breathing, e.g.

> **bĕláh** (*split*)
> **dárah** (*blood*)

The " h " closes the syllable, and consequently preserves the vowel-sound (see WARNING, par. 4) just as effectively as any other consonant.

When the following word begins with a vowel the " h " often sounds as if it were the initial consonant of the next word, e.g.

> **Sudah itu** (*After that*).

Par. 16. " g ", " ng " and " ngg ".

(a) The Malay " g " is always hard, as in " gate."
It never has the " j " sound as in " gem," e.g.

> **gágak** (*a crow*)
> **gíla** (*mad*)

(b) The combination " ng " represents a single sound, the sound of " ng " in English " singer," (NOT hard, as in " finger ") e.g.

> **singa** (*lion*)
> **léngah** (*loiter*)
> **tángan** (*hand*)
> **ngánga** (*yawn*)
> 'Ngah (abbreviation of **těngah** (*half*) ; a pet name given to the second or third child in a family).

(c) The combination " ngg " represents the sound of " ng " in English " finger," e.g.

> **singgah** (*breaking a journey*)
> **pinggan** (*plate*)
> **langgar** (*knocking against*).

Note that the " ng " and " ngg," being single sounds, belong to the syllable which follows, not to the syllable which precedes. Consequently the preceding syllable may be regarded as an open syllable, e.g.

> **tangan** should be divided thus : **ta + ngan.**

This may be noticed with other medial combinations of consonants, e.g.

minta (*ask*) is not **min** + **ta** but **mi** + **nta**
simpan (*keep*) is **si** + **mpan**
tumpah (*spill*) is **tu** + **mpah**
bungkus (*wrap up*) is **bu** + **ngkus**.

That is why the vowels of the first syllables have their full value.

Remember this point in talking. The vowels of such syllables make an appreciable contribution to the melodious softness of Malay speech.

Par. 17. " ny ".

The combination " ny " represents a single sound, the " gn " of French " signer ", e.g.

> **nyamok** (*mosquito*) [two syllables only]
> **nyanyi** (*sing*)   [two syllables only]
> **–nya** (*of him*)   [one syllable only]

Par. 18. " r ".

The pronunciation of " r " varies from a guttural " r " to a trilled " r." Except in dialect pronunciation, it is always sounded in all positions.

In English a final " r " is not sounded, but it usually changes the quality of the vowel which it follows, e.g. the " a " in " car " is longer than the " a " in " cat ", because of the " r " which follows it. This does not happen in Malay.

> In **bĕsár** (*large*), the " a " is not lengthened, and the " r " is sounded.

N.B. " ĕr " is frequently reversed in pronunciation, e.g.

> **kĕrbau** (*buffalo*) is usually pronounced **krĕbau**
> **kĕrtas** (*paper*) is usually pronounced **krĕtas**

(The most accurate transliteration would be **kĕrĕbau, kĕrĕtas.**)

Such syllables are *never* pronounced like the English syllables, " cur ", " burr ", " sir ".

Par. 19.   Arabic sounds.

It is not necessary for the beginner to learn the pronunciation of these, since (except in religious contexts) Malays usually assimilate them to Malay sounds, but the following notes will explain variations of spelling which might otherwise be found confusing.

" Kh " is like the " ch " in " loch," but it is frequently pronounced as " k ", or as " h ", e.g.

> **Ápa khábar ?**—*What (is) the news?*   (the usual greeting).

" Dl," " th," " l " and " dz " are all used as transliterations of the same Arabic letter " dlad ", e.g.

> **redla, retha** or **rela** (*wish*)
> **hathir, hadzir** or **hadlir** (*present, at hand*).

Educated Malays pronounce it like the " th " of " this," pronounced with the tip of the tongue behind the teeth instead of between the teeth.

" L " and " tl " are used as transliterations of the Arabic letter " tla," e.g.

> **tlohor** or **lohor** (*noon*)

Educated Malays pronounce it as " z " or " thz."

" Aa " and " 'a " are used to transliterate the Arabic vowel " 'ain," which is pronounced with a tightened throat, resulting in a strangled sort of sound, e.g.

> **saat** (*moment*)
> **'alam** (*universe*).

It is often pronounced as an ordinary " a."

" Gh " is used to transliterate the Arabic letter " ghain."
It is a partner to the sound " kh," in the same way that
" d " is a partner to " t."

Turn " lock " into " loch " to get the " kh " sound. Do
the same thing to " log " to get the " gh " sound, e.g.

> **mashghul** (*sorrowful*)
> **ghaib** (*vanish*)

In colloquial Malay, however, the sound is usually written
and pronounced as a throat " r ", e.g.

> **raib** (*vanish*)

Par. 20. A few reminders.

1. Avoid the vowel sounds of these English words :
   cat, cart, cake, cocoa.

2. Remember the glottal check for final " k."

3. Pronounce a final " h ".

4. Remember that there is no strong stress in Malay.
   Do not stress the second syllable of a disyllabic word
   if the first syllable is an open syllable, with any vowel
   other than " ĕ," If there is any stress, it falls on the
   first syllable, e.g.

> **túlang** (*bone*)
> **kósong** (*empty*)
> **pátut** (*seemly*)
> **sárong** (*a sheath*)

5. Remember that the vowel of a closed final syllable (particularly the vowel " a ") is clearly heard, e.g.

> **makan** (*eat*) : the second syllable is *not* telescoped, as is the second syllable of " Duncan."
>
> **tinggal** (*be left, remain*) is *not* pronounced like the English word " tingle."
>
> **karat** (*rust*) is *not* pronounced like the English word " carat."

6. Speak smoothly, and without undue emphasis. Emphasis is marked by word-order and intonation, rather than by urgency of tone.

CHAPTER II

PRONUNCIATION PRACTICE

Par. 21.

This chapter is intended to give you abundant practice in pronunciation before you begin considering the structure of the language. The words given in Exercises 1 and 2 supply the vocabulary for the first half dozen written exercises, where they are used in phrases and sentences. Their meanings therefore will become familiar to you through repetition, and you will be wise to concentrate, for the present, on pronunciation rather than meaning.

In Exercise 1 the pronunciation of every word is analysed. If you go through each one with care you will find that you have a model for nearly every combination of sounds that you are likely to meet. The only exception are the words containing Arabic sounds, (see par. 19)

Remember **that** pronunciation varies considerably according to locality. The suggestions here given are intended merely as a help to students who have not yet the opportunity of listening to the living tongue spoken by Malays. If you chance to be using this book in Malaya you can ignore the right hand column. Ask an educated Malay to read over the list of words to you two or three times. Then, if you like, read through the right hand column and see if you agree with it. It is unlikely that you will do so on every point.

In Exercise 2 less help is given, because most of the sounds have already been dealt with in Exercise 1.

Exercise 1

Read through the following words, pronouncing them with great care.

Kĕpála – *head*

The stress is on the middle syllable. The Malay " l " is never quite as hard as in " tall " ; the tip of the tongue is further forward. The final " a " may be like the " a " in " above " or may approximate to the vowel sound in " curve," or in French " feu ".

mata – *eye(s)*

Stress, if any, on the first " a ". Do not pronounce it as in the English word " matter " (i.e. the " a " of " cat ") nor yet as in "martyr" (i.e. the " a " of " cart "). In the first word the lips are too stretched, in the second they are not stretched enough. It is near the dialect " a " of Lancashire.

hidong – *nose*

Remember to round the lips for the second syllable. More like the first syllable of French " longtemps " than like the English " long ".

mulut – *mouth*

Remember to push the lips well out, further forward than for English " boot '. The second " u " a little shorter, but still with well-rounded lips. Final " t " very light, with the tip of the tongue behind the teeth.

bibir – *lip(s)*

The first " i " like the " ee " in English " seen ". The second " i " a little shorter.

muka – *face*
Well-rounded " oo ". Final " a " as for **kĕpala.**

pipi – *cheek(s)*
Even stress.

gigi – *tooth, teeth*
Both " g's " hard.

gusi – *gum(s)*
Sharp " s ", hard " g ", rounded lips for the " oo ".

lidah – *tongue*
Sound the final " h " ; shorten the " a " in front of it, but do not destroy its sound.

kĕrongkong – *throat*
Stress on the first " o ". Lips more rounded than for English " long ".

dahi – *forehead*
Sound the " h " very lightly.

kĕning – *eyebrow(s)*
Stress, if any, on second syllable. The first syllable is definitely heard, but with a completely characterless vowel, almost like the first syllable of English " connive ".

tĕlinga – *ear(s)*
Stress on the middle syllable. The " i " is fairly long since it is an open syllable. The " ng " is a single sound (like " singer," *not* like " finger ") and belongs to the third syllable. The indeterminate vowel of the first syllable is less clearly heard than in **kĕning** because the second consonant is an " l ". (Before " l " and " r ", " small e " is at its " smallest ".)

leher – *neck*
The medial " h " is clearly sounded, since it comes between identical vowels.

bahu – *shoulders*
Stress, if any, on the first syllable. The " h " is sounded very lightly if

at all, but it must always be sounded when the context requires it in order to avoid confusion with **bau** (*odour*).

bĕlakang – *back*   Stress on the middle syllable. Try to get the " a " of it right—not " cat " nor " cart ". The " -ang " almost like English " -ung ".

tuboh – *body frame*   Rounded lips for the " oo ". Sound the final " h ". Be sure to make the " o " a single sound, not the double sound of English " go " (go + oo).

pĕrut – *stomach*   First syllable usually very short because the second consonant is an " r " (see **tĕlinga**). Light " t ".

badan – *body*   Stress, if any, on the first syllable. *Do not* stress the second syllable. If you do, you turn the first " a " into " ĕ ".

nyawa – *life, spirit*   Only two syllables. The " ny " is one sound, like French " gn ".

hati – *heart, liver*   Tongue behind the teeth for the " t ". The final " i " is more tense than the " y " of " party ".

pinggang – *waist*   Even stress. The " ang " almost like English " ung ". The " ngg " hard like the " ng " in English " finger ". Since it is really one sound (par. 16c), the first syllable is an open syllable and the " i " is nearer to the " ee " of " seen " than to the " i " of " sin ".

tangan – *hand(s)* — Remember that the " ng " is like English " singer " (*not* like " finger "). Do not telescope the final closed syllable.

kaki – *foot, feet* — Be careful with the " a " – not " cat " and not " cart ". Make the " i " more tense than an English final " y ".

jari – *finger, toe* — Stress if any on the first syllable. For the " j " see par. 14. Be careful with the " a " – not " cat " and not " cart ".

lĕngan – *arm* — The stress is even between the two syllables " lĕ + ngan ". Remember, again, " singer " not " finger ", because there is no second " g ". Do not telescope the final syllable.

kuku – *nail(s), claw(s)* — Even stress ; well-rounded " oo's ".

lutut – *knee(s)* — Second " u " slightly shorter than the first. Final " t'" very light, with tongue behind the teeth.

rambut – *hair* — The " a " has not the tinge of short " u " which it would have in a final " -am ". The " mb " is felt as one sound, so that the syllable in front of it may be counted an open syllable. A Malay usually pronounces " ĕmbun " (*dew*) as though it were spelt **mbun**. The same happens with the combination " mp " ; the first syllable of **simpan** (*to keep*) is " see- " rather than " sim ". A Malay usually pronounces **ĕmpat** (*four*) as though it were spelt **mpat**. In the same way **ĕntah** (*perhaps so*) is pronounced **ntah**.

janggut – *beard*   The first syllable, again, is open because " ngg " is one sound. For the " j " see par. 14. The " u " slightly shortened. The " t " very light.

suara – *voice*   The " u " is a semi-consonant (i.e. it is almost equal to " w ").

tulang – *bone(s)*   " –lang " almost as English " lung ".

urat – *nerve, sinew*   Final " t " very light. Do not telescope the final closed " a ".

sĕndi – *joint, muscle*   Even stress, " sĕ + ndi ", but be careful to keep the first vowel quite colourless.

kulit – *skin, leather*   Slightly shortened " i " but not quite as short as in English " it ". Very light " t ".

Exercise 2

Read through the following words, pronouncing them with care. Remember the general rule that the stress, if any, falls on the first syllable of a two-syllabled word, if that syllable is an open syllable (i.e. if it ends in a vowel, other than ĕ.)

For the stress on words of three or more syllables, see par. 2 and par. 5a.

rumah – *house*

batu – *stone, rock*

tangga – *house-ladder, staircase*   Like " finger " because of the double " g ".

kayu – *wood*   The " y " equals two " i's ".

halaman – *courtyard; space round a Malay house*
Stress on second syllable. The colloquial pronunciation is **'laman.**

paǥar – *fence*
Do not forget the second " a ".

tembok – *wall (of masonry)*
The glottal check makes the " o " shorter *in time ;* it pulls it up with a jerk but does not alter its sound, which is like a French " o ", not an English " o ". Note that the " e " is a " full e ". Closer than the " e " in English " bend ", more like the " é " in " café ".

dinding – *wall (partition)*
The first " i " is more open than the second, almost " dee– ". Even stress.

bumbong – *roof*
The first syllable is open in prounuciation : " boo– ". Even stress.

bilek – *room*
Glottal check. " Full " e ", but shortened *in time.*

lantai – *floor*

meja – *table*
The " full e ". Remember to keep it a *single* sound, *not* like the English diphthong in " rate " (ré + eet)

kĕrusi – *chair* [or **kĕrosi**]
First syllable very short, because the following consonant is an " r ".

ǥambar–*picture*
Closed final " a ".

pinǥǥan – *plate*
pi + nggan. Like " finger ", because of the two " g's ".

manǥkok – *bowl, cup*
ma + ngkok. Glottal check ; do not let the final " k " come through.

chawan – *cup*
For the " ch " see par. 14. Even stress. Sound the final closed syllable clearly, giving the vowel its full value.

B*

piring – *saucer*

sĕkolah – *school*   Stress on the " o ", a *single* sound, not like the English diphthong in " coat " (ko + oot).   Sound the final " h ".

bangku – *bench*   ba + ngku.

buku–*knot, joint; book*

papan – *plank, wood*   Closed final " a " again.

kĕbun – *garden, plantation, estate*   Almost even stress.   The " u " is short, much like English " put ".

tali – *string, cord*   Not the " a " of English " tar " – lips more stretched.   Tongue forward for the " l ".   Tense " i ".

pĕti – *box*   Even stress.

bakul – *basket*   Even stress.   Do not telescope the final syllable.

tong – *barrel, bin*   Nearer to French " ton " than to English " tong ".

buah–*fruit*   Sound the " h ".

pokok – *tree*   *not* rhyming with English " cocoa ". Glottal check.

daun – *leaf*   A disyllable, both vowels clearly heard.

bunga – *flower*   " bu + nga "   " Singer "   *not* " finger ".

hitam – *black; dark in colour*   " h " very light.

puteh – *white*   Sound the " h ".   Keep the " e " a single sound.

kuning – *yellow*   Lips rounded and well forward for the " oo " sound.

merah – *red*   Full " e ". Clear " a ". Sound the final " h ".

biru – *blue*

hijau – *green*   " au " is a diphthong, but the sounds are run closely together, so that the word is a disyllable. Sound the " h " very lightly if at all.

panjang – *long*   The first " a " is a little more open than the second, and slightly stressed. " –jang " rhymes with English "sung" rather than " sang ".

pendek – *short*   The first " e " is more open than the second. Glottal check.

bĕrseh – *clean*   Even stress. The " r " must be sounded, either after or before the " ĕ ". Full " e " in the second syllable.

kotor – *dirty*   Stress, if any, on the first syllable.

tinggi – *high, tall*   " ti -|- nggi ". Hard, like " finger " because of the double " g ".

rĕndah – *low*   Even stress. Remember to keep the " ĕ " neutral in sound, like the first " o " in English " condition " ; but the syllable itself carries more weight, and takes more time to pronounce, than the first syllable of the English word.

bĕsar – *large*   Sharp " s ". Stress on second syllable.

kĕchil – *small*   Almost even stress. Final " l " seldom heard, usually replaced by " k " (glottal check).

manis – *sweet*   Even stress. The " i ", although it is in a closed syllable, is longer than the " i " of English " sit ".

masam – *sour*   Even stress. The " a " of the final syllable is clearly heard, with no tinge of " u ", in spite of the final " m ".

elok – *fine, beautiful*   Continental " e " and " o " ; soft " l " ; glottal check. If you pronounce it like English " halo " without the " h " you will be making four mistakes. " Halo " has four vowel sounds, " elok " has two.

chantek – *pretty*   Continental " e " but shorter (in time) than in " elok ", because of the glottal check.

kĕras – *hard*

lĕmbut – *soft, gentle*   Even stress. Very light " t ". The " u " a little shorter than in English " boot ", but not quite as short as in " foot ".

pĕnoh – *full*   Stress on second syllable, but the first syllable quite clearly heard. Sound the final " h ".

kosong – *empty*   Stress, if any, on the first syllable. *Not* the " o " of English " cocoa "

kurus – *thin*

gĕmok – *fat*

ini – *this, these*   First syllable open, therefore " ee ".

itu – *that, those*

Exercise 3

Read aloud these groups of words. (Do not bother about their meanings).

1. bila *when*, bĕla *look after*, *rear*, bĕlah *split*.
2. balas *requite*, bĕlas *pity*.
3. bĕlut *eel*, belut *desert*, *betray*, balut *wrap*.
4. bĕrat *heavy*, barat *west*.
5. rĕndah *low*, renda *lace*.
6. mĕrak *peacock*, merah *red*.
7. pĕta *map*, *plan*, petak *section*, *in a rice field*.
8. sarong *sheath ;* sĕrang *onslaught ; petty officer on a ship* ; serong *awry*.
9. buta *blind*, botak *bald*.
10. bulu *fur*, *nap*, buloh *bamboo*

CHAPTER III

I. The Attributive Adjective

II. The Predicative Adjective (omission of copula)

Par. 22. I. The attributive adjective.

The attributive adjective follows the noun.

There is no change, either in noun or adjective, to show gender[1], number[2] or case. Nor is there, in Malay, a definite[3] or an indefinite[4] article corresponding exactly to the English " the " or " a ".

The " adjective + noun " phrase is therefore easily constructed by placing the adjective after the noun.

Examples.

meja běsar	large table, or large tables.
bunga puteh	a white flower, or white flowers.
kěrusi ini	this chair, or these chairs.
bangku itu	that stool, or those stools.

The vocabulary for the following exercises will be found in the lists given in Chapter 2. *Say* the phrases to yourself as you read them or write them. Refer constantly to the rules for pronunciation.

Exercise 4

Translate into English.

1. Tulang panjang.   2. Kěrusi tinggi.   3. Mangkok

---

[1] For amplification of this statement see Footnote 6.
[2] For amplification of this statement see par. 100–1.
[3] For modification of this statement see par. 31, 88 and 158.
[4] For modification of this statement see par. 47.

puteh. 4. Bilek kotor. 5. Halaman běsar. 6. Piring běrseh. 7. Sěkolah kěchil. 8. Hidong panjang. 9 Suara lěmbut. 10. Rambut hitam. 11. Bibir merah. 12. Buah masam. 13. Bumbong tinggi. 14. Tembok rěndah. 15. Daun hijau. 16. Bunga biru. 17. Gambar elok. 18. Leher panjang. 19. Muka chantek. 20. Dahi tinggi. 21. Tangan kotor. 22. Papan hitam. 23. Mangkok kěchil. 24. Kuku pendek. 25. Bakul pěnoh. 26. Kayu hitam. 27. Pinggan puteh. 28. Janggut panjang. 29. Lantai hijau. 30. Chawan merah. 31. Buku ini. 32. Rumah kosong. 33. Meja ini. 34. Kulit itu. 35. Papan itu.

Exercise 5

Translate into Malay.

1. A white plank. 2. Empty bowls. 3. White hands. 4. Clean nails. 5. A short cord. 6. Big baskets. 7. Hard wood. 8. A small picture. 9. Large leaves. 10. A clean school. 11. Large books. 12. Blue plates. 13. A short beard. 14. Green fruit. 15. Clean floors. 16. High walls. 17. Long roofs. 18. White planks. 19. A high house. 20. A large rock. 21. Sweet fruit. 22. Pretty flowers. 23. A thin arm. 24. Low benches. 25. Fat cheeks. 26. Small rooms. 27. Empty baskets. 28. Dirty floors. 29. A small mouth. 30. A red bowl. 31. This face. 32. Those faces. 33. That head. 34. These tables. 35. Those eyes.

II The Predicative Adjective (omission of copula)

Par. 23. The Predicative Adjective.

There is no word for the verb " to be " in Malay,* when it is merely a copula, or link, joining a word to its description.

* But see par. 53.

From this it follows that any one of the phrases (noun + attributive adjective) in Exercise 4 may, if the context requires it, be taken as a complete statement (noun + predicative adjective, with no copula to join them).

Thus, in addition to the meanings given in the key, the following meanings might have been added:

1. The bone is long, *or* the bones are long, *or* the bone was long *or* the bones were long. 2. The chair is high etc.

In practice, however, ambiguity seldom arises since the predicative use of the adjective is usually indicated either by placing the adjective in front of the noun (par. 24) or by using one of the demonstrative adjectives **ini** and **itu** (par. 30) after the noun.

Par. 24.

When the adjective is used predicatively, it may be put in front of the noun if it is necessary to emphasize it.

Panjang meja ini " Long, this table is ", i.e. " This is a *long* table " or merely, " This table is long ".

This rule applies throughout the language. Any word which it is necessary to emphasize is brought to the beginning of the sentence. English usually indicates emphasis by added stress. Malay, which has no marked stress of syllable or of word, indicates emphasis by position in sentence or phrase.

It is possible to emphasize the adjective still further by attaching to it the particle " –lah ".

Panjang-lah   " That's a *long* table ".
    meja itu

Exercise 6

Translate :

1. Bangku tinggi. 2. Rěndah tembok itu. 3. Kotor-lah bilek ini. 4. Sěkolah běsar. 5. Rumah kěchil.

6. Bĕrseh rumah itu. 7. Panjang-lah tali ini. 8. Bunga chantek. 9. Mulut bĕsar. 10. Kotor pinggan itu. 11. Masam buah ini. 12. Bumbong rĕndah.

Exercise 7

Translate : (If two ways are possible, give both).

1. White flowers. 2. The fruit is sour. 3. The roof is high. 4. Fine houses. 5. The picture was large. 6. Dirty hands. 7. The book is blue. 8. A clean floor. 9. The basket was empty. 10. A long arm. 11. The chair is low. 12. Red fruit.

Par. 25.

When two adjectives follow a noun, the first is attributive, and the second predicative, i.e. the first is attached to the noun, and the second makes a statement about the noun, e.g.

1. **Papan puteh panjang**[5] The white plank is long.

2. **Gambar bĕsar elok** The large picture is fine.

Par. 26.

Two attributive adjectives are usually separated by the word **yang** (" who ", " which ", par. 154–9) or by **lagi** (" moreover "), e.g.

a long white plank   **papan puteh yang panjang.**

small green leaves   **daun hijau yang kĕchil.**

lovely blue flowers   **bunga biru yang elok.**

---

[5] In practice, the two adjectives seldom come together because the attributive adjective is usually followed by a demonstrative adjective: *Papan puteh itu panjang.*

a fine large picture **gambar elok lagi běsar** or
gambar yang elok lagi běsar.

[Note : In modern Malay the use of two or more attributive adjectives in succession is becoming common.]

Tne word *yang* may be inserted before any adjective which is used attributively. It lends emphasis, and balance, e.g.

kěrusi yang tinggi   A high chair.

Exercise 8

Translate : (Remember that an adjective which precedes the noun is predicative).

1. Rěndah tembok puteh itu. 2. Meja panjang itu rěndah. 3. Bilek itu kěchil. 4. Rumah ini tinggi. 5. Bakul hijau itu kosong. 6. Manis buah merah itu. 7. Panjang-lah tali itu. 8. Buku hitam itu běsar. 9. Daun kěchil itu hijau. 10. Kosong mangkok ini. 11. Bakul yang běsar lagi elok. 12. Bakul běsar itu elok.

Exercise 9

Translate.

1. The tall house is large. 2. Green fruit is sour. 3. Small green leaves. 4. The black book is small 5. A large clean courtyard. 6. The blue flowers are pretty. 7. The long string is white. 8. The white cup is small. 9. The houses were small and low. 10. Small low houses. 11. A long thin hand. 12 This cord is blue.

CHAPTER IV

I. The Demonstratives " ini " and " itu "
II. Possession

Par. 27.

Below is a vocabulary of the new words used in this chapter.

You will notice that the vocabulary is broken up into groups of words. Roughly speaking these groups correspond to what in English we call parts of speech. (see Appendix). The first column consists of nouns or pronouns, the second of adjectives, the third of verbs, and the fourth of adverbial words. But in dealing with the basic Malay word (i.e. the simple word, with no prefix or suffix attached) such distinctions are artificial. *It is only context that determines the function of such a word in any particular phrase.* The same word, without any change of form, may do the work of a noun, an adjective, or a verb, according to its setting.

Thus *patah* which, in the list below, is given an adjectival meaning (" broken "), will sometimes be found as a noun, meaning " a word ", " one broken-off scrap of language ". And at other times it will be a verb. Moreover, when it is a verb it may correspond to any of the verb forms found in the paradigm of e.g. a French verb ; it is singular or plural, it is past, present or future, it is active or passive, according to the context in which it is found. There are words which act as auxiliaries of time, and there is a supple system of prefixes and suffixes that enables the Malay verb to convey, in one word, shades of meaning which in English might require to be expressed by phrases three or four words long. But it is

51

C

true, nevertheless, that the simple root word, without auxiliary or affixation, is itself made to carry all possible shades of verbal statement.

It is for this reason that the meaning of a word is given in the vocabulary, in its simplest form, e.g. *makan* – ("eat"). Decide from the context whether you should translate it " to eat ", or " is eating ", or " ate ", or perhaps as a noun, " food ".

As you go through the vocabulary, pronounce the words with care even if you are reading them silently.

But do not, at this stage, attempt to learn the lists by heart. Come back to them later, when many of the words will have become familiar through usage.

VOCABULARY

ĕmak *or* 'mak .	. mother
bapa *or* bapak .	. father
abang	. elder brother
kakak	. ,, sister
adek	. younger brother or sister
anak	. child (son or daughter of)
anak pĕrĕmpuan[6]	. daughter
anak laki-laki[6] .	. son
kanak-kanak	. young child ; baby
budak	. child, girl, boy, young person
tukang	. workman
tukang kayu	. carpenter
tukang kĕbun	. gardener
roti	. bread
teh (*or* ayer teh)	. tea
kopi (*or* ayer kopi)	. coffee
susu (*or* ayer susu)	. milk
gula	. sugar
lada.	. pepper
anjing	. dog

anak anjing	.	. puppy
kuching	. .	. cat
burong	. .	. bird
kĕra	. .	. monkey
gajah	. .	. elephant
lĕmbu	. .	. ox
lĕmbu jantan[6]	.	. bull
lĕmbu bĕtina[6]	.	. cow
tikus	. .	. rat
ekor	. .	. tail
rumput	. .	. grass
ayer	. .	. water ; juice
sungai	. .	. river
laut	. .	. sea
matahari	. .	. sun
bulan	. .	. moon, month
kain	. .	. cloth ; *sarong*
sarong	. .	. sheath
kain sarong	.	. Malay *sarong*, a tubular cotton skirt worn by men and women
baju	. .	. coat ; Malay *baju*, a loose coat of silk or cotton material
punya	. .	. (shows possession. See par. 36)
sahaya (*or* saya) (see vocab.)		. I (*sometimes* we)
dia (*or, written,* ia)		. he, she, it, they
—nya	. .	. of him, of her, of it, of them.

laki-laki[6]	. .	. male (of people)
jantan[6]	. .	. male (of animals and sometimes of children)
pĕrĕmpuan[6]	.	. female (of people)
bĕtina[6]	.	. ,, (of animals)
masin	. .	. salt (of sea water)

[6] Note that Malay nouns do not change to indicate sex. When it is necessary to make the distinction, one of these four adjectives is used.

tawar	.	.	.	fresh (of water)
				tasteless (of food)
bulat	.	.	.	round
koyak	.	.	.	torn
rĕtak	.	.	.	cracked
pĕchah	.	.	.	broken, shattered
patah	.	.	.	broken, snapped off (of rigid things, e.g. a mast).
putus	.	.	.	broken, severed (e.g. of a rope)
sakit	.	.	.	ill, sick
sakit hati		.	.	annoyed, vexed
baik	.	.	.	good
ta' baik	.	.	.	not good
jahat	.	.	.	wicked, vicious (of people and animals)
jinak	.	.	.	tame, tamed.
suka	.	.	.	like
makan	.	.	.	eat
minum	.	.	.	drink
jatoh	.	.	.	fall
ada .	.	.	.	there is, there are, there was, there were (See par. 53-6)
sudah	.	.	.	has; has become, *and so, is*
lagi .	.	.	.	more, in addition, moreover
tidak or ta'		.	.	not (See par. 74)
jangan	.	.	.	don't (See par. 78)
–lah	.	.	.	(a particle that emphasises the word to which it is attached.)
di-atas	.	.	.	on (See par. 57-61)
di-dalam .		.	.	in (See par. 57-61)

I. The Demonstratives " ini " and " itu "

Par. 28.

You have already used the words " ini " and " itu " as demonstrative adjectives, after the noun, e.g.

anjing ini	this dog *or* these dogs.
kuching itu	that cat *or* those cats.

Par. 29.

Any descriptive words which belong to the noun (i.e. any attributive adjectives or adjectival phrase) must come *before* the " ini " or " itu ", e.g.

bilek kěchil ini	this little room.
pagar tinggi itu	that high fence.
kain merah itu	that red cloth.
rumah yang puteh itu	that white house.

Note that in English, too, the demonstrative adjective is separated from the noun.

Par. 30.

Any adjective which comes *after* the " itu " is predicative (i.e. it makes a statement about the noun that precedes the " itu "), e.g.

kěra itu jahat	that (*or* the) monkey is wicked.
chawan itu rětak	that (*or* the) cup is cracked.
gajah ini jinak, ta' jahat	this elephant is tame, it is not vicious.
burong itu sakit	that bird is sick.

Note that in English, too, the demonstrative adjective comes next to the noun.

Par. 31.

The adjectives " ini " and " itu " (particularly the latter) are at times the equivalent of the English definite article " the ". There is the implication that the thing to which the noun refers has been under discussion, or is familiar to the hearer, or, as in the last example, is well known to everybody, e.g.

Di-atas meja ada pěti. Pěti itu kěchil.
On the table there was a box. The box was small. (*or* It was a small box).

Buku yang merah itu
The red book.

Pokok lada itu kira² tiga kaki tinggi-nya.
The pepper-bush is about three feet in height.

Par. 32.

When the words " ini " and " itu " precede the noun they are not adjectives but pronouns[7], e.g.

Ini meja   This is a table.

The two words form a complete statement.

The complement is not often a noun. It is usually an adjective or a pronoun, e.g.

Itu-lah yang elok   That would be the best thing.

Itu dia   That's he *or* That's it (usually to be translated, " There he is ! ").

Since the adjective, in such an expression, is predicative, it will sometimes be found in the emphatic position, before the pronoun, e.g.

Elok-lah itu   That's a lovely thing.

Note, however, that *Elok-lah!* without the " itu " would be the Malay equivalent of " That's fine ! " (i.e. " It fits in with my plans ").

[7] Colloquially, however, the adjective *ini* is sometimes heard before the noun : *ini meja* for " this table ".

II. Possession

Par. 33.

The second of two nouns shows possession[8] : e.g.

    rumah tukang   the workman's house

    dinding bilek   the wall of the room

or else it is used adjectivally to indicate material, purpose etc., e.g.

    rumah batu   a house of stone, a concrete house

    rumah papan   a plank house.

    chawan kopi   a coffee cup[9]

Par. 34.

In the same way a pronoun placed after a noun is in the genitive case, e.g.

    rumah saya   my house (lit. the house of me).

    rumah dia   his (or her) house.

But these genitive pronouns are frequently omitted if they can be inferred from the context.

Par. 35.

Note, however, that " -nya " is the usual form of the possessive of the third person pronoun, singular and plural, masculine feminine and neuter, e.g.

    Ahmad susah hati. Bapa-nya sakit
    Ahmad is sad. His father is ill.
    Tikus itu běsar, ekor-nya panjang
    The rat was large, its tail was long.

Note, however, that in certain phrases two parallel nouns which in English would be joined by a conjunction are, in Malay, placed side by side, without a conjunction. e.g. *Pinggan mangkok*—" plates and bowls " i.e. " crockery " (See par. 95b).

[9] But *sa-chawan kopi* for " a cup of coffee " (See par. 52).

When the owner has not been previously mentioned, use *dia*, not *nya*, e.g.

Pěti saya hitam, pěti dia puteh.
My box is black, his is white.

Par. 36.

The last example shows the correct way of expressing the equivalent of the English possessive adjectives (" my ", " her " etc.).

Since the Malay words which are used to translate the English adjectives are themselves personal pronouns (*saya* " I " *dia* " she "), it is only by virtue of their position, following the noun, that they show possession.

Consequently, when the Malay expression corresponds to an English possessive *pronoun* (" mine ", " hers " etc.) the Malay noun must be repeated, in order to turn the Malay pronoun into a genitive (i.e. in order to make it show possession. See par. 33). Thus:

That house is mine

becomes, in Malay,

Rumah itu rumah saya.
(Lit.   That house is the house of me)

In practice, however, the expression most commonly used is:

Rumah itu saya punya.

which may possibly be translated literally as:

That house, I own it.

Similarly:

Rumah itu Hamid punya
That house is Hamid's.

Rumah itu siapa punya?
Whose house is that?

When the thing owned is not mentioned by name this is a convenient construction. (See footnote 72 for alternatives).

But the word **punya** is commonly misused in the bazaar Malay of the towns. Be on your guard. Use it only when the English equivalent is a possessive pronoun (mine, yours, whose?), or a possessive noun (i.e. apostrophe s) not followed by the name of the thing possessed (e.g. Hamid's).

Par. 37. Miscellaneous examples.

1. *Tukang gigi itu sakit.*
   The dentist is ill (*or* That dentist is ill).

2. *Ayer laut itu masin.*
   Sea-water is salt.

3. *Tulang lĕngan–nya sudah patah.*
   His (*or* her) arm is broken.

4. *Susu itu puteh.*
   Milk is white.

5. *Orang pĕrĕmpuan suka minum teh.*
   Women like tea (lit. " like drinking tea ").

6. *Budak laki–laki itu rambut–nya pendek, budak pĕrĕmpuan rambut–nya panjang.*
   The boy's hair is short, the girl's hair is long.

7. *Anak anjing itu kĕchil.*
   That (*or* The) puppy is small.

8. *Ini baju kanak–kanak itu.*
   This is the child's coat.

9. *Panjang ekor lĕmbu jantan itu.*
   What a long tail that bull has !

10. *Kain[10] sarong abang saya sudah koyak.*
    My brother's sarong is (*lit.* has become) torn.

11. *Tali pinggang-nya 'dah (i.e. sudah) hilang.*
    His belt is lost.

---

[10] *Kain sarong.* The word *sarong* is never used by a Malay in this sense without the word *kain*. On the other hand the word *kain* used alone frequently stands for *kain sarong*.

12. *Lĕmbu bĕtina itu makan rumput.*
The cow is eating grass.

13. *Anjing tidak minum ayer masin.*
Dogs do not drink salt water.

14. *Kĕra itu jahat.*
That monkey is mischievous.

15. *Adek saya sakit kĕpala.*[11]
My sister has a headache.

16. *Budak yang kĕchil itu baju–nya 'dah koyak.*
The little boy's (or girl's) coat is torn.

17. *Pinggan rĕtak, chawan pĕchah*[12].
The plate is cracked and the cup is broken

18. *Bakul pĕnoh, tong kosong.*[12]
The basket is full but the bin is empty.

19. *Dia sakit gigi*[11].
He has toothache.

20. *Ĕmak sakit hati*[11].
My mother is annoyed.

21. *Jangan minum ayer yang kotor itu.*
Don't drink that dirty water.

22. *Kain kuning ini ta' baik.*
This yellow material is not good.

23. *Jinak anak kuching Maimunah itu.*
Maimunah's kitten is friendly.

Exercise 10

1. Abang saya sakit.
2. Tĕlinga gajah bĕsar.
3. Kulit anjing itu kotor.
4. Kĕpala burong ini kĕchil.

---

[11] Note this idiom with *sakit*. *Sakit gigi*—" ill, in the teeth " *Sakit hati*—" hurt in the heart ". i.e. vexed, annoyed. Also *sakit dĕmam*—" ill with fever " ; *sakit batok*—" ill, with a cough ", equivalent to the English expressions " to have fever " etc.
[12] Note the omission of a conjunction. (See par. 95).

5. Jangan makan roti itu.
6. Bapa Ahmad tinggi, leher-nya panjang.
7. Ini rumah tukang kayu.
8. Kěrusi yang pěchah itu kěrusi saya.
9. Anjing Husain kěchil, kěra-nya běsar.
10. Anak Měriam gěmok, ěmak-nya kurus.
11. Fatimah kakak Hasan.
12. Ayer sungai tawar.
13. Mat sakit pěrut.
14. Budak jatoh, gigi-nya patah.
15. Ada bakul di-atas bangku.
16. Ada buku di-dalam pěti.
17. Kanak-kanak yang sakit itu adek Zainab.
18. Běsar mangkok biru itu.
19. Chawan kopi yang kuning itu saya punya.
20. Kěras roti ini.

Exercise 11

1. The root of that house is high.
2. That little dog is black.
3. There were some cows in the plantation.
4. Ahmad's kitten is fat.   It likes milk.
   (*say* likes to drink milk).
5. Don't drink river water.
6. The girl has a headache.
7. The green coffee cup is broken.
8. The dog's ears are long, and his tail is short.
9. The sugar bowl is cracked.
10. An elephant's neck is short.
11. Grass is green.
12. My belt is broken.
13. That's the gardener's daughter.
14. This long white table is not clean.
15. The moon is round.

CHAPTER V

I. Cardinal Numbers
II. Numeral Coefficients
III. Use of " ada "

VOCABULARY

Do not attempt to learn it by heart until the words have become half-familiar to you through their use in sentences. Remember, too, that Malay words are " very opals "— it is only when you have seen them in many lights that you will begin to realise their possibilities.

orang	. . .	people, persons
biji .	. . .	seed
batang	. . .	rod
kĕping	. . .	piece
puchok	. . .	shoot (of a plant)
masa	. . .	time, period
nyiur ⎫ kĕlapa ⎭	. . .	coconut
nanas	. . .	pineapple
pisang	. . .	banana
rokok	. . .	cigarette
pintu	. . .	door
sĕnapang .	. .	gun, rifle
pisau	. . .	knife
nĕgĕri	. . .	country, state, town
tanah	. . .	land, earth
gunong	. . .	mountain,
kĕdai	° . .	shop, booth
sen	. . .	cent
nama	. . .	name

62

bĕrkek	.	.	. snipe
kĕreta	.	.	. cart, car
jarum	.	.	. needle
surat	.	.	. letter, writing
payong	.	.	. umbrella
kĕrtas	.	.	. paper
bĕrapa ?	.	.	. how many ?
Mĕlayu	.	.	. Malay
lĕpas	.	.	. let go (as prep. " after ")
potong	.	.	. cut
hisap (mĕnghisap)			. smoke (cigarettes, etc. See par. 119).
kĕrja	.	.	. work
jahit	.	.	. sew
dudok	.	.	. sit, dwell
suroh	.	.	. bid, tell to do something
masok	.	.	. enter, come in
sampai	.	.	. arrive (as prep. " up to " or " until ")
datang	.	.	. come
tahu	.	.	. know
tĕrbang	.	.	. fly
jual	.	.	. sell
bĕli .	.	.	. buy
hĕndak or 'nak			. intend, wish ; as auxiliary, " will "
mahu	.	.	. wish ; will
bacha (mĕmbacha)			. read
tulis	.	.	. write
chari	.	.	. seek
buat	.	.	. make, do
kĕrat	.	.	. sever, cut
sĕkarang	.	.	. now
tadi	.	.	. just now

di–	. . .	at, *or* in, *or* on (before place words only. See par. 57)
di–bawah	. .	below, underneath
pada	. .	at, on, (before time words) ; **to** ; according to (see par. 57)
kapada	. .	to (persons) ; towards (see par. 57)
–kah?	. .	interrogative particle

I. Cardinal Numbers

Par. 38.

The Malay system of numbering is simple and straightforward.

Cardinals 1–10.

1	sa–, satu[13]. **suatu**	7	tujoh
2	dua	8	dělapan (in speaking shortened to " lapan ")
3	tiga		
4	ěmpat	9	sěmbilan
5	lima	10	sa–puloh
6	ěnam		

Par. 39.

The equivalent of the English suffix " –teen " is " –bělas ".

Cardinals 11–20.

11	sa–bělas	16	ěnam–bělas
12	dua–bělas	17	tujoh–bělas
13	tiga–bělas	18	dělapan–bělas
14	ěmpat–bělas	19	sěmbilan–bělas
14	lima–bělas	20	dua–puloh

[13] Note the following phrases

satu satu	one by one
lěpas satu, satu	one after the other
lěpas sa–orang sa–orang	one (person) after another
ta' satu, satu	if it isn't one thing, it's another
sa–sa–orang	anybody, everybody
pada suatu (or *satu*) *hari*	one day
bada suatu masa	once . . . , once upon a time
sa–hari dua	a day or two
dua–dua	two at a time *or* both

Par. 40.
As already shown, multiples of ten are formed by adding " puloh " to the units.

10	sa–puloh	60	ĕnam puloh
20	dua puloh	70	tujoh puloh
30	tiga puloh	80	dĕlapan puloh
40	ĕmpat puloh	90	sĕmbilan puloh
50	lima puloh	100	sa–ratus

Par. 41.
Intermediate numbers are formed by the addition of the unit.

21	dua puloh satu	54	lima puloh ĕmpat
32	tiga puloh dua	65	ĕnam puloh lima
43	ĕmpat puloh tiga	76	tujoh puloh ĕnam

Par. 42.
Multiples of a hundred are formed by adding " ratus " to the units.

100	sa–ratus	300	tiga ratus
200	dua ratus	400	ĕmpat ratus

Par. 43.
Multiples of a thousand are formed by adding " ribu " to the units.

1,000	sa–ribu	2,000	dua ribu

Par. 44.
The remaining multiples are :

laksa	ten thousand	⎱ not used
kĕti	a hundred thousand	⎰ colloquially
juta	a million.	

50,000	lima laksa (*or* lima puloh ribu)
600,000	ĕnam kĕti (*or* ĕnam ratus ribu)

7,000,000   tujoh juta

9,876,543   sĕmbilan juta dĕlapan kĕti tujoh laksa ĕnam
               ribu lima ratus ĕmpat puloh tiga
               or, usually,
               sĕmbilan milion dĕlapan ratus tujoh puloh
               ĕnam ribu, lima ratus ĕmpat puloh tiga.

Par. 45.

Note that there is no equivalent of the English
conjunction " and " in compound numbers :

four hundred and one . . ĕmpat ratus satu
five thousand eight hundred lima ribu dĕlapan **ratus**
and seventy three . . tujoh–puloh tiga.

Par. 46.

In the same way the conjunction " or " is omitted, in
rough estimates.

two or three . . . dua tiga
thirteen or fourteen . . tiga ĕmpat–bĕlas (lit.
                          three– or four– teen)
forty or fifty . . . ĕmpat lima puloh
five or six hundred . . lima ĕnam ratus
six or seven thousand . ĕnam tujoh ribu

II. Numeral Coefficients

Par. 47.

In English we speak of two hundred " head " of cattle.
A Malay speaks of so many " tail " of cattle.   Moreover,
he uses many other classifying expressions of the same
sort, when enumerating material objects.

The classifier, or coefficient, comes immediately after
the numeral.

> **e.g.** dua ekor tikus⎫
>   *or*   ⎬two rats (i.e. two tail of rats).
>   tikus dua ekor⎭

The word *satu* usually appears as *sa-*(pronounced *sĕ-*) when it combines with a coefficient.

> e.g. gajah sa–ekor . one elephant (*or, sometimes,* an elephant).

Note that *sa* + coefficient placed after the noun is usually a numeral.

Placed in front of the noun, it means " a ", i.e. " a certain one ", " a definite one ".

> **e.g.** Ada sa–ekor   There was a (certain) bird.
> burong

Par. 48.

The following are the numeral coefficients most commonly in use. (N.B. The classification is by no means rigid, as will be seen from some of the examples below).

orang   for human beings.

ekor   for other living creatures.

buah   for large things, e.g. houses, cars, ships.   Also books, rivers, chairs, and some fruits.

biji   for smaller things, e.g. eggs, fruits, nuts, cups.

batang   for rod-like things, e.g. walking sticks, trees. pencils.

hĕlai (or *'lai*) for things that occur in thin layers or sheets, e.g. paper, cloth ; also for feathers, and hair

kĕping   for pieces, slabs, fragments, e.g. of wood, stone, bread ; also land, and paper.

puchok   for letters, firearms, needles.

bilah   for bladed things, e.g. knives, spears.

Par. 49.

Of less common occurrence are the following.

bĕntok	for rings, hooks.
bidang	for mats, widths of cloth.
kuntum	for flowers.
kaki	for long stemmed flowers.
urat	for threads.
pintu	for houses (in a row).
tangga	for Malay houses (each with its house-ladder).
patah	for words and proverbial expressions.
butir	for jewels, seeds, fruits.
puntong	for stumps, butt-ends (e.g. of firewood, cigars, teeth).
potong	for slices, of bread, etc.
utas	for fishing nets.

Par. 50. Examples.

1.	*Sa–orang tukang kĕbun*	a (certain) gardener.
2.	*Tukang kĕbun sa–orang*	one gardener.
3.	*Budak dua orang*	two children.
4.	*Dua orang pĕrĕmpuan China*	two Chinese women.
5.	*Tiga ekor kĕra*	three monkeys.
6.	*Kĕreta ĕmpat buah*	four cars.
7.	**Buah nyiur lima biji*	five coconuts.
8.	*Ĕnam batang rokok*	six cigarettes.
9.	*Kain sarong tujoh hĕlai*	seven sarongs.
10.	*Dĕlapan kĕping papan*	eight planks.
11.	*Sĕnapang sĕmbilan puchok*	nine rifles.
12.	*Sa–puloh bilah pisau*	ten knives.

*Note : The word " buah " in Example 7 above is not a coefficient. The word is usually used before the names of fruits :

> e.g. *buah nanas* . pineapples.
> *buah pisang* . bananas.

For the same use of a generic term before a particular term compare the following :

orang China	. Chinese (people).
nĕgĕri China	. China (the country, China).
tanah Mĕlayu	. Malaya (the Malay land).
burong bĕrkek	. snipe (the snipe bird).
bunga mĕlur	. jasmine.
ikan tĕnggiri	. mackerel.

Par. 51.

It is not necessary to use the coefficient when the context does not require specification, or numerical definition. e.g.

1. *Saya 'nak bĕli rokok*   I want to buy (some) cigarettes.

2. *Dia makan rokok*   He is having a cigarette.

3. *Tukang kĕbun ada*   The gardener is here.

4. *Burong tĕrbang*   Birds fly *or* a bird flies.

but

Ada sa–ekor burong yang pandai bĕrchakap.
There was a (certain) bird that was able to talk.

Par. 52.

Notice such expressions of measurement as the following, which are akin to numeral coefficients.

sa–chawan kopi	a cup of coffee.
(but	
chawan kopi or	
sa–biji chawan kopi	a coffee cup).
sa–kĕreta tahi lĕmbu	a cartload of manure.
(but	
sa–buah kĕreta lĕmbu	a bullock cart)

III. The verb *ada*

A. When *ada* is not used.

Par. 53.

The word *ada* is **not** used to translate the verb " to be " when it is merely a copula (i.e. a link between a substantive and its description. See par. 23). e.g.

1.	He is good	*Dia itu baik.*
2.	He is a carpenter	*Dia kerja tukang kayu* or, simply, *Dia tukang kayu.*
3.	The trees in that plantation are coconut palms	*Pokok yang dalam kebun itu ia-lah pokok kělapa.*

Par. 54.

Neither is it necessary to use *ada* to translate the verb " to be " when it is an auxiliary, used with the present participle of another verb to form a compound tense. e.g.

1.	She is sewing	. *Dia měnjahit* (par. 119).
2.	He is sitting	. *Dia dudok.*

(If there is need to stress the continuance of an action, the words *sědang* and *těngah* may be used. See par. 112d).

B. When *ada* is used.

Par. 55.

Ada renders the verb " to be " when it is a verb expressing existence, or presence. The form of the English sentence is usually " There is . . ." " There are . . ." " There was . . ." " There were . . ." (corresponding to French " Il y a ") e.g.

1.	There are five birds on that tree . .	*Ada burong lima ekor di-atas pokok itu.*

2. In India there are high mountains . .   *Di–nĕgĕri India ada gunong yang tinggi* (Lit. which are high).

3. Is the carpenter there ? Tell him to come in.   *Tukang kayu ada ? Suroh dia masok.*

4. Is there any milk ? Yes, there is.   *Ada susu ? Ada.*

Note the use of the word " *ada* " in questions ;

> *Ada–kah tahu nama orang itu ?*   Do you know that person's name ?

This is comparable with the above examples, " Does this state of things exist—that you know that person's name ? " (Cf. Fr. Est–ce que . . . ?).

Par. 56.

Because of the impact of English idiom, *ada* has come to render the verb " to have " when it shows possession. In writing, the form of the Malay sentence is " There is to me..." Here it is performing the same function as in par. 55 above i.e. showing existence or presence. e.g.

The raja had one child . .   *Ada kapada raja itu anak sa–orang.*

I have forty-five books .   *Ada kapada saya empat-puloh lima buah buku.*

But in conversation, such sentences frequently take the same form as the English sentence i.e. the possessor becomes the subject of the sentence, and *ada* becomes, apparently, a transitive verb. e.g.

Have you a car, Hasan ? Yes, I have. *Hasan ada kĕreta ? Ada.* But it is often possible to omit the subject (e.g. " Ada kĕreta ? ") and so retain the Malay idiom.

Note : Other words which indicate possession are :
> *bĕroleh, mĕmpunyaï, taroh, simpan.*

Pěrumpamaan (Proverb).

 Biar lambat asal sělamat.
 Slow and steady wins the race.

 (Literally : Allow slow provided-that safe).

Exercise 12

1. Tiga puloh dua.
2. Dělapan–bělas.
3. Empat puloh lima.
4. Dua ribu ěnam ratus sěmbilan puloh satu.
5. Sa–puloh juta.
6. Tiga laksa.
7. Tujoh kěti.
8. Ada tiga ekor burong di–atas bumbong.
9. Di–dalam pěti ada mangkok hijau dua biji.
10. Orang China itu běli rumah batu sa–puloh pintu.
11. Tukang kěbun měnghisap rokok.
12. Tadi sahaya běli rokok dua puloh batang.
13. Bapa Husain 'nak měnjual kěreta.
14. Ada kěreta dua buah di–bawah rumah.
15. Tukang roti ada–kah?—Ada—Běli dua biji roti.
16. Abang saya měmběli pisau sa–bilah, tiga batang kayu rul (*rulers*), dua puchok jarum yang panjang.
17. Ada buah nanas yang elok di–kědai itu. Běrapa biji mahu běli?
18. Tadi datang sa–orang Mělayu 'nak měnjual kain sarong dua hělai.
19. Saya ada sa–buah rumah běsar di–někěri Běrma.
20. Ada sěnapang?—Ada—Běrapa puchok?—Dua–bělas puchok.
21. Di–dalam kěbun itu ada sa–batang pokok nyior.
22. Saya hěndak sa–kěping roti.
23. Běrapa biji tělor di–dalam bakul?—Lima–bělas biji.
24. Adek hěndak tulis sa–puchok surat.
25. Ada kěrtas dua tiga kěping di–atas meja bulat itu.

26. Fatimah dudok měnjahit baju, Sharifah měmbacha buku.
27. Bapa hěndak běli sa–hělai baju.
28. Ada sa–ekor kuching hitam di–atas tangga rumah papan itu.
29. Kakak hěndak tiga kěping kěrtas tulis.
30. Hashim chari sa–lai daun pisang buat payong.

Exercise 13

1. Eleven. 2. Forty-five. 3. Three hundred and one.
4. Five thousand seven hundred. 5. Eight thousand two hundred and fourteen. 6. Two needles. 7. A Malay.
8. Fifteen elephants. 9. The gardener. 10. A (certain) carpenter. 11. One workman. 12. Seventeen rifles.
13. Seven bullock carts. 14. Are there (any) cigarettes?—
Yes, there are nine. 15. The child has two stones.
16. There is a piece of paper on that low table. 17. My father wants to sell a piece of land. 18. Aminah's brother has a shop in Singapore. 19. I want two or three needles.
20. Buy two white coats. 21. There are six children under the house. 22. Their father is a dentist. 23. There are thirty coconut trees on that estate. 24. Don't sell that car. 25. How many cents each are those pineapples? 26. Rats eat bread.

Conversation No. 1

Měnjual Ikan

(Any words which have not yet been used will be found in the alphabetical vocabulary at the end).

Pěnjual[1] ikan :   Ikan! Ikan! Ênche'[2] mahu ikan–kah?
Orang rumah :   Mahu[3]. Mari–lah. Ikan apa di–jual[4] ?
Pěnjual ikan :   Ikan bawal pun[5] ada, ikan těnggiri pun ada.

c•

Orang rumah : Bĕrapa sa–kati ikan bawal itu?

Pĕnjual ikan : Sa–kati 'lapan puloh sen.

Orang rumah : Mahal sangat itu. Ĕnam puloh sen sa–kati, saya ambil.

Pĕnjual ikan : Ta' boleh ĕnche'. Saya bĕli di–pasar pun[5] mahal. Untong sadikit sahaja.

Orang rumah : Saya tawar. Tujoh puloh sen. Bagi–kah, tidak ?

Pĕnjual ikan : Ta' apa–lah. Ĕnche' mahu bĕrapa kati?

Orang rumah : Bagi dua kati. Ini dia duit sa–ringgit ĕmpat puloh sen.

Translation.

Selling Fish

The fish-seller : Fish ! Fish ! Do you want any fish?

The housewife : Yes. Come here please. What fish have you?

The fish-seller : I have pomfret, and mackerel.

The housewife : How much a *kati* is the pomfret?

The fish-seller : 80 cents a *kati*.

The housewife : That's very dear. I'll take it if you will give it to me for 60 cents a *kati*.

The fish-seller : I can't, madam. I myself paid a high price for it in the market. I'm making very little profit on it.

The housewife : Well, I'll offer you a little more. 70 cents. Will you let me have it, or not ?

The fish-seller : All right. How many *kati* do you want ?

The housewife : Give me two *kati*. Here's $1.40.

Notes.

1. pĕnjual . . A noun formed from the root *jual*– " sell ". For the prefix *pĕ*-, *see* par. 132.

2. ĕnche' . . As you go through the conversations note the many equivalents for the pronoun " you ". To address a person incorrectly is a grave discourtesy ; see par. 86.

3. mahu . . Note the omission of the pronoun, when there is no need to express it. (see Chapter IX for personal pronouns).

4. di-jual . . For the verbal prefix *di*– see par. 115–116.

5. pun . . For the ' balance word ' *pun* see par. 150.

CHAPTER VI

I. The place-prepositions " ka– ", " di– ", " dari ".

II. Other prepositions.

VOCABULARY

hari	. .	. day
minggu	. .	. week
tahun	. .	. year
pulau	. .	. island
pinang	. .	. betel nut
apa?	. .	. what?
khabar	. .	. news
Apa khabar?	.	. How do you do? (lit. What news?)
těmpat	. .	. place
sampah	. .	. rubbish
masa	. .	. time, period
chabai	. .	. long pepper, chilli
parit	. .	. ditch
pasar	. .	. market
ikan	. .	. fish
chěrita	. .	. story
pěnjual	. .	. one who sells (see Chap. XIV)
těpi	. .	. edge
pěkan	. .	. town, shopping centre
měntega	. .	. butter
pějabat	. .	. office, department
kasut	. .	. shoes
tuan	. .	. master
lebar	. .	. wide

lama	. . .	long (of time), old
tinggal	. . .	remain, live
pulang	. . .	return to starting place
lari .	. . .	run away
simpan	. . .	put away, keep
naik	. . .	go up
turun	. . .	go down
sorong	. . .	push
tarek	. . .	pull
tidor	. . .	sleep
kĕluar	. . .	go out
bĕri ⎱ bagi (coll.) ⎰	.	give
rasa.	. . .	feel, perceive ; feeling
pĕrasaan .	. .	feeling (see Chap. XIV)
bohong	. . .	lie
jatoh	. . .	fall
minta	. . .	ask for (a thing or an action)
tanya	. . .	ask a question
nanti	. . .	wait (*as future auxiliary* " will ")
sandar ⎱ (See par. bĕrsandar ⎰ 123) .		lean
pinjam	. . .	borrowing
buang	. . .	throw away
dapat	. . .	find, get ; succeed
pukul	. . .	strike
pukul tiga	. .	three o'clock
jalan	. . .	road ; travel
lĕbeh	. . .	more
tĕngah	. . .	mid, middle
balek	. . .	reverse
di–luar	. . .	outside
di–sini	. . .	here
di–situ	. . .	there

di–sana	.	.	. yonder
mari	.	.	. hither, here
mari !	.	.	. here ! (i.e. Come !)
ka–sana ka–mari		.	. hither and thither

I. " ka– ", " di– ", " dari."

Par. 57.

There are three prepositions of place :

ka–	.	.	. to
di–	.	.	. at, on, in
dari		.	. from

Note that the first two are proclitic. Neither can stand alone. It must be attached to the word which follows it.

That the following word must be a place-word.

When the following word is not a place word :

> *ka–* is replaced by *kapada* (sometimes shortened to *pada*) e.g. *ka–Singapura* but *kapada budak itu*. *di–* is replaced by *pada*, e.g. *di–Singapura* but *pada masa itu*.

[Note, however, the accepted expression *Dari suatu masa ka–suatu masa.* In modern Malay the preposition *di–*, also, is used with increasing frequency before expressions of time, e.g. *Di–masa itu* – At that time.]

The preposition *dari* may be replaced by *daripada* before a word which is not a place-word, but the change is not obligatory, except before the enclitic pronouns *–nya*, *–ku*, *–mu*. (See par. 173, 4.)

Par. 58.

Place words may be :

(a) Nouns. e.g.
       rumah, nĕgĕri, meja.

(b) Adverbs. e.g.
   sini, situ, sana.

(c) Nouns of position such as *atas* (top) *bawah* (bottom) *balek* (reverse) which combine with the locative prepositions to form compound prepositions, or compound adverbs.

Examples :

(a) 1. *Tiga bulan dia tinggal di–rumah sakit*[14].
      He stayed in the hospital three months.

   2. *Orang pĕrĕmpuan itu datang dari Pulau Pinang.*
      The woman came from Penang.

   3. *'Mak saya pulang ka–nĕgĕri-nya.*
      My mother returned to her own country.

(b) 1. *Budak itu lari ka–sana ka–mari.*
      The child was running hither and thither.

   2. *Dudok di–situ.*
      Sit there.

   3. *Apa khabar dari sana ?*
      What is the news from that part of the world ?

   4. *Bilek makan di–mana ?*
      Where is the dining room ?

(c) 1. *Ada sa–buah kĕreta di–bawah rumah.*
      There is car under the house.

   2. *Sorong pĕti ka–bawah tĕmpat tidor.*
      Push the box under the bed.

   3. *Sa–ekor tikus lari kĕluar dari bĕlakang tong sampah.*
      A rat ran out from behind the rubbish bin.

---

[14] *Rumah sakit*—" hospital ". Malay has many of these compound words. In accordance with the rule of emphasis, it is the first word that is the key word. e.g. *rumah sakit*—" a house for the sick " ; but *sakit kĕpala*—" sickness of the head, a headache ". So *jarum chuchok*— " a bodkin " (lit. " a needle for piercing ") but *chuchok jarum*—" to thread a needle."

4. *Ada pokok tinggi dua batang di–balek tembok.*
There were two tall trees behind the wall.

5. *Ada orang di–luar kĕdai.*
There are some people outside the shop.

Par. 59.

As was stated in paragraph 57 :

Kapada replaces *ka–* before a word which is not a place-word.

Pada replaces *di–* before a word which is not a place-word.

(*Daripada* replaces *dari* before *–nya, –ku,* and *–mu* but before other words the change is not obligatory).

Examples:

(a) *Kapada* (or *pada*) instead of *ka–* :

1. *Bĕri surat ini kapada Che' Mat.*
Give this letter to Che' Mat.

2. *Lĕpas itu, dia sampai kapada suatu sungai yang lebar.*
After that, he came to a wide river.

(But *ka–suatu sungai* is also commonly used.)

3. *Bĕri tahu kapada–nya* (or less formal, *Bĕri dia tahu,* or *Bĕri tahu dia*).
Tell him (lit. " give to know ").

(b) *Pada* instead of *di–* :

1. *Pada masa itu, anak laki–laki–nya dudok di–Ipoh.*
At that time, his son lived at Ipoh.

2. *Pada pĕrasaan saya dia bohong.*
I think he is lying (lit. " In my feeling ").

3. *Pada suatu hari hilang–lah anak lĕmbu itu.*
   One day, the calf disappeared.

Par. 60.

(a) Note the following distinction :

  1. *Saya bĕli chabai di–kĕdai Pa' Abas.*
     I buy chillies at Pa Abas' shop.

  2. *Ada dua orang Mĕlayu di–dalam kĕdai Pa' Abas.*
     There are two Malays in Pa Abas' shop.

(b) Be prepared for the omission of the place-preposition when the case-relationship is clear from the context.

Examples:

  1. *Dia pulang rumah* (i.e. *ka–rumah*).
     He went home.

  2. *Hari itu saya dudok rumah* (i.e. *di–rumah*).
     That day I stayed at home.

  3. *Batu itu jatoh parit* (i.e. *ka–parit* or *ka–dalam parit*).
     The stone fell into the ditch.

  4. *Pada pukul tujoh dia kĕluar rumah.*
     At 7 o'clock, he went out of the house.

(c) On the other hand, the place-preposition *ka–* is frequently taken as sufficient indication of " motion towards ", and the verb is omitted.

Example:

  Saad ka–mana ?—Saya ka–pasar.
  Where are you going, Saad ?—I'm off to market.

Par. 61.

The compound place prepositions are given below, with *di–* only.

The *di-* is replaced by *ka-* to express " motion towards ", and by *dari* to express " motion from ".

di–atas . . .	on
di–bawah . . .	under
di–hadapan (in speech *dĕpan*) . . .	in front of
di bĕlakang ⎫ *di–balek* ⎭ . .	behind
di–sebelah . . .	at the side of, beside.
di–antara . .	between
di–tĕngah . .	in the middle of

II. Other Prepositions.

Par. 62.

Below is a list of other prepositions, or words used prepositionally.   It is intended for reference.

daripada . . .	than (after a comparative) ; out of (followed by a number).
dĕngan . . .	with (accompaniment, instrument, manner. Often used where " and " or " by " would be used in English).
hampir ⎫ often with ⎫ *dĕkat* ⎭ *dĕngan* ⎭	near.
sa–kĕliling . . .	around.
tĕntang . . .	concerning.
bĕrtĕntang (often with *dĕngan*) . .	opposite to.
hingga . . ⎫ *sampai* . . ⎭	until, up to, as far as
tĕrlĕbeh dahulu dari pada . .	before (of time)

kĕmudian daripada	
lĕpas . .	} after
sa–tĕlah (written)	

bagi . „ . . for (indicating recipient. Modern Malay uses *untok* in this sense)

sa-lama . . . for (duration of time) ; during

sĕbab . .	
oleh sĕbab . .	} because, owing to.
karna or *kĕrana* .	
oleh kĕrana .	

oleh . . . . by (agent) ; because of.

hanya . . . except, only

mĕlainkan (after a negative) . . except, but

akan (*lity.*) . . . towards (not in front of place-words).

Par. 63.

Do not rely entirely on vocabularies for the translation of English prepositions into Malay.

(a) Most of the English prepositional verbs are rendered by Malay verbs which require no preposition. e.g.

to go or come up	.	*naik*
to go or come down	.	*turun*
to go in	. .	*masok*
to put (something) into		*masokkan* (see Chap. XIII)
to go or come out	.	*kĕluar*
to ask for	.	*minta*
to wait for	.	*nantikan* (see Chap. XIII)

(b) An English preposition may be rendered in various ways in Malay, according to the context. e.g. " for "

1. Buy some fish for me . *Bĕlikan saya ikan*
(See Chap. XIII).

D

2. I stayed there for five years   *Lima tahun saya dudok di–situ.*

3. This is a story for children   *Ini chĕrita bagi kanak-kanak.*

4. What's this for ?   *Ini buat apa?*

(c) A Malay preposition may be rendered in various ways in English, according to context. e.g. *dĕngan*

1. *Potong dĕngan pisau* .   Cut it[15] *with* a knife.

2. *Pĕgang dĕngan tangan kiri*   Hold it *in* your left hand

3. *Pĕti ini pĕnoh dĕngan sampah*   This box is full *of* rubbish.

4. *Dia bĕrchĕrai dĕngan bini–nya*   He is divorced *from* his wife

5. *Dudok dĕkat dĕngan dia* .   Sit next *to* him.

6. *Saya suka makan roti dĕngan mĕntega*   I like bread *and* butter.

7. *Bĕrsumpah dĕngan nama Allah*   To swear *in* the name of Allah.

8. *Pĕrgi dĕngan kĕreta api*   To go *by* train.

Par. 64. Miscellaneous Examples:

1. *Chawan jatoh dari atas meja.*
   The cup fell from the table.

2. *Tarek batu yang bĕsar itu dari bawah rumah.*
   Pull that big stone from under the house.

3. *Jangan buang sampah ka–dalam parit.*
   Don't throw rubbish into the ditch.

4. *Sa–orang China dudok di–tĕpi jalan.*
   A Chinese was sitting at the edge of the road.

---

[15] Note the omission of the pronoun object cf. *kĕrat dua*—" Cut it in half ", *Dĕngar–lah*—" Listen to me ". Be on the look out for this ; it is an example of the economy of words referred to in the Introduction.

5. *Dia lĕbeh tinggi daripada abang—nya* (for comparison see par. 107.)
He is taller than his brother.

6. *Potong dĕngan pisau yang dĕkat pĕti hijau itu.*
Cut it with that knife that is beside the green box.

7. *Kĕdai itu hampir dĕngan sungai.*
The shop is near the river.

8. *Dĕkat rumah itu ada pokok kĕlapa dua batang.*
Near the house there are two coconut palms.

9. *Tĕntang itu saya hĕndak bĕri tahu.*
I will inform you about that.

10. *Rumah—nya bĕrtĕntang dĕngan kĕdai kopi yang bĕsar itu.*
His house is opposite the big coffee-shop.

11. *Kaki budak itu kotor hingga lutut.*
The child's legs are dirty right up to the knees.

12. *Dia tidor sampai pukul sĕmbilan.*
He slept until 9 o'clock.

13. *Di—antara rumah dĕngan sungai ada pagar.*
Between the house and the river there is a fence.

14. *Hanya dua biji tĕlor sahaja yang pĕchah.*
Only two eggs are broken.

15. *Sĕmua tukang ada, mĕlainkan dia sa—orang yang ta' ada.*
All the workmen were present, except him.

Pĕrumpamaan.

Ringan tulang, bĕrat pĕrut.

Literally : When the bones are light, the stomach is heavy.
i.e. He who would eat must work.

Exercise 14.

Translate.

1. Di–těpi sungai ada sa–buah rumah yang elok.
2. Sorong kěrusi panjang itu ka–bělakang meja.
3. Pada suatu masa ada tiga ekor tikus dudok di–dalam sa–buah pěti yang běsar.
4. Bapa di–mana?—Dia kěluar tadi, hěndak ka–pasar.
5. Lěpas makan, ia masok tidor.
6. Ada halaman běsar děpan rumah.
7. Ayer dalam tong itu kotor. Buangkan.
8. Těrlěbeh dahulu daripada itu saya tinggal di–Raub.
9. Tarek meja itu ka–sa–bělah těmpat tidor.
10. Apa khabar?—Khabar baik—'Nak ka–mana?—'Nak ka–pěkan.

Exercise 15.

Translate.

1. The dog ran behind the shed.
2. There is a low table in the middle of the room
3. The house is near the river.
4. I waited until 7 o'clock.
5. He likes bananas (say " likes to eat ").
6. The school is opposite the Land Office.
7. His shoes are larger than mine.
8. There are twenty five houses on the island.
9. Where is the basket?—It's on the chair.
10. The bench is between the door and the wall.

Conversation No. 2.

Kasehan Mat!

Ahmad : 'Mak ! 'Mak ! Mat[1] jatoh parit.[2] Sakit kaki Mat.

Mak. :   Kasehan ! Mari 'mak tengok. Tunjok di–mana
          sakit.

Ahmad :   Di–sini. Pada ibu jari. Mělechet.

Mak. :   Itu ta' měngapa. Mari–lah mak chuchikan
          děngan ayer hangat, kěmudian buboh ubat
          sadikit. Esok hilang–lah sakit. Lusa boleh
          běrlari[3].

Translation.

Poor Mat!

Ahmad :   Mother ! Mother ! I fell into the ditch. I've
          hurt my foot.

Mother : Poor darling ! Let me see it.   Show me where
          it hurts.

Ahmad :   Here. On my big toe. The skin's broken.

Mother : Oh, that's nothing.   Let me bathe it with hot
          water and then put some medicine on it.
          Tomorrow the pain will be gone, and the day
          after you will be able to run about again.

Notes.

1. *Mat* (short for *Ahmad*   The child uses his own name
   and for *Muhammad*)   instead of " I ".

2. *jatoh parit*   .   .   " Fell into . . ." Note omission
                               of preposition in conversational
                               style.

3. *boleh běrlari*   .   .   i.e. " *You* will be able . . ."
                               Again, note omission of pro-
                               noun. Personal pronouns of
                               the first and second person are
                               usually avoided.

CHAPTER VII

I. *Adverbs:* (a) *place* (b) *time* (c) *interrogation*
   (d) *degree* (e) *manner.*
II. *Formation of Adverbial expressions.*

VOCABULARY

Words included in the lists of adverbs are not included in this vocabulary unless the ground-word requires explanation. They are all to be found in the alphabetical vocabulary at the end.

kějap	. .	a wink
hadapan	. .	front
siang	. .	daylight
malam	. .	night, darkness
saat	. .	moment
jarang	. .	at wide intervals (of time, or space)
kěrap	. .	at frequent intervals (of time, or space)
kali	. .	time, occasion
baharu	. .	new
tua .	. .	old, of years deep (of colour)
muda	. .	young, pale (of colour)
macham	.	} sort, kind
jěnis	.	
sěbab	. .	reason
harus	. .	current, stream
baji	. .	wedge
pagi	. .	morning
pětang	. .	early evening, afternoon
mula	. .	beginning
duit	. .	money, small change

děmam	.	.	. fever
kaseh	.	.	. love
kasehan	.	.	. pity
těrima kaseh	.		. thank you
běnang	.	.	. thread

kanan	.	.	. right
kiri .	.	.	. left
habis	.	.	. finished, used up
běnar	.	.	. true, correct
sunggoh	.	.	. true, genuine
děras	.	.	. swift
kuat	.	.	. strong, powerful
sěnang	.	.	. easy, comfortable
mudah	.	.	. easy
susah	.	.	. difficult, troublesome
rapat	.	.	. close to, against
chěrmat	.	.	. careful, tidy, neat
lambat	.	.	. slow
jauh	.	.	. distant
tumpul	.	.	. blunt

bělah	.	.	. split
běrjalan[16] .		.	. to go, travel
běrjalan kaki	.		. to walk
bělajar	.	.	. learn
pěrgi	.	.	. to go
chabut	.	.	. pull out
lipat	.	.	. fold
buka	.	.	. open
tutup	.	.	. shut
děngar	.	.	. hear
těrima	.	.	. receive
bagai	.	.	. like, as
sěngaja (*or* sahaja)		.	. purposely
lěkas	.	.	. quickly, immediately

[16] See par. 123e.

I. Adverbs.

Par. 65.

Lists given in this chapter are intended for reference only. It will be seen that many of the words have already occurred as other parts of speech. It cannot be too often emphasized that the Malay word is not a fixed part of speech but the embodiment of an idea. The function of a word in a particular sentence is decided by the context.

(a) Adverbs of place.

Par. 66.

Most of these have already occurred in combination with the locative prepositions. All the compound place-prepositions given in par. 61 become place-adverbs when they are not followed by nouns.

Examples:

1. *Nanti di–bawah, sa–kějap lagi saya turun.*
   Wait downstairs, I'll be down in a moment.

2. *Dia lari ka–děpan.*
   He ran forward.

3. *Simpan kěreta di–bělakang.*
   Leave the car at the back.

   (N.B. *di–balek* cannot be used in this way. It is always prepositional i.e. it must always be followed by a noun. e.g. *di–balek rumah*—behind the house).

Other adverbs of place are :

jauh . . . far	
děkat . . . near	
barang di–mana . anywhere	
rata–rata . . . everywhere	
sa–bělah měnyabělah. on both sides	
sa–bělah kanan (kiri) . on the right (left)	

(b) Adverbs of Time.

Par. 67.

The following is a list of time words and phrases.   For longer expressions of time, see par. 193.

sĕkarang . . .	now; presently
sĕkarang ini . .	now, at this moment
kĕmudian (*usually pronounced* kĕmdian) ⎫ lĕpas itu . . ⎬ then, afterwards sa–tĕlah itu . (*written*) ⎭	
dahulu . . .	before, previously
kalmarin (*usually pronounced* kĕmarin) .	yesterday (*sometimes* a little time ago)
kalmarin dahulu .	the day before yesterday
sa–malam . .	yesterday, last night, the night before last (See footnote 77)
tadi . . .	just now
pagi ini . . ⎫ pagi tadi . . ⎬ this morning	
malam tadi . ⎫ malam sa–malam ⎬ last night	
hari ini . . .	today
malam ini . ⎫ malam sĕkarang ⎬ tonight (*usually pronounced* 'karang)	
esok (*or* besok) . .	tomorrow ; in the future
lusa . . .	the day after tomorrow
tulat . . .	two days ahead
sĕgĕra . . .	soon, quickly
saat lagi . ⎫ sa–bĕntar lagi . ⎬ presently, in a moment sa–kĕjap lagi . ⎭	
bĕlum . . .	not yet

kadang–kadang	.	sometimes
sělalu . .	.	always; constantly, habitually; immediately (E. coast)
sěntiasa . .	.	always
ta' pěrnah .	.	never
pěrnah? . .	.	ever? (as interrogative, but often used positively in modern Malay)
jarang . .	.	seldom
kěrap kali .	.	often
sa–kali . .	.	at one time, altogether
sa–kali sa–kali .	.	occasionally
dua kali . .	.	twice
siang . .	.	by day
malam . .	.	by night
baharu . .	.	only now, only then, i.e. not until, only just; (usually with *sahaja*) as soon as (see footnote 29)
lama . .	.	for a long time

(c) Adverbs of interrogation.

Para. 68.

bila? . .	.	when?
di–mana? (ka–, dari)	.	where? (whither? whence?)
sa–bělah mana?	.	where?
'tang mana? .	.	whereabouts?
(i.e. těntang mana?)		
bagai–mana? .	} how?	
macham mana?		
apa sěbab? .		
apa fasal? (*or* pasal)		
awat? (i.e. apa buat)	} why?	
buat apa? .		
měngapa? .		
kěnapa? .		

(d) Adverbs of degree.

Par. 69.

tĕrlampau ⎱ *before* tĕrlalu ⎰ *the word qualified*	very, too
sa-kali . . (*after the word*)	very, most of all, very much, exceedingly
sa-kali-kali (tidak)	(not) at all
bĕlaka . . (*after the word*)	completely, without exception
habis . . (*before the word*)	utterly, completely

amat   .   .
    (*before the word*)
 sangat   .   .
    (*before or after*) ⎰
	very, too

ta' bĕrapa	not very
kurang . .	less (*with an adjective,* " not ")
lĕbeh kurang .	more or less, approximately.
lagi . . .	more, still, also
bagini . . bagitu . . ⎰	thus, to such a degree
sa-(panjang) ini	as (long) as this
hampir . . dĕkat-dĕkat . ⎰	almost
sahaja, hanya .	only, merely, just
chuma (*usually with* sahaja) . .	only
istimewa (*written*)	especially
nĕschaya (*written*) tĕntu . . ⎰	certainly
bĕnar (*after the ad-* *jective it qualifies*)	truly, indeed
chukup (*before the ad-* *jective it qualifies*)	enough, sufficiently
sa-dikit (*or* sikit)	a little, rather

| barang kali | . | . perhaps |
| makin . . . makin | | . the more . . . the more |

lagi pula . . ⎫
dan lagi . . ⎬ moreover

itu pun (spoken) ⎫
di–dalam pada itu ⎬ nevertheless
  pun (written) ⎭

(e) Adverbs of manner.

Par. 70.

A descriptive adjective may be used as an adverb of manner without change of form.

Examples:

1. (a) adjective . *Harus sungai itu děras.*
                The current of the river is swift.

   (b) adverb   . *Kěreta běrjalan děras.*
                The car travels swiftly.

2. (a) adjective . *Tali ini kuat.*
                This rope is strong.

   (b) adverb   . *Tarek kuat.*
                Pull hard.

There are, however, many adverbial expressions compounded from other parts of speech. The simplest of them is formed by putting the preposition *děngan* before an adjective.

Examples:

1. *Děngan sěnang sahaja dia chabut baji itu.*
   He pulled out the wedge quite easily.

2. *Lipat kain meja itu děngan chěrmat.*
   Fold that table cloth neatly.

3. *Dia buat děngan sěngaja.*
   He is doing it purposely.

(Note. For adverbs of negation, see next Chapter.
           For the adverbs *juga, pun, pula* see Chapter **XVI**).

II. Formation of Adverbial Expressions.

Par. 71.

Although there is no adverbial termination in Malay, comparable to " –ly " in English, there are certain recognised methods of forming adverbial phrases from other parts of speech.

Most of these methods are illustrated by the examples given below.

The basic word is usually a noun or an adjective. This word is frequently duplicated and combined with one or more of the words *děngan, sa–* and *–nya*.

The construction is fluid, and the same root word will appear sometimes in one combination, sometimes in another. There is no need, therefore, to learn the phrases by heart. They are given here in order that they may be recognised in written Malay. For conversation the two simple forms given in par. 70 are preferable.

Examples of adverbial phrases:

a. *baik–baik* . . carefully, well
   jimat–jimat . . cautiously
   pagi–pagi . . early
   pětang–pětang . every afternoon, in the afternoon
   sia–sia
   chuma–chuma } in vain
   mula–mula . . to begin with, at first

b. *sa–běnar* . . truly
   sa–kali . . together, at once
   sa–mula . . over again (from the beginning)

c. *sa–kali–kali* . . exceedingly ; *after neg.* at all
   sa–hari–hari . every day
   sa–habis–habis . utterly

d. *sa–sunggoh–nya*
   sa–běnar–nya } genuinely, in all truth
   sa–baik–nya . . as well as possible

e. *sa–lĕkas–lĕkas–nya* . as quickly as possible
   sa–kurang–kurang–
     nya   . . at the very least
   sa–lambat–lambat–
     nya   . . at the very latest

f. *dĕngan   sa–boleh–*
    boleh–nya . . with all his might
   dĕngan   sa–bulat–
    bulat–hati–nya . with all his heart, in all sincerity

g. *dĕngan   sa–habis–*
    habis chĕrmat . as carefully as possible
   dĕngan   sa–kuat– with all his might, with great
    kuat hati . . determination
   dĕngan   sa–pĕnoh–
    pĕnoh harap . with the fullest confidence
   (much used in letters and
    petitions)

h. *dĕngan kĕras–nya* . harshly
   dĕngan mudah–nya . easily

i. *dĕngan sa–bĕntar* . in a moment, at once

Par. 72.

Note that some adverbs may be qualified by the demonstrative adjectives *ini* and *itu*.

Examples:

   sĕkarang ini   . . now, at this very moment
   sa–lama itu   . . all that time
   sa–lĕkas itu   . . as quickly as that; so quickly
   sa–jauh ini   . . as far as this
   dĕmikian itu   . . thus

This is not illogical, seeing that all the other formative words (*dĕngan*—a preposition, *sa–*—an adjective, *–nya*— a genitive pronoun, *hati*—a genitive noun) point to the substantive nature of the basic word of the adverbial phrase.

Cf. *sa–panjang malam* . The–unbroken–length of the
night. i.e. all night long.

Par. 73—Miscellaneous examples:

1. *Dia baharu bĕlajar bacha.*
   He is only just learning to read.

2. *Pĕti itu sampai sahaja, dia buka*[17].
   He opened the box as soon as it arrived.

3. *Baharu sahaja saya tahu di–mana dia tinggal.*
   I have only just learned where he lives.

4. *Ini–lah rumah tĕmpat*[18] *saya dudok pada masa itu.*
   This is the house where[18] I lived at that time.

5. *Saya nanti tiga hari, baharu–lah dia datang.*
   I waited three days before he turned up.

6. *Budak itu jahat. Makin tua makin kĕras hati*[19].
   He is a naughty boy. The older he grows the more
   obstinate he becomes.

7. *Mĕngapa susah hati ?*[19]—*Sĕbab duit saya*[20] *hilang.*
   Why are you sad ?—Because I have lost my money.
   (lit. " Because my money is missing ").

8. *Kĕras sangat roti ini. Pisau pun tumpul. Sĕbab itu
   lambat saya potong.*
   The bread is very hard, and the knife is blunt, too.
   That's why I am so slow.

9. *Chakap kuat sadikit. Saya ta' dĕngar.*
   Speak a little louder. I can't hear you.

10. *Orang sudah balek bĕlaka.*
    Everybody has gone home.

[17] Notice the omission of the pronoun object.

[18] Note that *di–mana?*—" Where ? " is the interrogative form only.
(including indirect questions as in sentence 3) " Where " as an adverbial
relative, as in sentence 4, is always rendered by *tempat* (see par. 155 and
footnote 63). So, also, " when ", as an adverbial relative, meaning " the
time when ", is *waktu* or *masa*, not *bila*. For " where " used as connecting relative see Footnote 63.

[19] Notice compound words as they occur. Some of them will be found
under the appropriate words in the alphabetical vocabulary, but many
of them can be understood without explanation.

[20] *Saya* is not the subject of *hilang.* It is genitive, depending on *duit*

11. *Habis kĕrja, datang dĕngan sĕgĕra.*
As soon as you have finished your work, come as quickly as you can.

12. *Chuma dia sa-orang sahaja yang pĕrgi.*
He was the only one who went.

Pĕrumpamaan :

Malu bĕrtanya, sĕsat jalan.

If you are shy about asking, you'll lose your way.

Exercise 16.

1. Anak Aishah tiga orang dĕmam bĕlaka.
2. Kalmarin saya tĕrima surat dua puchok.
3. Nanti dahulu. Sa-bĕntar lagi saya pĕrgi ka-pĕkan.
4. Lambat sangat dia bĕrjalan. Barang kali sakit kaki.
5. Kĕrap kali dia datang ka-rumah saya.
6. Di-tĕpi jalan ada sa-buah rumah yang kosong, sa-bĕlah mĕnyabĕlah-nya ada parit batu.
7. Kain itu lipat baik-baik, kĕmudian baharu simpan dalam pĕti.
8. Kĕrtas ta' ada. Bagai-mana 'nak tulis surat?
9. Bĕnang ini ta'bĕrapa kuat, sĕlalu sahaja putus.
10. Jarum 'dah (i.e. sudah) patah. Macham mana 'nak jahit?

Exercise 17.

1. At this moment he is sitting on a bench at the edge of the river.
2. I don't often go to Penang (*say* " seldom ").
3. Don't go too fast. There's a ditch on each side.
4. He has only just come home.
5. This is the shop where I buy (my) fish.
6. Why is this table close against the wall ? Pull it a bit towards the middle.
7. Split this piece of wood (and) make two wedges.
8. Don't (be so) noisy. I want to sleep.
9. I don't know where she lives.

10. Yesterday I gave him a piece of cloth as long as this. Today he is asking for some more.

Conversation No. 3.

Di-Pasar.

Halijah :   Saya 'nak[1] běli kělapa.

Pěnjual :   Ada yang elok[2] ini.

Halijah :   Ta' mahu yang itu. Běsar sangat[3]. Běrapa harga kělapa ini ?

Pěnjual :   Lima sen sa–biji[4].

Halijah :   Mahal–lah itu. Di–kědai China, dapat[5] tiga sen sa–biji.

Pěnjual :   Kělapa kědai China itu ta' baik. Sudah lama.

Halijah :   Ěmpat sen saya běli sa–puloh biji[6].

Pěnjual :   Ambil–lah sa–puloh biji ěmpat puloh lima sen.

Halijah :   Ta' mahu[7]. Ěmpat sen sa–biji, lěbeh ta' mahu.

Pěnjual :   Ta' apa. Apa ěnche' 'nak běli lagi ?

Halijah :   Pisang apa itu ?

Pěnjual :   Pisang mas, pisang tandok, dua jěnis.

Halijah :   Pisang mas itu běrapa sa–sikat ?

Pěnjual :   Lima sen. Ěnam sikat, dua puloh lima sen.

Halijah :   Baik–lah. Saya ambil ěnam sikat. Pisang tandok itu sědap di–goreng agak–nya.

Pěnjual :   Sědap–lah ěnche' ! Mahal sadikit. Tiga sen sa–biji. Běsar sa–kali.

Halijah :   Mahal sangat. Ta' mahu–lah. Běli lain kali. Běrapa sěmua tadi ?

Pěnjual :   Kělapa ěmpat puloh sen. Pisang mas dua puloh lima sen. Ěnam puloh lima sen sěmua ěnche' !

Halijah :   Nah ! sa–ringgit, tolong tukar.

Pěnjual : Pulang[8] tiga–puloh lima sen, ěnche.

Halijah : Těrima kaseh.

In the Market

Halijah : I want to buy some coconuts.

Salesman : I have some fine ones (Lit. " There are (here) these fine ones ").

Halijah : I don't want those. They are very big. What's the price of these ?

Salesman : Five cents each.

Halijah : That's dear. In the Chinese shop you can get them for three cents each.

Salesman : The coconuts in the Chinese shop are not good. They are old.

Halijah : I'll buy ten, if you'll give me them at four cents.

Salesman : Take them. Ten for 45 cents.

Halijah : No. Four cents each, I won't give more.

Salesman : Very well. What else do you want to buy ?

Halijah : What bananas are those ?

Salesman : Golden bananas, and horn bananas, two sorts.

Halijah : How much are these golden bananas a bunch ? (Lit. a comb.)

Salesman : Five cents. Six bunches for 25 cents.

Halijah : Very well. I'll take six bunches. Those horn bananas would taste good if they were fried I should think ?

Salesman : Very good. They are rather dear. Three cents each. But they are very big.

Halijah : That's very dear. No, I won't have any of those. Another time. How much was all that, just now ?

Salesman : The coconuts 40 cents. The golden bananas
25 cents. That's 65 cents altogether.

Halijah : There you are. There's a dollar, change it for
me will you ?

Salesman : That's 35 cents change.

Halijah : Thank you.

Notes.

1. 'nak . . .	Short for *hĕndak*.
2. yang elok . .	For *yang* as the equivalent of the English expression " one " or " ones ". see par. 154.
3. Bĕsar sangat.	" They are very big ". Note omission of pronoun.
4. lima sen sa–biji .	The numeral coefficient is the usual equivalent for English " so much *each* ".
5. dapat . .	For " You can buy them ". This " general 2nd person ", which is so common in English, is never used in Malay. When a pronoun is necessary in such a sentence *kita* is used (see par. 85 and p. 237). The *dapat* here may be thought of as passive " They are obtained ", or more likely, a verbal noun " There is getting of them ".
6. sa–puloh biji .	" Ten ". The coefficient is always used with the numeral when the noun is omitted.
7. ta' mahu .	For " answers ", see par. 91.
8. pulang . .	Note that *pulang* is used here of the money returning to its original place.

CHAPTER VIII

VOCABULARY.

pĕnghulu	. .	headman
bola	. .	ball
buaya	. .	crocodile
kampong	. .	gathering ; homestead ; village
nasi	. .	cooked rice
bĕras	. .	husked rice
padi	. .	rice, unhusked
ubi	. .	tuberous root
ubi kĕntang	.	potato
wayang	. .	a theatrical performance
juru	. .	a skilled workman
bahasa	. .	language ; courtesy
juru bahasa	.	interpreter
bichara	. .	discussion ; court case
rantai	. .	chain
hujan	. .	rain
ayam	. .	fowl
daging	. .	meat, flesh
dĕnda	. .	a fine
ringgit	. .	dollar
topi	. .	hat
almari	. .	cupboard
gunting	. .	scissors, to cut with scissors
kabut	. .	haze, hazy

ĕmbun	.	.	dew
kapal	.	.	ship
wang	.	.	money
kĕrani	.	.	clerk
kita	.	.	we (including the listener)
awak	.	.	you
jam	.	.	watch, clock
paku	.	.	nail, spike
busok	.	.	rotten, decayed
malas	.	.	lazy, reluctant
sĕdar	.	.	conscious (of), aware
takut	.	.	frightened
hidup	.	.	alive
burok	.	.	worn out, shabby
halus	.	.	fine, delicate
bimbang	.	.	anxious
payah	.	.	difficult
gĕlap	.	.	dark, obscure
sĕjuk	.	.	cold
rosak	.	.	spoilt, out of order
lewat	.	.	late, unpunctual
marah	.	.	angry
suam	.	.	lukewarm
kĕring	.	.	dry
basah	.	.	wet
bisu	.	.	dumb
bising	.	.	noisy
tĕrok	.	.	severe, of illness
rĕput	.	.	rotten, crumbling
Hindu	.	.	Indian
bodoh	.	.	stupid
hangat	.	.	hot
binasa	.	.	ruined, spoilt
nampak	.	.	be visible, catch sight of, see

tengok	. .	look at
main	. .	play
boleh	. .	can, be able
běla	. .	bring up ; look after
sudah	. .	completed, finished (*as auxiliary* has, had).
masak	. .	cook, cooked, ripe
lengah *or* lenga	.	loiter
tolak	. .	push aside
běrtolak	. .	set out
isi .	. .	contents
gulai	. .	curry
jadi	. .,	become
kěna	. .	make contact, incur
měmbaiki	.	mend
aleh	. .	move, shift
luka	. .	wound
bangun	. .	get up
chakap	. .	speech ; *běrchakap* ; speak
basoh	. .	wash
pakai	. .	wear, use

I. Negative Adverbs

Par. 74—Tidak.

Tidak (not) has already been used.

The abbreviation *ta'* (pronounced, and sometimes written *tak* [21]) is commonly used in conversation before adjectives and sometimes before verbs.

Tidak negatives the whole statement. It merely denies it, without implying the contradiction of an opposite statement or thought. (Contrast *bukan* par. 75).

[21] *'Dak* is another form of abbreviation, used colloquially, as a one-word answer.

Example :

Mat 'nak main bola pĕtang 'karang ?'—'Dak. Ada kĕrja.

Are you going to play football this evening, Mat ? No, I've some work to do.

Examples.

1. *Pěnghulu tidak*   The *penghulu* did not come
   datang sa–malam.   yesterday.

2. *Bapa tidak běri tahu.*   My father didn't tell me.

3. *Gunong itu ta'*   The mountain cannot be seen
   nampak dari sini.   from here.

4. *Buah nanas ini*   These pineapples are no good.
   ta' baik. Sudah busok.   They are rotten.

Par. 75—Bukan.

Bukan generally negatives one word only, and implies a contradiction of, or an alternative to, a previous statement, question or thought. It is essentially emphatic. The word which it qualifies comes immediately after it.

Examples.

1. *Baju–nya merah —*   His coat is red—No, it's green.
   Bukan merah. Hijau.

2. *Bukan jahat, dia*   He isn't wicked, he's lazy.
          malas.

3. *Bukan dia yang*   It wasn't he who came, it was
   datang. Abang–nya.   his brother.

4. *Bukan ěmak saya*   It is not my mother who is
   yang sakit. Ěmak   ill, but his.
   dia.

In a negative question, *tidak* asks for information, *bukan* asks for confirmation.

Examples.

1. *Běnar, tidak ?*   (With a falling intonation).
   Is that true or is it not ?   (I want to know).

2. *Běnar, bukan ?*   (With a rising intonation).
   It's true, isn't it ?   (You know it is).

Bukan sometimes has the enclitic *–nya* attached to it.
D*

Examples.

1. *Bukan–nya saya ta' sĕdar.*	It wasn't that I didn't realize it. (Far from it !).
2. *Mari tengok buaya.* *Mĕngapa takut ?—* *Bukan–nya hidup.*	Come and look at the crocodile. Why are you frightened ? It isn't alive. (It isn't as if it were alive).

Note that in such sentences the *bukan* does not qualify one particular word. It is itself the subject of the sentence, with the whole of the rest of the sentence as complement : " The ' notness ' of it is—that I failed to realize it."

Par. 76—Tiada, t'ada, ta'ada.

Tiada, a literary form, is equivalent either to (a) *tidak* (not), or to (b) *tidak ada* (is not, are not).

When it is the equivalent of *tidak* it is represented in the colloquial language by the form *t'ada.* e.g.

> *Dia t'ada kata apa-apa.*
> He didn't say anything.

When it is the equivalent of *tidak ada* it is represented in the colloquial language by the form *ta' ada.* e.g.

> *Ta' ada rumah bĕsar di–kampong itu.*
> There are no large houses in that village.

Note the following phrases, used in written as well as spoken Malay.

ta' dapat tidak *ta' dapat tiada* *ta' boleh tidak* *ta' boleh tiada*	lit. " cannot not " i.e. must, cannot help but, certainly.
tidak apa (lit. there is not anything) *tid' apa* *ta' apa* } colloquial	Very well ! (but used by the Malays in a much wider variety of circumstances than the corresponding phrase in English).

Examples.

1. *Kalau tidak bĕla rumah, ta'dapat tiada lĕkas burok.*
   If you don't look after your house, it is bound to fall into disrepair before very long.

2. *Ta' apa—lah. Esok saya datang.*
   Very well. I'll come to-morrow.

Par. 77—Bĕlum.

Bĕlum (usually in conjunction with *lagi*) means "not yet" but it is used much more frequently than that expression is in English. It is used whenever there is the possibility of the negative being turned to a positive.

Examples.

1. *Bapa sudah sampai ka–Singapura ?*
   —Bĕlum tahu lagi.

   Has your father reached Singapore ?—I don't know.

2. *Sudah dia²² datang ?*
   —Bĕlum. Dia lambat. Barang kali sakit.

   Has he come?—No. He's late. Perhaps he is ill.

3. *Saya bĕlum pĕrnah tengok kĕrtas sa-halus ini.*

   I have never seen such fine paper as this.

4. *Nasi sudah masak ?*
   —Bĕlum lagi.

   Is the rice cooked ?—Not yet.

II. Prohibitions and Commands.

Par. 78—Jangan.

Jangan ("Don't") expresses a prohibition.

Example.

Jangan minta gula.
Gula ta'ada.

Don't ask for sugar. There isn't any.

²² See paragraph 83.

The brusqueness of a direct prohibition is frequently softened by the addition of the enclitic *–lah*.

Example.

Pĕrgi ka–pasar, bĕli ubi kĕntang.   Jangan–lah lengah.
Go to the market for some potatoes.   Now don't loiter.

Jangan sa–kali–kali is a very strong form of prohibition.

Example.

Jangan sa–kali–kali aleh tong sampah itu.
Don't move that rubbish bin whatever you do.

A very strong positive command is expressed by *jangan tidak* (lit. "don't not"), or *jangan tidak–tidak*, or *jangan tiada*.

Example.

Habis kĕrja jangan tidak pulang lĕkas.
When you have finished your work, be sure to go home as quickly as you can.

Note that *jangan* is used not only for a direct prohibition (i.e. "don't") but also for an indirect prohibition (i.e. "in order that . . . not" or "not to . . .").

Examples.

1. *Katakan adek jangan dia pĕrgi jauh.*
   Tell your sister not to go far.

2. *Suroh dia lĕkas balek jangan kita lambat bĕrtolak.*
   Tell him to come back at once, so that we shan't be late setting out.

3. *Jangan dia bising.   Ĕmak –nya sakit tĕrok.*
   Don't let them make a noise. Their mother is seriously ill.

Note that *jangan* is used also as the equivalent of an optative (or subjunctive–of–wish) as in "God save the King".

Examples

1. *Jangan kita těrlewat sampai.*
   I hope we shan't arrive too late (lit. May it not be that . . .).

2. *Jangan ta' ada gula lagi, ta'.*
   I hope there's some sugar left !

Par. 79.

Other less peremptory prohibitions in frequent use are :

ta' payah . . " don't trouble to ".
ta' usah . . " there is no need to ".
(sometimes *usah*)

Examples.

1. *Ta' payah měnulis surat sěkarang ini ; esok pun boleh.*
   Don't bother about writing the letter immediately, later will do.

2. *Ta' usah-lah bimbang. Anak ta' běrapa sakit.*
   Don't be anxious.   Your child is not very ill.

Par. 80.

In the same way a positive command is frequently put in the form of a suggestion, introduced by the word *Baik,* or *Elok* (" it would be well to "), or *Boleh* (" can " or "may").

Examples.

1. *Baik Esah pulang. Sudah jauh malam.*
   You had better go home, Esah.   It's late.

2. *Elok-lah Hashim makan nasi sěkarang. Sa-běntar lagi kita běrtolak.*
   Have your meal now, Hashim.   We shall be going soon.

3. *Boleh Mat simpan kěreta.*
   Put the car away, Mat.

Mari is used to introduce suggestions of this sort which include the speaker.

Example.

Mari kita pĕrgi tengok wayang gĕlap.
Let's go to the cinema.

Par. 81.

The expression *hĕndak–lah*, at the beginning of a sentence, is a polite command expressed as a wish. It is frequently employed in public notices.

Examples.

1. *Hĕndak–lah orang sakit masok pintu yang di–bĕlakang.*
   Patients are requested to enter by the door at the back.

2. *Hĕndak–lah pĕnghulu bĕri tahu kapada anak kampong bahawa nasi dĕngan gulai boleh di–dapati dĕngan pĕrchuma di–sĕkolah Mĕlayu.*
   Please inform the villagers that curry and rice are supplied, free of charge, at the vernacular school.

The more colloquial expression *mahu–lah* is used in the same way.

III. " Jadi " and " Kĕna."
Par. 82.

The words *jadi* and *kĕna* are very common in the spoken language.

Note the following idiomatic uses.

Jadi

1. *Bapa–nya jadi juru bahasa dalam bichara itu.*
   His father acted as interpreter in the case.

2. *Hari hujan.   Ta' jadi kita bĕrjalan.*
   It is raining.   We shan't be able to go for a walk

3. *Saya lambat balek, jadi nasi sĕjuk.*
   I arrived home late, and so (it came about that) my food was cold.

4. *Tujoh–bĕlas lagi lima jadi dua–puloh dua.*
Seventeen and five make twenty-two.

5. *Yang di–sangka tiada mĕnjadi.* (Prov.).
It is the unexpected that happens.
(Lit. " What is thought-of does not come to pass).

6. *Pĕkan ini tĕmpat saya jadi.*
I was born in this town.

Kĕna

1. *Dia kĕna²³ dĕnda dua–puloh ringgit.*
He was fined $20.

2. *Kain baju habis basah kĕna hujan.*
My clothes are soaking wet, I was caught in the rain.
(lit. They incurred rain).

3. *Jikalau lewat sampai, tĕntu kĕna marah.*
If we are late arriving, they'll surely be angry with
us. (lit. we shall incur anger).

4. *Meja ini kaki–nya 'dah patah; kĕna panggil tukang kayu.*
The leg of this table is broken, I shall have to get the
carpenter to mend it.

5. *Kain saya sudah koyak, kĕna paku.*
My sarong is torn ; I caught it on a nail.

6. *Baju–nya ta' kĕna dĕngan kain–nya.*
His coat does not go well with his sarong.

7. *Si–Hasan ada kĕna–mĕngĕna dĕngan saya.*
Hasan is related to me.

8. *Awak ta' ada kĕna–mĕngĕna dĕngan hal ini, jadi awak
jangan champor tangan.*
You are not concerned in this affair, so don't
interfere.

²³ Note that this construction with *kĕna* is a common equivalent of
an English passive verb, in conversational style, See footnote 34. For
the passive of the Malay verb, see Chapter XII. For *tĕrkena* meaning
" to be deceived ", see par. 131 B.3.

IV. Order of Words.

Para. 83.

a. The order of words in a Malay sentence is roughly the same as in an English sentence i.e. subject—verb—object. e.g.

    I called him . *Saya panggil dia.*

b. But since it is by position in the sentence that a Malay word receives emphasis, the usual order of " subject—verb—object " will be changed when the object is brought to the beginning of the sentence for that reason.

    Dia saya panggil.

    Him I called—i.e. It was he that I called.

See footnote 65 for literary examples.

Note that of two pronouns which precede a verb, the first is the object, the second the subject.

c. When there is an auxiliary or a modal verb the subject, if there is no emphasis on it, is frequently placed after the first of the two verbs, and thus made less obtrusive. (See Chap. IX). e.g.

    1. *Sudah dia datang*
       He has come.

    2. *Boleh saya buat.*
       I can do it.

d. A subject may be separated from its verb by an adverb of time. e.g.

    1. *Saya bělum tahu.*
       I do not yet know *or* I do not know.

    2. *Dia lagi tidor.*
       He is still sleeping.

    3. *Che' Din baharu kěluar.*
       Che' Din has just gone out.

e. An adverbial phrase of time usually precedes the verb, an adverbial phrase of place follows the verb.   e.g.

Lima tahun saya dudok di–nĕgĕri Siam.
I lived in Thailand for five years.

f. *Ada*, as a verb of existence, usually precedes its subject.   e.g.

Ada tujoh orang budak di–tĕpi sungai.
There are seven children by the river.

Pĕrumpamaan :
Pĕlĕpah di–bawah luroh, pĕlĕpah di–atas jangan tĕrtawa.
When the lower frond drops, let not the upper frond laugh. (Because its turn will come next).

Exercise 18.

1. Buah nanas itu bĕlum masak. Baik jangan makan.
2. Almari itu sudah burok sangat. Jangan aleh, takut kaki–nya rĕput.
3. Rumah pĕnghulu tidak jauh dari sini.
4. Jangan pakai ayer hangat, nanti warna turun.— Bukan–nya ayer hangat. Suam sahaja.
5. Jangan bĕri budak itu main gunting, nanti luka dia.
6. Pagi tadi saya bangun pukul ĕnam. Ĕmbun bĕlum kĕring lagi.
7. Halijah kĕna hujan, baju–nya habis basah.
8. Saya bĕlum pĕrnah naik kapal tĕrbang.
9. Lampu ini rosak, kĕna ganti.
10. Pokok ini pokok nyior ?—Bukan. Ini pokok pinang. Pokok nyior pĕlĕpah–nya panjang.
11. Simpan pĕti di–dalam almari. Ta' payah mĕmbuka. (see par 119c).
12. Orang Hindu ini bisu ? —Bukan–nya bisu. Dia ta' tahu chakap Mĕlayu.

13. Adek di–mana? Saya 'nak suroh dia pĕrgi bĕli ikan. Bagi dia wang lima puloh sen ini. Jangan dia lengah.

14. Besok jangan lewat datang. Kĕrja banyak. Kĕrani bĕsar sakit.

15. Hari hujan. Tidak dapat main bola.

16. Dia bĕlum datang lagi. Kita 'nak nanti–kah tidak ?

17. Emak 'Long kata jangan mandi di–sungai. Ayeı sungai dĕkat kampong itu tidak bĕrseh.

18. Hari sudah malam. Baik kita pulang.

Exercise 19.

1. I don't like sour fruit.

2. There are no crocodiles in this river.

3. Don't bother to wash that coat. It isn't really dirty. I only wore it for an hour or two.

4. He is very stupid.—It isn't that he's stupid, he's lazy.

5. He is asking for money. Had I better give it him, or not ?

6. This table won't do. It is too low. We shall have to look for another.

7. Has he come ?—I don't know. I'll go and ask the clerk.

8. I want to make a bench. Is there any wood ? (No), there is not.

9. I have only just come to this town, so I don't know the names of the shop-keepers.

10. My wrist-watch is broken—Never mind. I'll lend you mine. I have another one.

Conversation No. 4.

Di-kampong Mĕlayu.

Munah : Mari tolong aku basoh kain.

Esah :   Di–mana ? Pĕrigi di–bĕlakang rumah itu
           ayer[1]–nya kĕroh.

Munah :   Mari kita mĕmbasoh[2] di–pĕrigi dĕkat bukit.

Esah :   Ta' takut–kah ? Sa–malam kata Pa' Busu dia
           jumpa kĕsan rimau di–situ.

Munah :   Bohong–lah itu. Sahaja dia 'nak mĕnakutkan[3]
           kita.

Esah :   Kalau ĕngkau[4] hĕndak mĕngajak[3] aku mĕm-
           basoh kain[5], baik kita pĕrgi siang–siang.
           Pĕtang ini aku[4] kĕna tolong Mak 'Ngah[6]
           mĕnumbok[7] padi.

Munah :   Baik–lah. Biar kita ajak adek aku si[4]–Kasim
           buat tĕman[8]. Dia pun[9] ta' ada kĕrja. Sĕkolah
           sudah tutup.

Esah :   Tunggu–lah sa–kĕjap, aku 'nak balek bĕri
           tahu ĕmak.

Translation.
A Village Scene

Munah :   Come and help me wash clothes.

Esah :   Where ?   The well behind the house is muddy.

Munah :   Let's go and do it at the well near the hill.

Esah :   Aren't you afraid ? Pa Busu says that he
           saw traces of tiger there yesterday.

Munah :   That's a fib. He just wants to frighten us.

Esah :   If you want me to help you wash, we had better
           go early in the morning. This evening I have
           to help Ma 'Ngah pound rice.

Munah :   Very well. Let's ask my brother Kasim to go
           with us. He hasn't anything to do. His
           school is closed.

Esah :   Wait a second.   I'll go back and let my mother
           know.

E

Notes.

1. pĕrigi . . . ayer–nya Notice the turn of phrase. "That well . . . the water of it is . . .". So *Budak itu rambut-nya panjang.*—"That child's hair is long". The whole is mentioned before the part. Cf. Ex. 18. 10.

2. mĕmbasoh . . For this verbal prefix see Chapter XII.

3. mĕnakutkan . . From *takut* and *ajak* respectively. mĕngajak The same verbal prefix.

4. ĕngkau, aku, si– . See next chapter.

5. kalau . . . kain . Lit. "If you are going to invite me to wash".

6. Mak 'Ngah . . *'Ngah* is short for *tĕngah*. *Mak 'Ngah* is a title for an aunt who comes second in the family. Practise pronouncing this abbreviation. There is no "n" or "ny" sound in it. It begins with the "–ng" of "singer".

7. mĕnumbok . . From *tumbok*. The same prefix again.

8. buat tĕman . . Notice this colloquial use of *buat*, "as a companion".

9. pun .   . . See para. 150. The "balance" in this case is between the girls being busy, and the boy being on holiday.

CHAPTER IX

I. *Personal Pronouns*
II. *Questions*
III. *Answers*
IV. *Requests*

VOCABULARY

datok; dato' . .	grandfather, chief, (mod.) a title of distinction
kĕnyataan . .	notice, announcement
guru . . .	teacher
murid *or* anak murid .	pupil
pĕlandok . .	mousedeer
gĕtah . . .	rubber
bangsal . .	shed
ayah . . .	1. father (polite)
	2. children's nurse, Malay or Indian (bazaar).
draiber . .	driver (car)
sais	groom (horse)
api . . .	fire
garam . .	salt
pĕlita . .	lamp
amah . . .	children's nurse, Chinese
kathi (kadzi, kadi)	judge (in Muslim law)
hakim . .	judge (High Court)
kawan . .	1. friend 2. flock
minyak . .	oil, fat
(buah) limau .	limes
chuchu . .	grandchild

masjid (*or* mĕsjid) . . mosque
duri . . . thorn

mati . . . dead ; stopped (of clock etc.)
mĕngantok . . sleepy
liat . . . tough
bĕtul . . . true, straight
banyak . . . many, much
lain . . . other, different
ta' sĕnang . . busy
panas . . . hot
layu . . . faded (of flowers or plants)
mana ? . . . which ?
salah . . . wrong

kĕluar(kan) . . put out, issue
siap . . . ready, make ready
tĕnggĕlam . . to sink
kĕnal . . . recognise, be acquainted with
hĕrti (*or* ĕrti *or* rĕti) . understand
pĕreksa . . . examine
tĕrangkan . . to make clear
bĕlayar . . . to sail
biar . . . allow, let
ajak . . . invite (somebody to do something)
tangkap . . . catch, capture
singgah . . . call in at (a place)
jumpa   }
bĕrjumpa }   . . come across, meet
padam . . . go out, be extinguished
padamkan . . put out, extinguish
panggil . . . call, summon
kasi (*bazaar*) . . give
bangun . . . get up

sa–bĕrang . . on the other bank (of a river)

I. Personal Pronouns

Par. 84.

Personal pronouns are used less in Malay than they are in English. They are frequently omitted if the meaning is clear without them.

Examples.

1. *Mahu jual kěreta ini ?—Mahu.*   Do (you) want to sell this car ? —Yes (I) do.

2. *Bapa ada lagi?— Ada.*   Is (your) father alive ?—Yes. (He) is.

Par. 85.

Below are given those personal pronouns most commonly in use. Nearly all of them may be either singular or plural. Several of them are substantives which have come to be used as pronouns. There is a wide diversity of usage according to locality.

First person singular[24]. **I, me**   *aku* (for abbreviated forms *–ku* and *ku–* see par. 173 and 178.) Malays, familiarly, to each other.

Sahaya or *saya* (see vocab.) Malays and non-Malays.

First person plural . **We, us**   *kita* This pronoun includes the listener.

---

[24] Others are : *hamba* (lit. slave), *hamba tuan*, *hamba datok* (Malays, inferior to superior) ; *beta* (in letters) ; *patek* (Malay commoner to member of ruling house) ; *kami* (royal, editorial, ladies of high birth) ; *kita* ; *těman* ; *kawan*.

kami
This pronoun excludes the listener.

sahaya (or *saya*). In the plural it is usually combined with *sakalian* or *sĕmua*.

Second person singular and plural[25] . **You** *ĕngkau.*
Familiar. Superior to inferior. Abbreviations are *hang* and *kau.*

awak. To equals.

kamu (for abbreviation *–mu* see par. 173).
Malays to each other. Familiar. Older to younger. Superior to inferior.

tuan
Polite. (see next paragraph).

ĕnchek or *ĕnche'* (see next paragraph).
Polite. Malays to each other, and non-Malays to Malays.

Third person singular and plural. **He, she it, they, him, her, them** . . . *Ia, dia* (accusative and genitive) or titles. In conversation, *dia orang* is often used for " they "; in writing, *mĕreka* or *mĕreka itu* or *orang itu.*

[25] Other are: *mika; sahabat beta* (in letters, lit. " friend of me "); the royal titles, *ĕngku, tĕngku,* and *tuanku* (the last for a reigning prince only).

Par. 86.

A note on the uses of certain second person pronouns.—

(a) *Ĕnche'* is a courteous form of address to any Malay, man or woman, who does not possess a higher title. Before proper names and titles, it is usually shortened to *Che'*.

(b) *Tuan* is used before the name *Sayid* (a name borne by descendants of the Prophet), and before the title *Haji* (fem. *Hajjah*) a title given to one who has made the pilgrimage to Mecca. When the name or title is omitted, the form of address is *Tuan*. In modern Malay the word is coming into general use, with *puan* as a corresponding feminine form.

(c) *Taukeh* is a courteous form of address to a Chinese of some substance.
Nonya is used in speaking to a Chinese woman of the same status.
Occupational titles such as *tukang* (craftsman), *amah* (nurse), are commonly used as forms of address.

Par. 87.

All the words given in paragraph 86 are really noun-words. If the Malay verb were inflected to show " person ", the verbs that follow these would show third person endings, not second person endings. Malays avoid the use of a direct second person address.

Beside these pseudo-pronouns the following types of words are used as substitutes for second person pronouns.

a. Proper names.

b. Words indicating relationship, real or assumed, e.g. *'Mak* to an elderly woman. (Non-Malays should not, as a rule, use these.)

c. Titles.

d. Words indicating occupation.

The English vocative becomes the direct subject of the Malay verb. (i.e. " Can you hear, John ? " becomes " Does John hear ? ").

Examples.

1. (To Husain) . . *Husain mĕngantok?*
Are you sleepy, Husain ?

2. (Ahmad, to his *'Mak jangan marah. Bukan*
mother) *sĕngaja Mat buat.*
Don't be angry. I didn't do it purposely.

3. (To a penghulu) . *Hĕndak–lah dato' pĕnghulu kĕluarkan kĕnyataan.*
You must issue a notice.

4. (Houseboy, to his *Tuan lambat balek. Kĕreta rosak*
employer) *tĕngah jalan ?*
You are late back, sir. Did you have a breakdown on the way ?

5. (To Omar, a house- *Boleh Omar siap makan sĕkarang.*
boy) Serve dinner now, Omar.

6. (To a Malay of *Ada–kah ĕnche' kĕnal tuan rumah*
either sex) *ini ?*
Do you know the person who owns this house ?

7. (To a teacher) . *Baik che' guru suroh murid pulang.*
You had better tell your pupils to go home.

8. (To Saad) . . *Saad jangan lupa siapkan tanah liat itu.*
Don't forget to get the clay ready, Saad.

9. (To Aminah)   . *Che' Minah bĕlum hĕrti? Biar saya tĕrangkan sa–kali lagi.*
Don't you understand, Che' Minah? Let me explain it again. (lit. more, one time).

Par. 88—The prefix " si-".

This prefix, originally an article, is used before the names of persons and of animals, and before descriptive adjectives used as names of persons or animals.   It denotes :

a. friendly familiarity.

e.g. (from Conversation 4).

Biar kita ajak adek aku si–Kasim.
Let's ask " our " Kasim to come along.

b. contemptuous depreciation.   e.g.

si–pandai itu.
Mr. Cleversticks.

c. personification.   e.g.

si–pĕlandok.
Mr. Mousedeer.

d. a particular member of a class.   e.g.

si–pĕnjual.
the salesman.

si–sakit.
the patient.

Note also, the expressions *si–anu* and *si–polan* (or *si-fulan*)—" So and so ".

II. Questions

Par. 89.

The interrogative particle is *–kah*, attached to the word which demands an answer.

Examples.

1. *Baju hijau–kah mem 'nak pakai ?*
   Is it the green dress you are going to wear, Madam ?

2. *Banyak–kah pokok gĕtah dalam kĕbun itu ?*
   Are there many rubber trees on that estate ?

3. *Dia–kah yang mĕmbuat ?*
   Was it he who did it ?

4. *Bĕtul–kah dia 'dah bĕlayar ?*
   Is it true that he has sailed ?

N.B. As in English, a question is frequently conveyed by intonation only. e.g.

> *Dia yang mĕmbuat ?*
> Was it he who did it ?

Par. 90.

Interrogative pronouns and adverbs require no additional interrogative particle.

Examples.

1. *Bila ĕnche' hĕndak balek ?*
   When do you intend to return ?

2. *Apa salah ?*
   What's wrong ? (*sc.* " with the idea ".) *Hence* Why not ? or Very well.

3. *Macham mana 'nak buat ?*
   How am I to do it ?

4. *Bĕrapa banyak kapal dapat bĕrlaboh di–sini ?*
   How many ships can anchor here ?

5. *Apa sĕbab Mahmud ta' bacha kĕnyataan ?*
   Why didn't you read the notice, Mahmud ?

6. *Mana boleh ?*
   How can it be ? (i.e. Of course not !).

III. Answers

Par. 91.

The words *ya* (yes) and *tidak* (not, no), used alone as direct affirmation and negation are considered abrupt.

An answer is usually given by the repetition of a relevant word from the question.

The word *ĕntah* as an answer implies doubt, usually with regard to a choice between alternatives. It is familiar, and somewhat abrupt.

The adjectives *bĕtul, sunggoh, bĕnar*, with or without the enclitic particle *–lah*, are frequently used as affirmative answers, instead of *ya*.

Examples.

1. Question : *Orang sudah tangkap gajah itu ?*
   Did they catch the elephant ?

   Answer : *Sudah.*
   Yes, they did.

2. Question: *Enche' 'nak bĕli daging lĕmbu?*
   Do you want to buy some beef?

   Answer: *Hĕndak.*
   Yes, I do.

3. Question: *Daging lĕmbu–kah enche' 'nak bĕli itu?*[26]
   Is it beef that you want to buy?
   Is it beef that you want to buy ?

   Answer : *Daging lĕmbu.*
   Yes, beef.

4. Question : *Ada–kah chukup kayu buat bangsal ?*
   Have you enough wood to make a shed?

   Answer : *Ada*, or *Chukup.*

5. Question : *Ayah 'dah siap ayer mandi ?*
   Have you put the bath ready, Ayah ?

   Answer : *Sudah*, or *Siap.*

[26] Note the change of order. The word for " beef " is emphasized by its position at the beginning of the sentence.

6. Question: *Těnggělam–kah kapal api*[27] *itu?*
   Did the ship go down?

   Answer: *Tidak těnggělam.*
   No, it didn't.

7. Question: *Tukang kěbun sudah potong rumput di-
   bělakang rumah?*
   Have you cut the grass behind the house?

   Answer: *Sudah* or *Bělum lagi.*
   Yes, *or* No.

8. Question: *Azizah suka běrjalan kaki?*
   Do you like walking, Azizah?

   Answer: *Ta' běrapa suka.*
   No, not very much.

9. Question: *Draiber kěnal tuan*[28] *itu tadi?*
   Do you know that person (whom we saw
   just now)?

   Answer: *Kěnal.*
   Yes, I know him.

10. Question: *Rumah ini kosong–kah?*
    Is this house empty?

    Answer: *Êntah. Biar aku pěrgi tengok.*
    I don't know. I'll go and have a look.

11. Question: *Mat kěn' apa?* (i.e. *kěna apa*).
    What's wrong, Mat?

    Answer: *Kěna běsi duri.*
    I got caught in some barbed wire.

---

[27] *Kapal api*—lit. fire ship, i.e. steam-ship. Another compound noun.
[28] *tuan*—used here as a noun.
The words *taukeh* and *nonya* are sometimes used in the same way, but
the word *ěnche'* is never used as a common noun.

IV.   Requests

Par. 92.

A polite request may be introduced by one of the following words :

choba literally " try ".
tolong   ,,   " help ".
minta   ,,   " ask for ".
sila   ,,   " welcome ".

There is no Malay equivalent of the English phrase " will you ? ".

Examples.

1. *Choba buka pěti ini.*
   Open this box, please (*or* Open this box, will you).

2. *Tolong tunjok rumah to' pěnghulu.*
   Will you show me which is the headman's house, please ?

3. *Minta garam.*
   May I have some salt please?

4. *Sila masok.*
   Come in, please.

Tolong is frequently preceded by *minta* and sometimes by *choba*.

Sila ! is the usual form of invitation to eat, or drink, what has been served.

Pěrumpamaan.

   Hěndak sa–ribu daya, ta'hěndak sa–ribu upaya.
   Where there's a will there's a way.

Lit.   Wishing, a thousand schemes (for doing), not wishing, a thousand means (of avoiding).

Exercise 20—Translate

1. Apa khabar tuan haji ?—Khabar baik, tuan. Lama kita ta' bĕrjumpa.

2. Choba ayah padam pĕlita. Saya mĕngantok, 'nak tidor.

3. Omar boleh buang pokok bunga yang mati itu, ganti dĕngan lain.

4. Bapa jangan–lah marah. 'Ngah ta' dĕngar bapa panggil.

5. Tuan hĕndak singgah di–rumah Tuan Smith ?— Ta' usah. Hari ini ta' sĕnang. Besok draiber boleh kasi dia surat.

6. Ĕnche' sudah bawa tanah liat itu ?—Sudah.

7. Tukang jahit (*or* " derzi ") sudah gunting kain kuning itu ?—Sudah, mem.

8. Boleh–kah taukeh datang bĕrjumpa dĕngan saya di– tĕpi padang pukul tiga pĕtang ?—Boleh tuan.

9. Amah siap ayer mandi. Jangan–lah panas sangat.

10. Baik kita balek lĕkas–lĕkas. 'Mak kata jangan lewat.

11. Tolong tuan kathi nanti saya di–rumah tuan hakim.

12. Bila Mahmud dapat tahu ?—Baharu sa-kĕjap ini saya dĕngar.

13. Kĕbun apa taukeh mahu bĕli ? Nyior–kah, gĕtah ?

14. Tuan haji kĕnal abang Tuan Sayid Shaikh ?— Ta' kĕnal.

15. Bunga ini layu, baik buang. Ada-kah lain ?—Ada.

16. Hasan boleh pĕrgi pĕkan bĕli minyak gas—Mem.

17. Hai kawan! Ada-kah nampak sa-orang Hindu bĕrjalan naik basikal ?—Ta' nampak.

Exercise 21

1. Good morning Haji. You have come very early.

2. Call the prisoner.—He is present.—Where do you live ?—I live across the river, sir.—How old are you ?—I am eighteen.—Is your father living ?—Yes, sir.

3. Tell the cook to come in.—Good morning, Ma'am—Good morning, Cook. Did you get some fish at the market ?—No, madam. You told me to get meat.

4. (To a Malay) Could you please tell me which is the judge's house ? (use " where ").

5. Would you like a drink, Timah ?—Yes, please. Do you like lime squash ?—Yes, please.

6. (To a Chinese) You've a fine house. You have lived in Malaya a long time, I expect ? (say " certainly "). Do you often go back to China ?

7. (To Mat) Don't talk so fast. It is very difficult to understand you. I have only just come to this country.

8. Where is Che' Jid ?—He isn't up yet.

9. You can put the car away now Hasan.—Very well, sir.

10. (To an elderly Malay) Good evening, sir. Where are you going ?—I am going to my grandson's house. Is it far ?—Not very far. It's exactly opposite the mosque.

Conversation No. 5

Nyaris ta'kĕna

'Mak Teh. :   Allah ![1] Tĕngku. Patek tĕrpĕranjat[2] bĕnar tadi.

Tĕngku 'Ngah : Mĕngapa, Mak Teh ?

'Mak Teh.:   Nyaris–nyaris[3] patek ta'jadi " Aruah 'Mak Teh ".

Tĕngku 'Ngah :   Fasal apa ?

'Mak Teh.:   Ada siku di–simpang tiga dĕkat jel, bukan ?

Tĕngku 'Ngah :   Ada.

'Mak Teh.:   Patek tĕngah[4] bĕrlenggang[5] dĕngan bakul sireh sama mĕmikirkan[6] anak patek, Si–Omar, bĕlum balek dari Jĕram.

Tĕngku 'Ngah :   Kĕmudian ?

'Mak Teh.:   " Kĕrut, kĕrut," bunyi kĕreta. Bĕlum sĕmpat patek mĕnoleh [7] dia patah[8] masok Jalan Jel.

Tĕngku 'Ngah :   Habis itu ?

'Mak Teh.:   Apa   lagi ?   Patek   mĕlompat, tĕrpĕlanting[2] bakul   sireh,   patek tĕrtiarap[2].

Tĕngku 'Ngah :   La ilaha ila Allah ![1]

'Mak Teh.:   Roda dĕpan–nya mujor ta' mĕnindeh[9] tangan patek.

Tĕngku 'Ngah :   Nasib baik ! Takut hilang sĕmangat Mak Teh. Baik–lah baring sa–kĕjaᴅ di–atas kĕrusi panjang.

'Mak Teh.:   Ta' usah–lah, Tĕngku.   Biar patek balek.

Translation

A Narrow Shave

'Mak Teh.: My word, Tĕngku, I've just had a terrible fright !

Tĕngku :   How was that, Mak Teh ?

'Mak Teh. : It was only by the merest shave that I wasn't killed (literally, "that I did not become the ghost of Mak Teh ").

Těngku : Why ?

'Mak Teh. : Well, there's a sharp turn, isn't there, where the three roads meet, near the jail ?

Těngku : Yes.

'Mak Teh. : I was swinging along with my basket of sireh leaves, and thinking that my son Omar hadn't come back yet, from Jěram.

Těngku: And what happened ? (lit. "Then ? ").

'Mak Teh. : There was the crunching sound of a car. Before I had time to look round, it swung into Jail Road.

Těngku : And then ?

'Mak Teh. : Well. I gave a leap, my basket of sireh went bowling away, and I found myself flat on my face.

Těngku : Good heavens !

'Mak Teh. : The front wheel just missed going over my hand.

Těngku : That was luck ! But you must be feeling faint. You had better come in and lie on a long chair for a bit.

'Mak Teh. : No thank you, Těngku.   I'll be getting home.

Notes

1. Allah! .   .   . By no means as strong an expletive as is " My God ! " in English. That would be better rendered by the expression used further on *La ilaha ila Allah.* " There is no God but Allah."

2. tĕpĕranjat . . From *pĕranjat* (startled). For the prefix see par. 124b " accidental completion ". So, too, *tĕrpĕlanting* and *tĕrtiarap*, further on.

3. nyaris–nyaris . The duplication of the word is here intensive. See par. 104d. " the closest possible shave ".

4. tĕngah . . For this use of the word see par. 112d.

5. bĕrlenggang . . For the prefix *bĕr-* see par 123.

6. mĕmikir . . From *pikir*.

7. mĕnoleh . . From *toleh*.

8. patah . . . Note this colloquial use of *patah*— to turn off, usually at a right angle. Also *patah balek*—to turn back.

9. mĕnindeh . . From *tindeh.*

CHAPTER X

I. *Conjunctions*

II. *Impersonal Expressions*

VOCABULARY

pěnchuri	. .	thief
usaha	. .	diligence
pědang	. .	sword, scythe
kambing	. .	goat
haus	. .	1. thirst 2. worn away, consumed
buah pala	.	nutmeg, mace
ribut	. .	storm
pantai	. .	shore
hulu (*or* ulu)	.	upper part, usually of river valley
bunyi	. .	noise
harimau	. .	tiger
pělěpah	. .	palm frond
mata-mata	.	policeman
manggis	. .	mangosteen
chiku	. .	sapodilla
rupa	. .	appearance
umor	. .	age
sědap	. .	pleasant ; good to taste
měntah	. .	raw, uncooked
nyata	. .	clear
rajin	. .	diligent
sama	. .	same
běrsama	. .	together
sěsak	. .	packed full
těrtutup	. .	closed

133

kĕroh	.	.	. muddy
ramai	.	.	. populous ; in large numbers
bengkok	.	.	. bent
ringan	.	.	. light (not heavy)

tembak	.	.	. shoot
panggang	.	.	. roast (dry) ; toast
taroh	.	.	. put
lalu	.	.	. go past
gĕlinchir	.	.	. slip
tĕrgĕlinchir	.	.	. slipped
kĕjar	.	.	. chase, pursue
ingat	.	.	. pay attention, bear in mind
(mĕ)lompat	.	.	. leap
hunus	.	.	. unsheath
hambat	.	.	. chase
mudek	.	.	. go upstream
hilir	.	.	. go downstream
bilang	.	.	. count ; say, tell (bazaar)
champor	.	.	. mixed, mixing
bĕrhĕnti	.	.	. stop (oneself)
bĕrĕnang	.	.	. swim
gugor	.	.	. drop, fall
bĕrpindah	.	.	. move house

| juga | . | . | . and yet, (see par 148) |

I. Conjunctions

(a) Subordinating Conjunctions
Par. 93.

Subordinating Conjunctions (e.g. if, when, after, because) are less common in Malay than in English.

English conversational style uses the complex sentence freely. e.g. " I will come when I am ready "; " He said it although he did not believe it ", " Bring it as soon as you receive it ".

In spoken Malay the complex sentence is much less used. A speaker will usually balance a pair of short simple sentences, and expect his hearer to infer the relationship between them. The context gives sufficient guidance as to whether the second action happened *because* of the first, or *after* the first, or *in spite of* the first, as the case may be. Hence, subordinating conjunctions are not very much used in conversation. Study the sentences given below. The conjunctions of the English translations are underlined. They do not appear in the Malay sentences. But note that the idea conveyed by the English conjunction is sometimes present in the other clause of the Malay sentence. See examples 1, 2 and 6.

Examples.

1. *Hari hujan, dia pĕrgi juga.*
   Although it was raining, he went.
   (Lit. The day was wet, he went all the same.)

2. *Orang itu tua, tĕtapi kuat bĕrjalan.*
   Although he is an old man, he is a good walker.
   (Lit. The man is old, but strong, walking.)

3. *Nampak kapal tĕrbang, lĕkas datang bĕri tahu saya.*
   As soon as you see the aircraft come and tell me.
   (Lit. The aircraft visible, quickly come and tell me.)

4. *Chakap kuat sadikit, boleh dia dĕngar.*
   Speak louder so that he may hear you.
   (Lit. Speak loud a little, he will be able to hear).

5. *Kuching ta'ada, tikus bĕrmain.*
   When the cat's away, the mice play.
   (Lit. The cat not there, the mice play).

6. *Matahari turun baharu–lah kita bĕrtolak.*
   When the sun has set, we will set out, or
   We will not set out until the sun has set.
   (Lit. The sun having set, newly (i.e. only then) we will set out).

7. *Sampan itu těnggělam–kah tidak saya bě‌’um dapat tahu.*
I don't yet know <u>whether</u> (or if) the sampan was sunk
or not.

Note that when *whether*, or *if*, introduces an indirect
question the Malay word required is not *kalau* but
–kah.

Par. 94.

The following is a list of the subordinating conjunctions,
to be used for reference, not for learning by heart.   Many
of them are literary and will not be used freely until the
later chapters are reached.   Read them through, and
come back to them as you need them.   For conversation,
as you have already seen, you will not need many of them.

jikalau *jika* . . . } *kalau*	if, whether
jikalau tidak . . .	if not, unless
sapěrti *sa–umpama* . . } *sa–olah–olah*	as if
walau (pun) *sunggoh pun . tětapi* }	even if, even though
sědangkan (literary) .	although . . .
supaya . ,, .	in order that
supaya jangan ,, .	in order that . . . not, lest
takut *takut kalau* : }	for fear that, lest
kalau–kalau .	for fear that, in case, that (after words expressing apprehension).
sa–lagi *sa–lama* : : }	as long as, during the time that

asalkan (coll. *asal*) .	provided that
dĕngan sharat–nya .	on condition that

bila (coll.) . . ⎫ *apabila* *apakala* . . ⎬ *tatkala* (of past time) ⎭	when. Not relative. See footnote 18.

sa–tĕlah (literary) . ⎫ *sĕrta* ,, . ⎬ *dĕmi* ,, . ⎭	as soon as, when

bila–bila . . ⎫ *barang bila* . . ⎬	whenever

sĕmĕnjak . .	since (of time)

oleh . . . ⎫ *sĕbab* or *oleh sĕbab* *kĕrana* or *oleh kĕrana* ⎬because *fasal* (or *pasal*) ⎭	because

sĕmĕntara ⎫ *sĕdang* . . ⎬ while *tĕngah* . . ⎬ *di–dalam* . . ⎭	while

hingga ⎫ *sa–hingga* . . ⎬ until[29] ; up to the point that *sampai* ⎭	until[29] ; up to the point that

sa–bĕlum . . ⎫ *antara bĕlum* . ⎬	before[29]

lĕpas ⎫ *sudah* . . ⎬ after *tĕlah* or *sa–tĕlah* ⎭ (literary)	after

[29] " Until," " before ": in spoken Malay these ideas are usually rendered by the idiomatic use of *baharu*. See par. 73, Examples 3 and 5, and par. 93, Example 6.

E*

(b) Co-ordinating Conjunctions.

Par. 95.

Co-ordinating Conjunctions (" and ", " but ")
These, too, are less used in Malay than in English.

Co-ordinating conjunctions are frequently omitted:

a. between clauses :

Examples.

1. *Saya tembak, ta' kĕna juga.*
   I fired but I missed it.

2. *Burong itu dia panggang, buboh atas pinggan.*
   She roasted the bird and put it on a plate.

3. *Lĕpas puteh, hitam ta' dapat.* (Prov.).
   To let go the white, and fail to get the black.
   i.e. To fall between two stools.

4. *Nasi sĕdap, gulai mĕntah.* (Prov.).
   When the rice is just right, the curry is half-cooked.
   i.e. Nothing is perfect.

Malay proverbs afford numberless examples of this balanced antithesis.

b. between words : e.g.

(i) between pairs of opposites :

baik jahat	. good and bad (*or* good or bad)
lambat bangat	. sooner or later
pĕrgi mari	. going and coming
pĕrgi balek	. there and back
kiri kanan	. left and right
lĕbeh kurang	. more or less

(ii) between similar pairs corresponding to English collective words :

> *itek ayam*   . poultry
>
> *ibu bapa*
> *ayah bonda* (pol.) } parents
>
> *pinggan*
>   *mangkok*. crockery
>
> *tanah ayer*   . native land
>
> *anak chuchu*   . decendants
>
> *laki bini* .   . husband and wife
>
> *anak bini*   . family (wife and children)
>
> *pĕriok bĕlanga* . pots and pans

(iii) between alliterative pairs, of like meaning (e.g. English " hale and hearty "), but sometimes of different origin.

> *kĕlam kabut*   . dark and misty
> (both Malay)
>
> *budi bahasa*   . kindness and courtesy, tact.
> (both Sanskrit)
>
> *kaum kĕluarga*
> (Arabic and
>   Sanskrit) } kith and kin
> *sanak saudara*
> (Malay   and
> Sanskrit)

(iv) between alliterative jingles comparable to English frequentatives such as " helter-skelter ".

> *lalu lalang*   . passing to and fro
> *bolak balek*   . backwards and forwards

dan *lagi* *lalu* *sěrta* (lit.) *sěraya* ,, *sambil* ,,	} and
tětapi *akan tětapi*	} but
atau	or else
atau . . . atau	. either . . . or
baik . . . baik . *sama ada . . . atau* .	} both . . . and *or* whether . . . or

Par. 97.

Translation of the conjunction " and ".

(a) Dan.

This is the word in most common use, but it is far less frequent in Malay than is the word " and " in English. It is not used for joining sentences. See b, c, and d below.

The word *dan* is not used:

    (i) in numbers :
        413   *ěmpat ratus tiga-bělas.*

    (ii) in fractions :
        $1\frac{1}{2}$ *satu sa-těngah* (see Chapter XVII).

    (iii) usually at the end of a series :
        Tables, benches, and chairs.
        Meja, bangku, kěrusi.

    (iv) between imperatives.
        Pěrgi chari kayu api.
        Go and look for some fire wood.

    (v) as shown above, between pairs of words which are commonly found together.

> *siang malam.*
> day and night.
>
> *jantan bĕlina.*
> male and female.

(b) Lalu—(then, going on).

This word is used as a conjunction to join two verbs when the two actions are performed consecutively, usually by the same agent.

Examples.

1. *Orang tua itu bangun lalu kĕluar.*
   The old man got up and (at once) went out.

2. *Tĕrgĕlinchir–lah dia, lalu jatoh.*
   He slipped and fell.

3. *Dia mĕngĕjar pĕnchuri itu, lalu di–tangkap–nya.*
   He chased the thief and caught him.
   (lit. " and then, catching happened ". **This** impersonal use of the verb with the prefix *di–* is explained in Chapter XII).

In conversation *langsong* (forthwith) is often used in the same way as *lalu*.

Examples.

1. *Dia masok langsong kĕluar.*
   He came in, then went out again.

2. *Dia kĕluar langsong ta' balek.*
   He went out and never returned.

(c) Sĕrta. (together with).

This word is used in written Malay as a conjunction to join pairs of adjectives, or nouns. (cf. *lagi*).

Rajin sĕrta usaha.
Diligent and hard-working.

Salam sĕrta ingatan.
Greetings and remembrances.

It is used also between two verbs when the actions are performed almost simultaneously, usually by the same agent.

Examples.

1. *Raja Suran sĕgĕra mĕlompat sĕrta mĕnghunus pĕdang-nya.*

   Raja Suran swiftly leapt aside at the same time drawing his sword.

2. *Naik-lah marah-nya, lalu ia mĕnchabut kĕris sĕrta mĕnikam abang-nya.*

   He flew into a rage, then drew his dagger and stabbed his brother.

(d) Sĕraya and Sambil. (together with)

These words are used in written Malay to join verbs which denote actions performed simultaneously by the same agent. *Sĕraya* (as a conjunction) is obsolete.

Examples.

1. *Pa' Pandir pun hampir-lah kapada kambing itu sĕraya bĕrkata, "Hai, Pa' lĕbai!"*

   He went up to the goat saying "Hi! Your Holiness!"

2. *Di-hambat juga oleh Pa' Pandir, sambil bĕrkata, "Nanti! Nanti! Kita pĕrgi bĕrsama-sama".*

   Pa' Pandir chased after them crying "Wait, wait, we'll go together".

(e) **Lagi.** (moreover) see par. 26.

Examples.

1. *tinggi lagi kurus.*
   tall and thin.

2. *khabar yang bětul lagi nyata*
   clear and reliable news.

II.   Impersonal Expressions

Par. 98.

The following impersonal expressions are very common both in spoken and in written Malay. They enable the speaker to avoid a personal expression of opinion.

agak-nya
(lit. the guess of it) } probably
rasa-nya
(lit. the feel of it)

rupa-nya
(lit. the appearance
             of it) } apparently
nampak-nya

khabar-nya   according to report
(lit. the news of it)

Their place in the sentence is either at the end or at the beginning.

Examples.

1. *Běrapa lama lagi ?—Dua tiga jam, agak-nya.*
   How much longer shall we be ?   Two or three hours, I should think.

2. *'Nak hujan rupa-nya.*
   I think it's going to rain *or* It looks like rain.

3. *Tuan hakim 'nak běrpindah khabar-nya.*
   I hear that the judge is going to move.

Par. 99.

Less common is the occasional use of a rhetorical third person statement, when the speaker is directly addressing the person concerned.   This is merely an extension of the usual substitution of third person for second person shown in paragraph 87.

Examples.

1. (From Conversation 6).

    Hai !   'Nak jadi apa budak ini !
    What's the boy coming to !

2. *Orang kĕdai apa ini!   Pĕkan sĕsak, kĕdai–nya[30]*
    tutup pula.
    You're a fine shop-keeper (lit. " What sort of a shop-keeper is this ? "). The town is choc-a-bloc and your (lit. " his ") shop is shut, if you please !

3. *Anak 'mak baik !*
    That's a good boy ! (*or* girl)

Pĕrumpamaan :

Busut juga di–timbun anai–anai.
Little and often in time makes a heap.

(Lit.   A hillock even can be heaped up by white ants).

Exercise 22

1. Sunggoh pun haus, lĕbeh baik jangan minum ayer sungai yang kĕroh itu.   Nanti sa–kĕjap barang kali bĕrjumpa mata ayer.

2. Buah manggis itu sĕdap sangat rasa–nya.

3. 'Nak dĕmam rasa–nya.   Baik balek lĕkas.

4. Kasehan budak itu !   Bĕlum sa–tahun umor–nya, ibu bapa–nya mati.

[30] Note that with this rhetorical use the third person persists through-out the sentence.   This is not the case with sentences such as those in paragraph 87. The pronoun *–nya* could not be used in any of those to refer to the person addressed.

5. Mudek dari sini hingga ka–Pantai Janggus, bĕrapa jam ?—Agak–nya tĕngah dua jam.

6. Sudah hilir sa–panjang hari, sampai–lah ia kapada suatu kampong yang amat bĕsar lagi ramai.

7. Isahak suka dudok dĕkat–dĕkat dĕngan pintu. Apa bila kĕreta lalu, lĕkas–lĕkas dia tulis nombor–nya (*number*). Pĕtang, sa–bĕlum masok tidor, dia bilang banyak–nya kĕreta yang lalu itu.

8. Ikan itu tawar rasa-nya. Lain kali Ah Heng champur buah pala sadikit, baharu-lah sĕdap.

9. Rotan itu liat. Mudah mĕmbengkok, payah mĕngĕrat (*from* kĕrat), patah ta' boleh langsong.

10. Minta pinjam kĕrusi tiga ĕmpat buah. Baik bĕsar, baik kĕchil, ta' apa.

11. Kuching itu kĕjar tikus. Sudah tangkap, 'nak makan.

12. Sa–malam ribut. Sampan dua buah tĕnggĕlam di–balek Pulau Bintang itu khabar–nya.

13. Orang tua itu sudah bĕrhĕnti dĕkat pintu masjid. 'Nak masok, agak–nya.

14. Dia pasang rokok, langsong buang.

15. Lambat sahaja dia bĕrjalan. Sakit kaki rupa–nya.

16. Buah chiku itu sapĕrti ubi kĕntang rʋpa–nya.

Exercise 23

1. How far is it from the mosque to the shore ?—About five miles there and back, I should think.

2. I hear there are many crocodiles in the upper reaches of the river.

3. Tomorrow, if it's fine (say " if it is not raining "), we'll go up river for a mile or two.

4. If you swim in salt water, your body feels light.

5. He said he would not wait any longer in case his father should be angry.

6. I want to borrow a few dollars—What for ?—To buy some wood to mend my sampan. If I don't, it will sink, one of these days.

7. Did you hear that noise just now ?—What noise ?— Like an aircraft (say " like the noise of . . .)—No, I didn't.

8. One day, a tiger drank from that spring, and straightway died.

9. There must have been a storm last night. Thirty or forty coconut fronds have fallen.

10. This is the house where I lived when I was a policeman.

Conversation No. 6

Emak děngan Anak

Aminah : Mat ! Chěpat–lah minum kopi. Matahari 'dah tinggi[1]. Bila lagi[2] 'nak běrgěrak ka– sěkolah ?

Ahmad : 'Mak, minta duit lima sen.

Aminah : Hai ! 'nak jadi apa budak ini ! Tadi sudah di–běri ayah lima–bělas sen, sěkarang dia[3] minta lagi.

Ahmad : Jangan–lah lokek, 'mak. Duit yang ayah běri tadi itu 'nak bělanja běli pensel, batang pen, kěrtas tulis. Kalau mak ta' tolong běri lima sen lagi, kěbulor–lah Mat waktu rehat.

Aminah : Nah ! Lima sen. 'Tapi ingat esok jangan minta duit 'nak běli kěrtas, batang pen, pensel lagi. Chěpat masok baju. Kalau tidak, nanti lewat sampai ka–sěkolah.

Ahmad :   Kalau 'mak 'nak ka–kĕdai pĕtang 'karang[4]
            tunggu–lah sampai saya lĕpas sĕkolah ugama,
            boleh saya[5] ikut sama.

Aminah :   'Mak ta' jadi[6] ka–kĕdai pĕtang 'karang.
            Pĕtang esok kita pĕrgi sama.

Ahmad :   Baik–lah, 'mak.

Translation

Mother and Child

Aminah :   Mat! Come and have your breakfast
            quickly. It's late. When in the world are
            you going to start for school?

Ahmad :   Mother, give me five cents, will you ?

Aminah :   What a boy you are ! Just now your father
            gave you fifteen cents and now you are
            asking for more.

Ahmad :   Don't be mean Mother! The money that
            Father gave me I am going to spend on
            a pencil, and a pen, and some paper. If you
            won't give me another five cents I shall go
            hungry when play-time comes.

Aminah :   Well, here you are. Here's five cents. But
            remember, don't come asking for money
            tomorrow, to buy them over again. Hurry
            up and put your *baju* on, or you'll be late
            for school.

Ahmad :   If you are going shopping this afternoon, wait
            until I come out of Koran school, then I can
            come with you.

Aminah :   I shan't be going this afternoon. Tomorrow
            afternoon, we'll go together.

Ahmad :   Good !

F

Notes

1. matahari 'dah tinggi . . . Lit. " the sun has become high " i.e. " is now high ". So, *Baju sudah koyak*. The coat is torn. But, *Baju itu elok*. That's a fine coat.

2. lagi . . . . The adverb here adds a touch of impatience.

3. dia . . . . Lit. " he ". See footnote 30.

4. 'karang . . . Lit. " presently," and so " the afternoon which is coming ".

5. boleh saya . . . Note the inversion of pronoun subject and modal verb. This is very common. See par 83.

6. **Mak ta' jadi** . . . Lit. " it will not be happening that I go ".

CHAPTER XI

VOCABULARY

pohon (kayu)	. .	tree
manusia	. .	mankind
akar	. .	root
pĕrtunjokan	.	a show (e.g. agricultural)
sayur	. .	vegetables
pasu	. .	bowl, basin
pĕrentah	. .	government, rule
pĕgawai	.	officer, government agent
daerah	. .	district
hasil	. .	revenue, rent
undang–undang	.	laws, ordinances
bĕndang	. .	padi–field
pĕlabohan	. .	harbour
tempoh	. .	allotted time, extension of time
sarang	. .	nest
laba–laba	.	spider
chap	. .	printing; sealing; " brand " (e.g. of cigarettes)
barang	. .	anything; any; goods
bĕsi	. .	iron
perak	. .	silver

149

ĕmas (*or* mas)	.	. gold
ubat	. .	. medicine
ombak	. .	. waves
pĕrahu	. .	. boat
(kain) sutĕra	. .	. silk
pĕnjara	. .	. prison
bulu	. .	. nap, feathers, etc.
tingkap	. .	. window (of Malay house)
kapak	. .	. axe
batok	. .	. cough
kacha	. .	. glass

sĕmua	. .	} all, every
sĕgala	. .	
sadikit	. .	. a little
bĕbĕrapa	. .	. several, some
lapar	. .	. hungry
chobak–chabek	.	. frayed, tattered
tĕbal	. .	. thick
nipis	. .	. thin
gĕntar–gĕmĕntar	.	. quivering
luas	. .	. spacious
tĕtap	. .	. fixed, constant

atur	. .	. arrange
bual	. .	. bubbling up
bĕrbual	. .	. to chatter
ambil	. .	. take (and keep)
gali	.	} dig
mĕnggali	.	
kutip	. .	. pick up, collect
jĕrit	.	} shriek
mĕnjĕrit	.	
jawab	. .	. answer
pungut	. .	. gather, collect
angkat	. .	. lift

gĕlĕtar   .   } quiver, shake
mĕnggĕlĕtar   .   }

tatkala . . . at the time when

I. Number (in nouns)

Par. 100.

The Malay noun may be singular or plural according to context.

Examples.

1. *Saya mahu bĕli payong.*
   I want to buy an umbrella.

2. *Rumah–nya di–bĕlakang pokok kayu itu.*
   His house is behind those trees.

3. *Di–jalan itu ada kĕdai.*
   In that street there are shops.

4. *Baik pĕrgi bĕli paku ; esok 'nak buat pagar.*
   You had better go and buy some nails.   We must put up a fence, to-morrow.

It is the singular, rather than the plural, that requires definition.

Example.

5. *Di–jalan itu ada sa–buah kĕdai yang bĕsar sa–kali.*
   In that street there is a very large shop.

Par. 101.

The plural is indicated, when it is necessary to do so, in the following ways :

a. by numerals and numeral coefficients.

Example.

    Orang Hindu itu sudah bĕli dua ekor lĕmbu bĕtina.
    That Indian has bought two cows.

b. by words expressing quantity, such as

> *banyak* (many) ; *sĕmua, sĕgala, sakalian* (all) ;
> *sadikit* (a few) ; *bĕbĕrapa* (several).

These words precede the noun, being substantival rather than adjectival.

Examples.

1. *Pada masa dahulu banyak kapal bĕlayar daripada pĕlabohan ini.*
   Many ships sailed from this port in days gone **by.**

2. *Sĕmua orang tua suka bĕrbual–bual.*
   All elderly people enjoy a chat.

3. *Sĕgala anak murid di–sĕkolah itu pandai bĕrĕnang.*
   All the pupils in that school can swim.

4. *Ada bĕbĕrapa jĕnis pohon kayu di–kĕbun itu.*
   There are several kinds of trees in that garden.

5. *Jikalau lapar, ambil sadikit buah pisang.*
   If you are hungry, take a few bananas.

c. by reduplication.

Example.

> *Tatkala itu makanan manusia hanya–lah dĕngan usaha pĕrĕmpuan–pĕrĕmpuan mĕnggali bĕbĕrapa jĕnis akar–akar yang bĕrubi.*

> In those days, people depended for food on the toil of women, who dug up many kinds of tuberous roots.

II. Reduplication

Par. 102.

The underlying idea of duplication, however, is not plurality, but indefiniteness.

Hence, it will not be used with a numeral : e.g.

> *Tujoh orang*   .   . seven people
> *Sĕmbilan ekor kuching*   . nine cats

Nor will it be used when the noun refers to a definitely specified plural : e.g.

Ada bunga di–atas meja.
There are some flowers on the table.

It implies unspecified variety : e.g.

Di–pĕrtunjokan itu ada bunga–bunga yang elok sa–kali.
There were all sorts of magnificent flowers at the show.

Par. 103.

All parts of speech except prepositions may be duplicated, if the meaning of the word permits. Usually the whole word is repeated, but there are some words in which the initial consonant only is duplicated and an " indeterminate ĕ " inserted. This shorter form is sometimes a variant for a simple form : e.g.

> *gasing* or *gĕgasing* . a spinning top
>
> *bĕrapa* or *bĕbĕrapa* . several

and sometimes, in speech, a variant for a fully duplicated form : e.g.

> *layang–layang* or *lĕlayang* a kite
>
> *mata–mata* or *mĕmata* . a policeman

Another type of duplication is the repetition of the ground word in a changed form. The idea of variety in unity is usually strongly present in such frequentative forms. e.g.

> *gilang–gĕmilang* . . dazzling, sparkling
>
> *bengkang–bengkok* . . twisting, zigzag
>
> *sayur–mɹyur* . . vegetables of all sorts

Par. 104.

The following shades of meaning may be differentiated, but with the exception of (d) they are all of them clearly

aspects **of** the underlying idea of indefiniteness.
Remember that duplication should *not* be used merely
to indicate plurality.

(a) Distributive plurality, embracing all possibilities.
Examples.

1. *Masa dahulu něgěri–něgěri yang di–bawah pěrentah
   raja těrlampau kuat.*

   Formerly countries which were under the rule of
   princes were very strong.

2. *Hěndak–lah pěgawai daerah kutip hasil–hasil yang
   di–tětapkan di–dalam pěraturan–pěraturan ini.*

   District officers must collect all such dues as are
   fixed in these regulations.

3. *Hěndak–lah anak murid jaga buku–buku jangan
   chobak–chabek.*

   Pupils should look after their books (i.e. any
   which they possess), and not allow them to
   become tattered and torn.

It is this same idea of indefinite plurality that underlies
the many duplicated names for insects and other
creatures. e.g.

ampai–ampai.	. jelly fish (because of their swaying tentacles)
kělip–kělip .	. fireflies (because of their intermittent light)
angkut–angkut	. the mason bee (because of its repeated journeys)

and the duplicated indefinite pronouns, conjunctions,
and adverbs : e.g.

siapa–siapa .	. whoever ; anybody
apa–apa .	. whatever ; anything
mana–mana .	. whatever, whichever, any
di–mana–mana	. wherever, anywhere.

bila–bila   .   . whenever
angsur–angsur   . by instalments

(b) Repetition.

Examples.

1. *Kĕra itu mĕnjĕrit–jĕrit.*
   The monkey shrieked (and went on shrieking).

2. *Saya bĕrtanya–tanya, ta' dapat jawab juga.*
   I asked over and over again but got no answer.

3. *Hari–hari Pa' Mahmud ka–bĕndang.*
   Every day old Mahmud goes down to the rice-fields.

(c) Resemblance—(sometimes fanciful). e.g.

mata	. eyes	*mata–mata* policeman
puteh	. white	*puteh–puteh* whitish
buat	. do	*buat–buat* make a pretence of doing.
apit	. press between flat surfaces	*apit–apit* a pincer trap for rats.
jala	. a net	*jala–jala* trellis work.
gading	. tusks	*gading–gading* boat ribs.

(d) Intensity. e.g.

lama–lama dahulu
long ago.

dĕngan bĕsar–bĕsar hati
with great pride.

potong halus–halus
cut it very fine.

Note.   Reduplication is sometimes indicated by the figure " 2 " written as an index.   e.g. *bĕsar-bĕsar* or *bĕsar.*[2]

In this book, however, duplicated words are written in full, in order to avoid confusion with index figures used to indicate notes.

III.   Comparison

Par. 105.

There is no special form of the adjective or adverb to show comparative or superlative degree.   In the written language there is to be found a variety of phrases to express comparison, but in conversation the hearer is frequently left to infer comparison from context.   e.g.

Yang mana baik? . Which is the better? (of two things) *or*
Which is the best? (of more than two) *or*
Which are the best? (if the context requires it).

The answer is :

Yang ini baik . This is the better, *or*
This is the best, *or*
These are the best.

Par. 106.

Equality of degree (i.e. as . . . as).

This is expressed :

(a) by simple juxtaposition of words, usually with duplication of the adjective.

Examples.

1. *Buah ini manis–manis gula.*
   This fruit is as sweet as sugar.

2. *Budak sudah bĕsar–bĕsar gajah bĕlum bĕrsĕkolah
lagi !*
A great boy like that, and not yet going to
school!
(lit. as big as an elephant).

(b) by *sama* (or *sa–*) followed by *dĕngan* or *sapĕrti*
Either of the correlatives may be omitted.

Examples.

1. *Budak itu sama tinggi dĕngan bapa–nya.*
The child is as tall as his father.

2. *Rupa–nya sama elok sapĕrti rupa kain batek.*
It looked as effective as *batek* cloth.

3. *Minta tali sa–panjang ini.*
May I have a piece of string as long as this,
please.

4. *Pagar itu tinggi sapĕrti tembok pĕnjara.*
The fence was as high as a prison wall.

Par. 107.

Comparative degree (i.e. more . . . than).

Comparison is expressed :

(a) by **arrangement of words,** the two terms of the
comparison being placed side by side, in antithesis.
The statement is sometimes strengthened by the
use of *yang.*

1. *Kayu, batu, bĕrat batu,* or
Kayu batu, yang bĕrat batu.
Stone is heavier than wood.

2. *Itu, ini, baik ini.*
Of this and that, this is the better, *or*
This is better than that.

(b) by lĕbeh[31] (more) with daripada (than) as correlative.

Examples.

> 1. *Bĕsi lĕbeh bĕrat daripada kayu.*
>   Iron is heaver than wood.
>
> 2. *Kain bĕnang lĕbeh tĕbal daripada kain sutĕra.*
>   Cotton material is thicker than silk.

(c) by daripada alone.

Examples.

> 2. *Ini baik daripada itu.*
>   This is better than that.
>
> 2. *Daripada ta'ada, baik ada* (prov.).
>   Something is better than nothing.
>   (i.e. Half a loaf . . .)

Note :

1. Ascending and descending degree is expressed by *makin . . . makin,* or *makin . . . sa–makin.*

Example.

> *Makin tua, makin bodoh.*
> The older he grows, the more foolish he becomes.

2. When comparison is concerned only with increasing quality, with no reference to that quality in any other person or thing, the word *lagi* (more, in addition) is frequently used.

---

[31] A comparison showing inferiority may be expressed by *kurang . . . dari-pada.* e.g. *Kayu kurang bĕrat dari-pada bĕsi*—" Wood is less heavy than iron."

But note that *kurang* used without *daripada* merely negatives the adjective which it precedes, e.g. *kurang baik*—" not good, unsatisfactory ", i.e. " bad " ; *kurang elok*—" ugly ". The understatement of such phrases (" less good than it might be ") is more courteous than a direct negative (*tidak baik*—" not good ") would be. Compare the frequent answer, *Kurang pĕreksa* or *Bĕlum pĕreksa* or *Ta' pĕreksa pula* (sometimes clipped to *Pĕreksa pula*)—" I haven't sufficiently looked into the matter," instead of *Ta'tahu*—" I don't know ".

Example.

> *Tarek lagi kuat.*
> Pull harder.

Sometimes both words are used.

Example.

> *Hĕndak lĕbeh panjang lagi.*
> It must be longer still (i.e. more–long, in addition to the present length).

Par. 108.

Superlative degree.

(a) Relative Superlative. (i.e. most . . . of all).

This may be expressed :

> a. by order of words, sometimes emphasized by the use of *yang*.

Examples.

> 1. *Bĕsi, kayu, kĕrtas, ringan kĕrtas.*
>   Of iron, wood and paper, paper is the lightest.
>
> 2. *Kain bulu kambing, kain bĕnang, kain sutĕra, yang nipis kain sutĕra.*
>   Of woollen material, cotton material, and silk, silk is the thinnest.

> b. by *yang* combined with one of the adverbs meaning " very ".

Examples.

> 1. *Daripada sĕmua–nya, ini yang baik sa–kali.*
>   Out of all of them, this is the best.
>
> 2. *Daripada anak Che' Mahmud, Ali yang tĕrlĕbeh rajin.*
>   Of Che' Madmud's children, Ali is the most industrious.

(b) **Absolute Superlative** (i.e. merely intensive, not involving comparison with anything else).

This may be expressed :

a. by any of the adjectives meaning " very " (sometimes two or three of them used together), with or without *yang*.

Example.

> *Padang yang amat sangat luas.*
> A very large field.

b. by reduplication.

Example.

> *Tutup tingkap rapat–rapat.*
> Shut the windows very tightly.

c. by *sa–* with reduplication, often with *–nya*.

Example.

> *Sa–lambat–lambat–nya.*
> At the very latest.

d. by picturesque similes.

Example.

> *Gigi–nya sa–bĕsar kapak.*[32]
> He had very large teeth.
> (lit. His teeth were as large as axe-blades.)

Pĕrumpamaan.

> *Bujor lalu, lintang patah.*

What goes lengthwise gets through, what goes crosswise is broken (and gets through too).

---

[32] Similes of this sort are very common. They are often the most idiomatic way of rendering an absolute superlative. The following sentence was offered to a Malay for translation : " Do you see that tiny island, far far away, right on the horizon ? " and the result was this : *Ada-kah nampak, ja-a-u-uh, sa-bĕlah sana, di-kaki langit pulau sa-bĕsar kuman* ?   " . . an island, as big as a louse."

i.e. Nothing escapes his net. (Said of a grasping person).

Exercise 24

1. Buah manggis lĕbeh sĕdap daripada buah chiku.

2. Jangan takut. Abang buat–buat sahaja.

3. Di–kĕbun bapa saudara Che' 'Nah ada bĕrjĕnis–jĕnis pokok buah–buahan. Bila buah itu gugor Che' 'Nah suka bĕnar mĕmungut (*from* pungut).

4. Daripada gajah, harimau, kĕra, yang bĕsar gajah.

5. Masa dahulu raja–raja sahaja yang mĕmakai (*from* pakai) payong kuning.

6. Kĕna habiskan kĕrja ini, sa–habis–habis lambat–nya dalam tempoh dua bulan.

7. Urat sarang laba–laba itu halus–halus bĕnar.

8. Di–kĕdai Cheng Huat Hin ada tin rokok bĕrmacham–macham chap–nya.

9. Dalam pĕkan itu, kĕdai dia yang bĕsar sa–kali.

10. Baik–baik–lah angkat bakul ini. Ada macham–macham barang kacha yang halus, lĕkas pĕchah.

11. Jikalau sakit batok baik minum ubat.—Bukan–nya sakit batok ; dĕmam sahaja.

12. Malam tadi ombak bĕsar gunong. Pĕrahu t'ada kĕluar.

13. Ada–kah pĕrnah tengok rantai ĕmas sa–panjang ini ?

14. Sĕjuk rasa–nya. Mĕnggĕlĕtar pĕlĕpah pokok nyior. 'Nak ribut agak–nya.

Exercise 25

1. There are two goats on the padang. I expect they are Pa Man's.

2. Your house, Che Su, is a finer house than mine.

3. Be careful ! This paper is very thin.

4. Push the car right against the wall.

5. Did you ever see such big bananas !

6. There are all sorts of flowers in the garden.

7. If the child is hungry, give him a little bread and butter.

8. Clerks who are taking leave tomorrow must sign the book in the main office (*ofis.*).

9. Don't bring the coffee until you have taken away the dirty plates.

10. This plank is too thin.—Will this one do ?—No, it must be thicker still. I shall have to look in the shed.

Conversation No. 7

Tabib děngan Orang Sakit

Doktor :   Mari–lah masok.   Siapa yang sakit ?

'Mak si[1]sakit : Anak saya, Doktor.

Doktor :   Sakit apa ?

'Mak :   Saya ta'tahu 'nak khabar sakit dia[2] Puas[3] sudah saya[4] běrubat[5] děngan bomoh Mělayu[6], tidak mahu[7] baik. Kěmudian bapa saudara budak ini suroh saya choba ubat di–rumah sakit. Ini–lah[8] saya bawa dia minta pěreksa.

Doktor :   Elok–lah itu.

'Mak :   Jadi bagini, Doktor.   Anak saya badan–nya ta' těgap, děmam sahaja, pěrut dia kěmbong, kaki tangan běngkak. Makan ta'lalu, malam–malam měnangis (*from* tangis), tidor pun ta' lena[9]   Tolong–lah doktor běrikan dia ubat.

Doktor :   Boleh–lah. Baringkan dia, boleh saya[10]
            pĕreksa dahulu.

            .   .   .   .   .

'Mak :   Sakit apa, Doktor?   Boleh baik–kah?

Doktor :   Ĕnche' jangan susah. Sakit ini tiada
            mĕlarat. Boleh baik, jikalau makan
            ubat ini.

'Mak :   Bagaimana 'nak makan ubat yang di–
            bĕri itu ?

Doktor :   Makan dua chamchah teh, sa–hari tiga
            kali. Lagi satu minggu mari lagi, boleh
            saya bagi ubat lagi.

'Mak :   Tĕrima kaseh banyak–banyak, Doktor.
            Bĕrasa lĕga hati saya mĕndĕngar doktor
            chakap bagitu.

Translation

Lady Medical Officer and Patient

L.M.O. : Come in.   Who is it that is ill ?

Mother : My child, Doctor.

L.M.O. : What's wrong with him ?

Mother : I can't tell you what is the matter with him,
I have taken him to the Malay doctor until I
am tired, but he doesn't get any better.   Then
his uncle told me to try the medicine at the
hospital.   So I have brought him to be
examined.

L.M.O. : That's right.

Mother : It's like this, Doctor. The child's body does
not grow firm, he is always having fever, his
stomach is swollen, and his hands and feet are
puffy. He has no appetite, and he cries at

night and does not sleep soundly. Will you give him some medicine please ?

L.M.O. : Yes, I will give him something. Put him to lie down so that I can examine him first.

. . . . .

Mother : What is wrong with him, Doctor ? Can he be cured ?

L.M.O. : Don't worry. The illness won't go on indefinitely. He will get better, if he takes this medicine.

Mother : How is he to take the medicine that you have given me ?

L.M.O. : He is to take two teaspoonfuls, three times a day. In a week's time come back again, and I will give you some more medicine.

Mother : Thank you very much, Doctor. I feel relieved to hear you say that.

Notes.

1. Si–sakit . . Note that the *si* here is the equivalent of the English definite article. *si–sakit*—" the sick person ".

2. saya . . . dia . Lit. " I do not know, wishing to tell the illness of him."

3. puas . . Notice this idiomatic use of the word *puas* (satisfied, sated). Cf. *saya puas měnchari*—" I've looked everywhere " (lit. " until I am tired of looking ").

4. sudah saya   . Note position of subject pronoun after auxiliary (par. 83).

5. bĕrubat   .   . Lit. " have had him medicined." See par. 123.

6. Mĕlayu, tidak   note omission of conjunction.

7. Tidak mahu baik. Colloquial use of *mahu*. Cf. " This box will not shut "—*Pĕti ini ta'mahu tutup*.

8. ini–lah   .   . *Ini* here is a pronoun subject, and the whole of the rest of the sentence is the predicate. " This is my–bringing–of–him–for–you–to–examine–him."

9. Anak saya ... lena Note omission of conjunctions.

10. Boleh saya .   . Inversion of subject pronoun after modal verb. Cf. note 4.

CHAPTER XII

THE VERB

I.   Person, Number, Mood, Tense, Voice

II.   The simple verb

III.   The verbal prefix " di- "

IV.   The verbal prefix "mĕ- "

Par. 109.

The accidence of the Malay verb is very simple. There are no tables of inflections to be learned by heart, comparable to the forbidding " verb " pages of a Latin or a French grammar. On the other hand, this very fact gives the Malay verb an elusive character which makes it impossible to fit it into any scheme of syntax formulated under the usual headings of person, number, mood, tense, voice.

It is by a system of affixation (*di-, mĕ-, bĕr, pĕr-, tĕr- ; -kan, -i*) that the Malay verb achieves its subtlety of shading. The functions of these prefixes and suffixes are explained in this chapter and the following chapter.

Malays use these affixes freely, most of them in speaking as well as in writing. You have already come across several of them in the proverbs and the conversations. In the written language they are of much more frequent occurrence. Up to this point they have not been used, except occasionally, in the exercises, but from this point onwards the Malay-English exercises will be drawn chiefly from literary sources, in order to give you practice in recognising the affixes, and studying their functions.

Do not be too eager to use affixes in your own conversation, but listen for them when you are talking to Malays. The English–Malay exercises will continue to be in conversational vein, but they will not be confined to isolated sentences. Do not attempt to translate them word for word. Express the ideas simply and in logical order. Malay idiom is terse and direct.

The vocabulary at the beginning of each chapter is discontinued from this point. All words used in the examples and in the Malay–English exercises are to be found in the alphabetical vocabulary at the end of the book. If a word has a prefix, look it up under the initial letter of the ground word, e.g. for *mělompat* look up *lompat*.

When the prefix is *mě–* or *pě–*, the initial letter of the ground word is sometimes changed. You will have studied these changes before you reach the next exercise.

Remember, in using vocabularies and dictionaries, that there is no strict division of Malay words into different parts of speech.

I. Person, number, mood, tense, voice

Par. 110—Person and number.

The examples already given have made it clear that there is no change in the form of the Malay verb to indicate person or number.

Examples.

1. *Saya makan nasi* . I am eating (first person singular.)

2. *Arifin makan nasi* . Arifin is eating
(third person singular.)

3. *Budak makan nasi*. The children are eating
(third person plural.)

Par. 111—Mood.

The examples given in the chapters dealing with conjunctions, and commands, have shown that there is no change of form in the Malay verb to show what would be, in some languages, a change of mood.

Examples.

1. *Ibu bapa-nya datang* His parents came. (Indicative.)
2. *Sunggoh pun ibu* Although his . parents came.
   bapa-nya datang (Possible subjunctive.)
3. *Panggil adek* . . Call your sister. (Imperative.)

Par. 112—Tense.

(a) The Malay verb may be any tense.

Example.

   Dia pĕrgi . He goes *or* is going ; he went *or* was going ; he will go.

(b) Tense may be indicated by one of a number of words which act as auxiliaries :

To show past time :

   sudah } or both together } have
   habis   } has
   tĕlah . . . (written) had

To show future time—

   akan

   hĕndak }
   mahu   } . . with intention implied   } shall,

   nanti . . . mere futurity with no implication of intention } will

   kĕlak (written) . at end of sentence

(c) Tense may be indicated by adverbial expressions of time.

Examples.

1. *Tiap–tiap hari dia bangun pukul tujoh pagi.*
   He gets up at seven every morning.

2. *Sa–malam saya běli ikan kěring dua kati.*
   Yesterday I bought two *kati* of salt fish.

3. *Esok pětang abang saya datang dari Sungai Patani.*
   Tomorrow evening my brother will come from Sungai Patani.

(d) If it is necessary to stress the incompleteness of an action the word *sědang* (lit. medium) or the word *těngah* (lit. middle) may be used.

Examples.

1. *Sědang běrchakap, orang pěrěmpuan itu pengsan.*
   In the middle of speaking the woman fainted.

2. *Těngah běrmain, budak itu běrkělahi.*
   In the midst of playing, the children began to quarrel.

Par. 113—Voice.

There is not, in the Malay verb, the sharp distinction between active and passive voice that is seen in the English verb.

A Malay scholar[33] has suggested that the true subject of a Malay sentence is the verb.   That is to say, when the verb is used in its simple uninflected form, the statement made by the Malay sentence is

not that :

> Somebody, or thing, *does* something, or *is* something.   (i.e. active).

[33] Dr. C. O. Blagden, quoted by Sir Richard Winstedt: Malay Grammar, p. 65 footnote.

nor is it that :

> Something is done *to* somebody, or thing. (i.e. passive).

but that :

> There happens, something ; or, there exists some state.

If it is possible to think of the Malay verb in this way, it is clear that it is not possible to apply the words " active " and " passive " to it, with any precision.

Nevertheless at this stage it will be helpful to take the following statements as rough guides.

- a. The simple root form of the verb is more often active than passive.

- b. The passive is expressed in written (and sometimes in spoken[34]) Malay by *di–* prefixed to the simple root form of the verb.

II. The Simple Verb

Par. 114.

The simple uninflected form of the verb is used whenever the emphasis is on the action or condition expressed by the verb, rather than on the doer of the action, (i.e. the word which in English would be the grammatical subject.)

Hence, the simple verb is used :

- a. In conversation frequently, especially when the actor is in the 1st or 2nd person. (With a 3rd person subject the simple verb is often a shortened pronunciation of the *mě–* derivative in which the initial

---

[34] Passive sentences can sometimes be rendered colloquially by *kěna* (incur) in front of a word that is probably substantival. The " action received " is usually in the nature of a penalty. e.g. *Dia kěna pukul*— " He was beaten ". *Ular kěna palu*—" The snake was struck " (lit. " incurred striking ").

syllable is scarcely heard, e.g. *Dia 'mbacha surat khabar*—He is reading the newspaper.)

The exercises, being mainly in conversational style, have given numerous examples of this use of the simple verb.

b. When a verb expresses an involuntary state of mind, or a simple action which has involved little conscious thought. Most of the common intransitive verbs (mainly verbs of movement) come under this heading.

Examples.

1. *Suka orang mělihat budak běrmain.*
   People like to watch children playing.
   (There is pleasure for people in watching . . .)

2. *Datang–lah anak–nya minta duit.*
   His son came to ask for money.
   (There came his son asking for money.)

3. *Pěnchuri itu kěluar langsong lari.*
   The thief came out and straightway took to his heels.

c. For requests, commands, prohibitions (both direct and indirect) when there is no emphasis on the person who is to carry out the request or command.

Examples.

1. *Suroh panggil juru bahasa.*
   Tell (somebody) to call the interpreter.

2. *Minta tolong.*
   Help me, please (somebody or other).

3. *Jangan ludah.*
   Don't spit (anybody who reads this notice).

4. *Suroh bawa masok orang salah itu.*
   Order the prisoner to be brought in.

d. With the prefix *di–* to form a passive.

III. The verbal prefix " di-"
Par. 115.

Di– is used with the simple root form of the verb. Its effect is to turn the verb into a passive. But note that this 'passive with *di-*' is not used after a word of command. See example c. 4 above. Nor can it be used when the agent is in the 1st or 2nd person. The Malay passive with *di-* is not exactly the same thing as the English passive, where the object of the active transitive verb becomes the subject of the passive verb.

Example.

(active) The thief struck him (Subject + transitive verb + object.)

(passive) He was struck by the thief. (The object " him " has become the subject " he ").

The Malay construction is more in the nature of a so-called impersonal passive.

Di–pukul akan dia oleh pěnchuri.
Striking–was–done[35] towards him, by the thief.

It is the action that is stressed, not the doer of the action, nor yet the person to whom the action is done. The agent, being of secondary importance, comes after the verb, sometimes preceded by *oleh* which may be translated " by ". When the agent is a 3rd person pronoun it appears as *–nya*[36] which may be translated " by him ", " by her ", " by them ".

Par. 116.

This idiomatic passive form with *di–* is very common

[35] Cf. Lat. *Concurritur ad templum*—" There-was-a-rush towards the temple. (*lit.*" " Running-together was done ").

[36] Sir Richard Winstedt (Malay Grammar par. 40) considers that this *di-* before the root form of the verb, in such phrases as *di-lihat-nya is* merely an idiomatic use of the place preposition *di-* (" at " or " in "). Thus the *lihat*, being in the nature of a verbal noun, would naturally be followed by the genitive of the pronoun, *di-lihat-nya*—" in the seeing of him " i.e. " in his sight ".

in written narrative style, (see Example 1), but it is frequently used in conversation also. Note that it corresponds as a rule to an English *active* statement.

Di–angkat–nya pĕti itu.
He picked up the box.

Since there is no stress on the agent, the simple form of the verb with *di*– is frequently used in proverbial expressions and in public notices. (see Examples 1 and 2.)

Examples.

1. *Ayer tĕnang, jangan di–sangka tiada buaya.* (Prov.)
   Because the water is calm, don't think (i.e. let nobody think) that there are no crocodiles.

2. *Chukai hĕndak di–bayar di–Pĕjabat Hutan, antara pukul sa–puloh pagi dĕngan pukul ĕmpat pĕtang.*
   Customs duties must be paid at the Forestry Office (i.e. by anybody to whom this notice applies) between 10 a.m. and 4 p.m.

3. *Sa–tĕlah di–dĕngar oleh saudagar, maka di–suroh–nya tangkap akan si–miskin itu, kĕmudian di–bawa–nya ka–hadapan kathi sĕrta di–khabarkan–nya dari awal sampai akhir–nya.*

Free translation :

When the merchant heard this, he ordered the poor man to be arrested. Then he brought him before the kathi and related the whole story from beginning to end.

Literal translation :

When there–had–been–hearing by the merchant, (*maka*—a punctuation word, see Chap. xv.), there–was–telling by him to capture (lit. " towards ") the poor man. Then there–was–bringing by him

before the kathi together–with telling by him
from the beginning to the end.

IV. The verbal prefix " mě-".

Par. 117

You have already seen in the Notes on the
Conversations that the prefix *mě-* sometimes brings
about a change in the initial letter of the ground word.
The following table shows all the possible changes.
*Brackets round an initial letter indicate that that letter is
dropped in the derivative word.* The easiest way to
learn the rules is to memorize one example for each
initial letter.

Table of Mutations after the prefix " mě-"

Form of Prefix.

mě- before : l, m, n, ng, ny, r.

Examples.

layang	becomes	*mělayang,*	(fly)
masak	,,	*měmasak*	(cook)
nanti	,,	*měnanti*	(wait)
nganga	,,	*měnganga*	(open one's mouth)
nyanyi	,,	*měnyanyi*	(sing)
rampas	,,	*měrampas*	(plunder)

měm- before : b, (p).

Examples.

buang	becomes	*měmbuang*	(throw away)
pukul	,,	*měmukul*	(strike)

měn- before : d, (t), ch, j.

Examples:

dukong becomes *měndukong* (carry on the hip)
tipu   „   *měnipu*   (deceive)
chabut   „   *měnchabut*   (pull out)
jawab   „   *měnjawab*   (answer)

měng- before : vowels and g, h, (k).

Examples.

ajar   becomes *mĕngajar*   (teach)
eja   „   *mĕngeja*   (spell)
isi   „   *mĕngisi*   (fill)
ukor   „   *mĕngukor*   (measure)
gulong „   *mĕnggulong*   (roll up)
hantar „   *mĕnghantar*   (send)
kĕnal   „   *mĕngĕnal*   (recognise)

měny- before : (s)

Example.

simpan becomes *mĕnyimpan*   (keep)

Par. 118.

Mě- may be prefixed :

(a) to simple verbs. e.g.

   buka or *mĕmbuka* . to open

(b) to verbs lengthened by a suffix (see par. 126–8),
    the resulting derivative being a causative verb. e.g.

   datang . to come *mĕndatangkan* . to make to
                                         come.

   kĕna . to make   *mĕngĕnakan* . to bring
            contact   into   con-
                                      tact, to fix.

(c) to other parts of speech, in order to turn them into verbs (sometimes in conjunction with a suffix). e.g.

bĕlakang	. back	*mĕmbĕlakang* .	to turn one's back
elok .	. beautiful	*mĕngelokkan* .	to make beautiful
dĕkat .	. near	*mĕndĕkati*	. to approach
surat	. a document	*mĕnyurat*	. to write (a letter)

Par. 119.

The *mĕ-* derivative when it is verbal lays stress on the doer of the action, and is usually transitive; it indicates that somebody is doing something, and is thus essentially active. It can never be used in conjunction with *di-*, nor with *kĕna* when it is equivalent to an English passive.

Being thus closely linked with a noun, or a noun equivalent (the subject), the *mĕ-* derivative is usually, though not always, adjectival in nature. Used after a verb it can be thought of as the equivalent of the English present participle.

Below are set out in tabulated form the commonest uses of the prefix *mĕ-*. Read them, and come back to them for reference. but remember as you read that any classification by 'meaning', and expressed through the medium of another language, is necessarily artificial since, to a Malay, a change of affix represents a change of mental attitude rather than a change of meaning.

A tabular arrangement is used wherever this is possible because most students find such an arrangement helpful. Do not allow yourself to be misled by these subdivisions. You will come across many examples that will not fit into

any one of them, and other examples which would fit
equally well into either of two subdivisions.

Uses of the prefix "mĕ-".

a. To express continuance of action the *mĕ*–derivative
is used after such words as *dudok, sĕdang, tĕngah,
pĕrgi, datang.* This is comparable to the English
participial use in " Poor Mary sits a–weeping."

Examples.

1. *Dia sĕdang mĕnulis surat.*
   He is writing a letter.

2. *Maimunah   dudok   mĕnangis–nangis*[37] (from
   tangis.)
   Maimunah sat there weeping her heart out.

3. *Dia pĕrgi mĕnchari*[38] *bapa–nya.*
   He went to look for his father.
   (Lit.   He went, seeking . . .)

4. *Datang sa–orang mĕmbĕri tahu hal itu.*
   There came somebody bringing the news.

b. After the words *tĕmpat* and *hĕndak*[39], the *mĕ*–
derivative used as the equivalent of an English verbal
noun.

---

[37] Note that when the root word is duplicated the mutation is retained
in the second part of the word. Cf. *mĕngĕpak-ngĕpak*—" to flap the
wings " (from *kĕpak*—" wing ").
   This form of reduplication expresses repetition, or persistence. e.g.
mĕmbĕlah-bĕlah—" chopping away ". *mĕnanti-nanti*—" waiting and
waiting ".
   There is a parallel form of reduplication in which the prefix appears
only in the second half, e.g. *tĕmbus-mĕnĕmbus*—" holed through and
through".
   In such formations the underlying idea is usually not repetition but
variety. e.g. *pĕjabat   karang-mĕngarang*—" office   for all-sorts-of-
compositions " (Translation Bureau). *pĕrgi tembak-mĕnembak*—" to
go shooting " (any birds that you chance to find.) *kira-mĕngira*—" to
make calculations ". *tari-mĕnari*—" dancing ".
[38] But note that when *pĕrgi* is used in the imperative, it is followed by
the simple verb, probably also in the imperative, e.g. *Pĕrgi chari kayu
api*—" Go and look for some fire-wood " (lit. Go, seek . . .)
[39] When *hĕndak* and *mahu* are used as auxiliaries merely to show
future time they are usually followed by the simple verb, e.g. *Habis
kĕrja saya 'nak bacha buku*—" When I have finished my work I shall
read ".

Examples.

1. *Ini-lah almari těmpat měnyimpan pinggan mangkok.*

   This is the cupboard where the crockery is kept. (lit. the cupboard, place for keeping . . .)

2. *Dia panjat pokok, hěndak měngambil layang-layang yang těrsangkut itu.*

   He climbed the tree to get the kite that had caught in the branches (lit. intending the getting of . . .).

3. *Hěndak měnaiki tangga, ia ta' larat.*

   When he tried to go up the steps, his strength failed him.

c. The *mě-* derivative is commonly used after such adjectives as *pandai, jěmu, puas, mudah, susah, payah, suka hati ;* and the verb *suka*. This use may be regarded as participial.[40]

Examples.

1. *Pandai měnari* . . clever, dancing.
2. *Jěmu měnděngar* . sick, hearing.
3. *Mudah měndapat* . easy, getting.
4. *Payah měngangkat* . difficult, lifting.
5. *Suka hati měnengok* . pleased, seeing
6. *Suka mělihat* . . like, seeing.

[40] But it is possible to consider the *mě-* derivative here as a verbal noun, "clever at dancing," "sick of hearing". More definitely substantival is its use in the following example, where it is preceded by a preposition. *Maka běrhěnti-lah orang daripada měnikam ikan itu*—"They stopped spearing the fish". Comparable to this is the use of the *mě-* derivative in headings, e.g. *Měnanam Padi*—"Padi Planting" ; *Měnembak Buaya*—"Shooting Crocodile".

Clearly adjectival is its use in such phrases as *padi měnirus*—"the ear of padi when still wrapped in the leaf" (from *tirus*—"tapering"), and *surat měněgah*—"a patent" (from *těgah*—"to forbid") *kapal měnyusur* —"a coasting vessel" (from *susur*—"outer edge"), *kasau mělintang* "cross beams" (from *lintang*—"athwart".)

d. The *mě*– derivative is used when attention is drawn to the doer of the action by the use of the pronoun *yang* (see footnote 65.)

Examples.

1. *Saya yang měmanggil, bukan ěmak.*
   It was I who called you, not my mother.

2. *Ada yang měnulis surat, ada yang měmbacha kitab.*
   Some were writing, and some were reading.

e. The *mě*– derivative may be used simply as the finite verb of a statement.

Examples.

1. *Apabila dia naik, dia měmandang kiri–kanan*
   When he came up, he looked to right and to left.

2. *Sěgěra–lah burong itu měnuju ka–tingkap tuan putěri.*
   The bird swiftly made towards the princess's window.

Note :

1. The simple uninflected form of the verb, not the *mě*– derivative, is used for most intransitive verbs denoting simple actions which usually involve little conscious thought, e.g. *pěrgi, datang, naik, turun, jatoh, bangun.*

2. There are some *mě*– derivatives which are always used. The commonest of them are :

měnari .	. dance
měngantok	. be sleepy
měndideh	. be boiling
měnyaběrang	. cross to the other side (of water)
mělawat	. visit

Par. 120—Examples.

1. *Saya tiada pandai měngasah pisau.*
   I am not good at sharpening knives.

2. *Orang China rajin měnanam sayur–sayuran.*
   The Chinese are industrious market-gardeners.
   (lit. " industrious at planting vegetables ").

3. *Sěgala orang kampong di–suroh buat jambatan.*
   All the villagers were told to build a bridge.

4. *Bunga itu di–kata orang Mělayu bunga raya.*
   The Malays call that flower *bunga raya.*

5. *Di–mana ěnche' dapat měmběli dawat hijau itu ?*
   Where did you manage to buy green ink ?

6. *Dia bělayar ka–něgěri yang lain, hěndak měnchari kěhidupan–nya.*
   He sailed to another country, in order to earn a living.

7. *Leher kuching itu běrdarah. Agak–nya di–gigit anjing itu.*
   The cat's neck is bleeding. Perhaps the dog bit it.

8. *Ada dua ratus orang yang měnengok wayang itu.*
   Two hundred people saw the performance.

9. *Mudah měmikul pěti yang bagitu ringan.*
   It's easy to carry such a light box as that.

10. *Hěndak di–siapkan bangsal těmpat měnyimpan pěrkakas.*
    You must build a shed in which to keep your tools.

Par. 121.

Proverbs

(a) with the simple verb.

1. *Tahan jěrat sorong kěpala.*
   To set a noose–trap and run your own head into it.

2. *Kata itu biar–lah kota.*
   Let your word be your bond. (lit. fortress.)

3. *Ayer laut pun ada pasang surut.*
   Even the sea ebbs and flows (i.e. Nothing is certain.)

4. *Ingat antara bĕlum kĕna.*
   Look before you leap. (lit. Think, before you run into some difficulty.)

5. *Akal ta' sa–kali tiba.*
   Rome wasn't built in a day. (lit. A good plan does not come into your head at once.).

(b) with *di–*.

1. *Si–tidor di–makan si–jaga.*
   The sleeper is the prey of the wide-awake.

2. *Di–dĕngar ada, di–pakai tidak.*
   In at one ear, out at the other (lit. It is heard, but it is not carried out.)

3. *Sudah sĕmbunyi jangan di–sorok.*
   Leave well alone. (lit. Having hidden yourself, do not go further into concealment.)

4. *Di–pandang dĕkat, di–chapai ta' boleh.*
   So near and yet so far. (lit. When looked at, near, when reached for, ungettable.)

5. *Hak yang lĕpas, jangan di–kĕnang.*
   Don't cry over spilt milk. (lit. Do not hanker after things that you have lost.)

(c) with *mĕ–*.

1. *Ada–kah pĕrnah tĕlaga yang kĕroh, mĕngalir ayer yang jĕrneh ?*
   Does a muddy lake send forth a stream of clear water ?

2. *Jikalau měnampi jangan tumpah padi–nya.*
   If you are winnowing, don't let the grain be
   spilt (with the dust) (i.e. Unnecessary
   vehemence often defeats its own ends.)
3. *Těpok nyamok měnjadi daki.*
   The remedy is almost as bad as the disease (lit.
   you slap the mosquito, and it leaves your hand
   dirty.)
4. *Měnghalau měnyepak měnghela měnghěmbus.*
   Drive it and it kicks, lead it and it snorts (of a
   buffalo, or a stubborn person.)
5. *Měndirikan běnang basah.*
   To make a wet thread stand on end (i.e. an
   impossibility. *Mě–* is very common in
   metaphors of this type.)

Exercise 26

1. Hari–hari si–Ali pěrgi měngail ikan.
2. Saya hairan měnděngar khabar–nya.
3. Patut di–buang pokok yang kurang subor.
4. Pada suatu hari ada–lah sa–ekor anjing běrjalan
   ka–sana ka–mari. Tiba–tiba di–lihat–nya sa–kěrat
   daging.
5. Ubat yang di–běri itu pahit rasa–nya.
6. Pokok–pokok bunga habis di–makan kambing itu.
7. Di–něgěri Inggěris kalau musim dingin ayer kolam
   muka–nya měnjadi běku.
8. Sakalian kanak–kanak sudi měněrima hadiah.
9. Di–mana dapat běli rokok ?
10. Di–dalam karong ini ada kachang tanah dua ratus
    tiga puloh empat biji. Kalau di–ambil sa–ratus
    tujoh puloh ěnam biji, tinggal běrapa ?

Exercise 27

(Note. It is possible to use the *mě–* derivative in each
of the following sentences.)

1. She is a good dancer.
2. I am sick of writing letters.
3. The mother was delighted to see her child.
4. The child knows how to sew.
5. He went to the market to buy fish (use *hĕndak*).
6. Yesterday an Indian came to the office to ask for work.
7. This is the box that we keep the teaspoons in.
8. Don't be afraid of acknowledging a mistake.
9. He went to look for bait.
10. It was he who cut down the casuarina tree.
11. The fisherman was slow to understand.
12. It is easy to cut bread with a sharp knife.

Conversation No. 8

Tanya Ayah

Emak :   Hai! Mĕngapa Ismail lambat pulang dari sĕkolah ? 'Mak lama mĕnanti[1], nasi pun dĕkat 'nak sĕjuk.

Ismail : Lĕpas sĕkolah che' gu' tahan sa–kĕjap, 'nak bĕrchakap[2].

Emak :   Fasal apa ? Ada apa–apa 'Mail 'dah buat salah ?

Ismail : Ta'ada apa–apa, 'mak. 'Mak ini[3] sĕlalu fikir yang ta' baik–baik sahaja[4]. Che' gu' tanya apa 'Mail 'nak buat, tamat bĕlajar di–sĕkolah Mĕlayu itu.

Emak :   Apa 'Mail jawab ?

Ismail : 'Mail ta' tahu apa 'nak jawab, 'mak. 'Mail suroh che' gu' tanya ayah.

Emak :   'Mail tĕntu tahu apa 'Mail sĕndiri suka 'nak buat lĕpas bĕlajar[5] di–sĕkolah Mĕlayu.

Ismail : 'Mail suka 'nak pĕrgi sĕkolah Inggĕris, bĕlajar bahasa Inggĕris, jadi boleh bacha surat khabar macham ayah.

Emak : Mĕngapa 'Mail ta'bĕri tahu che' gu' bagitu ? 'Mail ini memang[6]–nya malu.

Ismail : Ayah yang patut katakan kapada che' gu', 'mak.

Emak : Baik–lah. Sa–bĕntar lagi ayah 'Mail balek dari ofis. Chakap–lah kapada ayah apa–apa yang 'Mail suka. Pĕrgi–lah basoh tangan. Makanan[7] 'dah[8] siap.

Ismail : Baik–lah, 'mak.

Translation

Ask your Father

Mother : Ismail ! Why are you so late coming home from school ? I have been expecting you for a long time. Your food is almost cold.

Ismail : My teacher kept me back for a bit after school. He wanted to talk to me.

Mother : About what ? Have you been doing anything wrong ?

Ismail : No, nothing at all. Mother, you *are* unfair. You always imagine the worst. He was asking me what I want to do when I finish at the Malay school.

Mother : What answer did you give him ?

Ismail : I didn't know what to answer him, Mother. I told him to ask Father.

Mother : But surely you know what you yourself want to do when you finish at the Malay school ?

Ismail :   I should like to go to the English school and learn English. Then I should be able to read the newspaper as Father does.

Mother : Why didn't you tell your teacher that ? Oh, 'Mail, you *are* a bashful creature !

Ismail :   It's my father who ought to tell my teacher that, Mother.

Mother : Very well. Your father will be back from the office presently. Tell him what you want. Now go and wash your hands. Your food is ready.

Ismail :   Yes, Mother.

Notes.

1. měnanti	To sit waiting.
2. běrchakap	" He wanted to talk with me." For the *běr–* prefix see par. 123(e).
3. Mak ini	Notice this conversational use of *ini*, with a note of protest.
4. fikir . . . sahaja	Lit. you always think only (of) things that are not satisfactory.
5. bělajar	From *ajar*, see par. 138.
6. memang	A conversational use, that can seldom be rendered by the dictionary meaning " of course ". The idea is "That's you all over!". Here, it reinforces the protest that is implied in the *ini*.
7. Makanan	For suffix see par. 133.
8 'dah	(For *sudah*) i.e. has been made ready.

CHAPTER XIII

THE VERB (Continued)

I.   The prefix " bĕr- "
II. The prefix " tĕr- "
III. The prefix " pĕ- "
IV. The suffix " kan "
V.   The suffix "-i "

I. The prefix " bĕr-".

Par. 122.

The prefix *bĕr-* is widely used, in the spoken as well as the written language. It is possible to label it " reflexive ", if that word is used in a comprehensive sense that embraces all aspects of " reflexion."

The prefix *bĕr-* expresses not only the simple reflexive idea, where the action " bends back ", immediately, to the doer of the action (e.g. French " je me lève "—I raise myself, i.e. I stand.) It expresses, in addition to this, many other shades of meaning. But in nearly all of them it is possible to trace some idea of " reflexion " towards the preceding substantive.

Par. 123.

It may be helpful to distinguish the following uses, but remember that there is no real cleavage between them. Moreover, the same derivative may have different meanings in different contexts.

(a) **Clearly reflexive**—to do a thing to or for oneself[41] or to get a thing done for oneself[42].

Examples.

bĕrsandar .	. to lean (oneself against something)
bĕrpindah .	. to move (oneself, from one place to another)
bĕrubah .	. to change, to become different
bĕrubah warna	. to change colour
bĕrkĕmas .	. to do one's packing
bĕrkĕmas kain[41]	. to pack one's clothes
bĕrpĕsan baju[42]	. to order a coat
bĕrgunting rambut	to get one's hair cut
bĕrchabut gigi	. to have a tooth out.

(b) **Reciprocal**—to involve oneself with others, or one thing with another. (Sometimes in conjunction with *-an*, with or without duplication.)

Examples.

bĕrkĕlahi .	. quarrelling (oneself with another, *or* one with another.)
bĕrjabat tangan	. to shake (lit. clasp) hands, with another.
bĕrchampor	. mixed (one thing with another) *or* mixing (oneself with others.)
bĕrkĕnaan .	. in connection with.
bĕrsambut–sambutan	exchanging visits.

(c) **Possession**—to have a thing for oneself, to possess, to be provided with. These derivatives will be formed usually from nouns and adjectives, and will themselves be adjectival.

---

[41] Cf. the reflexive-active use of the passive participle in Latin verse : *scissa comas* " tearing-for-herself the hair."

[42] Equivalent to the French " faire faire."

Examples.

bĕrbini	}	possessed of a wife ('be-wifed'), married.
bĕristĕri		
bĕrbaju	. .	wearing a coat, coated.
bĕrbaju panjang	.	wearing a long coat
bĕrkaki tiga	.	three-legged
bĕrharta	. .	propertied.
bĕrbangsa	. .	nobly born.
bĕrbahasa	. .	courteous.
bĕrkuda	. .	'be-horsed' i.e. on horse-back *or* possessing a horse.

Note that the root word admits of qualification.

(d) Repetition i.e. addition to what originally existed. (Usually with the ground word duplicated and often with its indefiniteness strengthened by the suffix *–an.* See par. 133a.)

Examples.

bĕratus–ratus	. in hundreds
bĕrsusun–susunan	in layers
bĕrtambah–tambah	more and more
bĕrgugus–gugus	. in patches, in clusters
bĕrpĕlantingan	. rolling over and over, rebounding.

(e) Verbal use i.e. as the equivalent of an English active, usually intransitive, finite verb. (The root-word is often substantival.)

Examples.

bĕrmalam	. . spend the night
bĕrsungut	. . mutter and grumble
bĕrkawal	. be on sentry duty
bĕrtanam padi	. be a *padi* planter
bĕrjual bĕli.	. be a merchant

Note : As with the prefix *mĕ–*, there are a few crystallized
       formations which are never found without the
       prefix. e.g.

> *bĕrĕnang* .   . to swim
> *bĕlayar*[43] .   . to sail
> *bĕlajar*[43] .   . to learn

II. The prefix " tĕr-".

Par. 124.

The underlying idea in this prefix is completion,
sometimes intentional, sometimes accidental. It may be
thought of as a perfect participle, or a perfect tense, but
the word " tense " is misleading because the Malay prefix
has no reference to *time*. It stresses only the realisation
of the act or the state.

The following aspects of the idea may be distinguished.

(a) Completion, in a state of completion.

Examples.

> *tĕrsandar* .   . leaning (i.e. leant against.)
> *tĕrkatup* .   . closed
> *tĕrsĕbut* .   . said
> *tĕrtulis* .   . written (i.e. on a certain date,
>   but note that *bĕrtulis* means
>   " in writing ", without any
>   reference to the completion of
>   the act, e.g. *bĕrtulis Mĕlayu.*)

(b) Accidental Completion.

Examples.

> *tĕrkĕjut*   .   } startled
> *tĕrpĕranjat*

[43] Note that the prefix does not usually take " r " when that letter
occurs in the root word. cf. *bĕkĕrja*.
In *bĕlajar*, an " l " replaces " r " for the sake of euphony.

tĕrgĕlinchir	.	slipped (active, but without volition)
tĕrsĕdeh–sĕdeh	.	sobbing (having the sobs shaken out of her, willy nilly)

(c) Ability to complete (usually negative).

Examples.

tiada tĕrbilang	.	beyond counting
tiada tĕrkata	.	that cannot be told
tiada tĕrhingga	.	that cannot be reached, boundless

(d) Superlative completion.

Examples.

tĕrbĕsar	.	. exceedingly large
tĕrmashhur	.	. renowned (from *mashhur* famous)
tĕrlampau	.	. exceedingly, excessively (from *lampau* excess)

III. The prefix " pĕ-" or " pĕr-".

Par. 125.

Pĕr- as a verbal prefix is limited in function, and the derivatives formed are few in number. Most of them are causative verbs formed with the suffix *–kan*. They frequently have the prefix *mĕ(m)* in front of the prefix *pĕr-*. Note that the *p* of the prefix in such words is not dropped (contrast par. 119).

Examples

pĕrhatikan or *mĕmpĕrhatikan*
to take note of

pĕristĕrikan or *mĕmpĕristĕrikan*
to marry (of the man)

pĕrbaiki or *mĕmpĕrbaiki*
to make good, to have (a thing) repaired

pĕrgunakan or *mĕmpĕrgunakan*
to make use of

IV.   The suffix "-kan"

Par. 126. With verbs which take two objects

With such verbs the suffix *–kan* is the remnant of a preposition, the word *akan*, denoting " towards ", " to." For this reason, an indirect object which would have been governed by the preposition *akan* in the original construction must be placed immediately after the suffix, i.e. between the verb and its direct object.

Examples.
1. *Bĕlikan saya rokok* . Buy (for) me some cigarettes.
2. *Bĕrikan dia surat itu* . Give (to) him that letter.

Note that when the *–kan* is omitted the indirect object still follows the verb.

Examples.
1. *Bĕli saya rokok.*
2. *Bĕri dia surat.*

If the indirect object is deferred, it must be preceded by a preposition.   e.g.
Bĕri surat itu kapada dia or *kapada–nya.*

Par. 127.   As a causative verbal suffix

(a) It turns intransitive verbs into transitive verbs, usually causative.

Examples.
datang   .   . to come.

datangkan . . ⎱
mĕndatangkan . ⎰ to cause, to make to happen.

(b) It forms causative verbs from adjectives.

Examples.

murah . cheap   *murahkan* . to cheapen
dalam . deep   *mĕndalamkan* . to deepen
rĕndah . low   *mĕrĕndahkan diri* to humble
                                           oneself.

Note: The suffix *–kan* attached to a verb which is already transitive is comparable to *–kan* with a two-object verb (i.e. *akan*). See par. 126.

Example.

Tutupkan pintu
Close the door (for the benefit of the speaker).

V.   The suffix "-i"

Par. 128.

This suffix represents an old locative (i.e. " place ") preposition.

(a) It is therefore frequently found with direct objects which denote place, corresponding to a prepositional phrase in English.

Examples.

Mĕnĕrusi kĕbun . to go through the garden.
Mĕndĕkati sungai . to approach the river.

(b) It turns nouns and adjectives into transitive verbs.
Examples.

nama . name	*namaï*[44]	. to give a name to.
baik . good	*mĕmbaiki*	. to make good, to repair.
susu . milk	*susuï*[44] *mĕnyusuï*	} to give milk to, to suckle.

Note : A verb will usually take either –*kan* or –*i*, the latter suffix being less common than the former. Some verbs, however, are found with both suffixes. When this is the case there is sometimes a distinction of meaning.

Examples.

mĕndĕkati . to draw near to (locative}.
mĕndĕkatkan . to bring (something) near (causative).

Other verbs, however, take either suffix without distinction of meaning.

Examples.

mĕnghidupi or *mĕnghidupkan*
to bring to life, to keep alive.

Par. 129.

You have now worked through all the verbal affixes.
Below is a summary of their functions, with references to the relevant paragraphs.

Try to find reasons for the affixes which you come across in the Malay exercises from this point onwards, but do not think of them as being subject to " rules." Remember, too, that there are no clearly marked dividing lines between parts of speech.

[44] Note the diæresis, to show that the two vowels are sounded separately.

G

Summary of Verbal Affixes

1. The simple verb. par. 114:

Usually active, sometimes passive. No stress on the subject.

2. *di*– with simple verb. par. 115:

Passive. Almost impersonal. Followed by the "subject" as agent, either with or without *oleh*. Third person only.

3. *mĕ*– par. 117–119:

Active. Stresses the subject. Sometimes a participle, sometimes a verbal noun, sometimes a finite verb, usually transitive.

4. *bĕr*– par. 122–3:

Mainly reflexive, including the idea of possession. Also as finite verb, usually intransitive.

5. *tĕr*– par. 124:

Shows completion, sometimes accidental. Usually passive.

6. *pĕ*– par. 125:

Not common. Usually combined with other affixes in the formation of causative verbs.

7. *–kan* par. 126–7:

Forms transitive verbs, and causative verbs; indicates a recipient.

8. *–i* par. 128:

Forms transitive verbs, usually followed by place-words as objects. Forms verbs from other parts of speech.

Par. 130—Examples.

The following piece is taken from *Hikayat Sang Kanchil*, one of the stories in *Hikayat Pĕlandok* (see par. 141).

Kanchil (" the small one "), and *pĕlandok* (" the wily one ") are names for the dwarf-deer or mouse-deer who plays, in Malay fable, the part which Reynard the Fox plays in European fable.

The extract includes punctuation words and balance words which will be explained in later chapters. For the present, do not bother about them.

The verbal affixes are underlined. They are discussed in the notes, below.

Pada sa–kali pĕrsĕtua Sang Kanchil bĕrjalan–jalan[1] mĕnchari[2] mangsa–nya ; tiada bĕrapa lama–nya lalu[3] sampai[4]–lah ia kapada sa–buah sungai, dan pada masa itu juga, dĕngan takdir Allah taala tĕrtumbang–[5]lah sa–pohon kayu bĕsar ka–dalam sungai itu, sa–konyong–konyong datang[6] mĕnimpai[7] sa–ekor buaya, lalu tĕrsĕpit–[8] lah ekor–nya pada kayu itu. Maka di–tĕpi sungai itu pula ada–lah sa–ekor kĕrbau sĕdang mĕminum[9] ayer. Sa–tĕlah di–lihat[10] oleh buaya, ia pun bĕrtĕriak[11], kata–nya, "Wahai, tuan hamba[12] Sang Sempoh[13], kasehan apa–lah[14] tuan hamba mĕnolongi[15] hamba akan mĕngangkatkan[16] batang kayu ini." Maka ujar kĕrbau, "Bĕtapa hal hamba hĕndak mĕnolongi[17] tuan hamba, Sang Bĕdal[13], karna hamba tiada mĕmpunyai[18] tangan hĕndak mĕngangkat dia." Maka kata buaya, "Cheh ! Kalau bagitu sia–sia–lah sahaja[19] tandok tuan hamba yang di–atas kĕpala itu, tiada–kah bĕrguna[20] ?

Translation

Once upon a time Sir Mousedeer was wandering about looking for food. Before very long, he came to a river, and at that very moment, by the will of Allah, Most High, a large tree fell into the river. Swiftly, it crashed down on a crocodile, and the crocodile's tail was caught under it. Now at the edge of the river there was a buffalo, drinking. When the crocodile saw him, he called out to him, saying " Hai, Sir Gorer, have pity on me, I pray you, and help me to lift this tree-trunk." Said the buffalo, " How should I help you, Sir Lasher, (because) I do not possess hands to lift it." The crocodile answered, " Well ! Well ! If that's how it is, it is for nothing then that you have those horns on your head ? Aren't they any use ? "

Notes

1. bĕrjalan–jalan   . Verbal use of bĕr–, par. 123 (e), with repetition indicated by duplication.

2. mĕnchari   . . The mĕ– prefix used participially, par. 119(a).

3. lalu   . . Almost otiose in this context : " He then came ".

4. sampai–lah   . Simple verb for action which involves little conscious thought, par. 114(b). Under this heading come most intransitive verbs of movement : pĕrgi, datang, naik, turun, etc.

5. tĕrtumbang   . " Accidental completion " par. 124(b).

6. datang   . . See note 4.

7. mĕnimpa   . . From timpa. Participial, " came crashing down ". The –i suffix

		here has no particular force, since *timpa* is itself transitive. It may, however, strengthen the locative idea that is in the verb " to crash down *upon* . . ."
8. tĕrsĕpit	.	Accidental completion. par. 124b.
9. mĕminum	.	Participial—continuance of action, par. 119(a).
10. di–lihat	.	The impersonal passive, because the crocodile was not a consciously active agent. The sight presented itself to him.
11. bĕrtĕriak	.	Verbal use of the *bĕr-* derivative, par. 123(e).
12. tuan hamba	.	Lit. " master of this slave ". A respectful mode of address. Translate : " you".
13. Sang Sempoh	.	*Sempoh*—to gore with the horns. Descriptive titles of this sort are common in animal fables. · They enable the speaker to avoid using the hearer's proper name. *Sang* is an honorific prefix much used in animal fables, and before the names of heroes and dignitaries.
14. apa–lah	.	See par. 161.
15. mĕnolongi	.	The *mĕ-* possibly participial, " Pity, as you help me." For the suffix see note 7.
16. mĕngangkatkan	.	The *mĕ-* derivative as a verbal noun after *akan*, " Help towards the lifting."

17. měnolongi . . Verbal noun after *hěndak* par. 119(b).

18. měmpunyaï . . The usual form of the verb, from *punya*. See par. 36.

19. sahaja . . Notice how frequently this word occurs with intensive force, comparable to the English use of "simply", or "just". It is usually pronounced *saja*.

20. běrguna . . Par. 123(c)

Par. 131.   Proverbial Expressions.

A. with *běr–*.

1. *Tiada akan pisang běrbuah dua kali.*
   The banana plant is not likely to bear fruit twice.
   (i.e. Don't expect too much.)

2. *Nanti ara ta' běrgětah.*
   When the fig tree loses its sap.
   (i.e. Never.)

3. *Makan běrkuah ayer mata.*
   To eat with tears for sauce.
   (i.e. To live sorrowfully.)

4. *Běranak tiada běrbidan.*
   To give birth to a child without calling in a midwife.
   (i.e. To take foolish risks.)

5. *Diam ubi běrisi, diam běsi běrkarat.*
   The potato, silently growing ; iron, silently rusting.
   (Similes for quiet progress, and unprofitable idleness.)

B. with *těr–*.
1. *Sudah těrantok baharu těngadah.*
   To look up after the collision has happened.
   (i.e. To lock the stable door after the horse has gone.)

2. *Pileh–pileh ruas, tĕrpileh pada buku.*
   Be fussy over choosing your piece (of sugar cane), and all you'll get will be the knot.
   (i.e. Go farther and fare worse.)

3. *Sa–kali jalan tĕrkĕna, dua kali jalan tahu.*
   Go once and be caught, go twice and know (better)
   (i.e. Once bit, twice shy.)

4. *Biar tĕrsenget, jangan tĕrtiarap.*
   Let (the boat) heel over, but don't let it capsize.
   (i.e. Take risks, but know when to stop.)

5. *Kĕra bĕrmain baji kayu, baji tĕrchabut ekor tĕrsĕpit.*
   The monkey plays with a wedge. The wedge comes out and his tail gets caught.
   (i.e. Don't meddle with what does not concern you.)

Exercise 28

a. Translate the following passage, which is a continuation of the piece given in par. 130. A few of the words have noun affixes. These will be explained in the next chapter.

b. Write explanatory notes on the words which have index numbers.

Sa–tĕlah di–dĕngar[1] oleh kĕrbau datang[2]–lah ia mĕnyusupkan[3] tandok–nya ka–bawah batang kayu itu, lalu[4] di–angkat–nya, maka lĕpas[5]–lah buaya itu tiba–tiba langsong[6] ia mĕnangkap[7] kaki kĕrbau yang mĕmbuat kĕbajikan itu.

Maka bĕrkata[8]–lah kĕrbau dĕngan sĕdeh hati–nya, "Adohai! Sampai–nya hati ("Have you the heart to . . . ") tuan hamba, Sang Bĕdal? Hamba mĕmbuat[9] baik, tuan hamba balas[10] dĕngan kĕjahatan. Shabash–lah budi tuan!

Ada–lah (see par. 146b) sĕgala hal ahwal itu sĕmua–nya tĕlah di–lihat oleh Sang Kanchil. Maka ia pun sĕgĕra mĕlompat ka–atas batang itu, sĕraya[11] bĕrkata, " Hai, Sang Kĕrbau yang dĕngu, sia–sia–lah sahaja bĕsar tuboh tuan hamba itu tiada mĕmpunyaï akal ; tiada–kah tuan hamba mĕndĕngar bahawa (" that ") sakalian manusia dan binatang di–dalam dunia ini mĕmbalas budi dan bahasa yang maha baik itu dĕngan jasa yang tĕrsangat[12] jahat lagi kĕbĕngisan ? (see par. 135a).

N.B.—In writing your notes do not feel that you are being asked to pigeon-hole the words under definite labels. All that you are doing is to say what you think was the idea that was in the writer's mind when he used the derivative.

Exercise 29

Translate.

1. Is there anybody in the village with a raft ?—Yes, Che' Ngah has just finished making a new one.—Do you think he would be willing to pole me down the rapids ?—Yes, I should think so. I'll go and ask him.

2. You won't be late to-morrow, will you ? It is important that we should get to Kuala Sĕrau before the case begins. Or, at any rate, before they call the witnesses. I hope the case won't be long drawn out.

Conversation No. 9

Siapa itu ?

Darus : Siapa itu ?

Osman : Di–sini nombor 321.
(or
Uthman)

Darus : Saya 'nak bĕrchakap dĕngan Che' Osman.

Osman : Ini dia.

Darus : Saya ini Darus.

Osman : Che' Darus–kah ? Apa khabar ? Lama ta'
bĕrjumpa. Apa hal ?

Darus : 'Nak bĕrkhabar istĕri saya sudah bĕrsalin
anak pĕrĕmpuan pada pukul 'lapan pagi tadi.

Osman : Sunggoh–kah? Suka hati saya mĕndĕngar.
Saya tahu Che' Darus bĕrkĕhĕndak sangat
kapada anak pĕrĕmpuan. Sĕkarang Tuhan
sudah sampaikan hajat. Apa nama di–bĕrikan
budak itu ?

Darus : 'Tok–nya bĕri nama Zainab, ganti nenek–nya
yang mĕninggal sa–puloh tahun dahulu. Elok–
kah nama itu, Che' Osman ?

Osman : Bunyi–nya sĕdap, lĕmbut pula pada tĕlinga.

Darus : Kalau bagitu saya tidak ubahkan nama itu.
Baik–lah, Che' Osman. Tinggal–lah.

Osman : Sĕlamat tinggal. Kita bĕrjumpa lagi.

Translation

Who's Speaking?

Darus : Who is that ?

Osman : Number 321.

Darus : I want to speak to Che' Osman.

Osman : Speaking.

Darus : Darus here.

Osman : Oh, Che' Darus, is it ? How are you ? I
haven't seen you for a long time. What did
you want to say to me ?

Darus : I just wanted to tell you that my wife had a
daughter, at 8 o'clock this morning.

Osman : Really ? I'm very glad to hear it. I know you very much wanted a girl. Now Tuhan Allah has granted your wish. What name have you given her ?

Darus : Her grandfather has given her the name Zainab, in memory of (lit. in place of) her grandmother who died ten years ago. Do you like it ?

Osman : Yes, it has a pleasant, soft sound. (lit. " The sound of it is pleasant. Moreover, it is soft to the ear.)

Darus : If you think that, I shan't change it. Well then, good-bye.

Osman : Good-bye. I shall be seeing you some time. (lit. we shall meet again.)

CHAPTER XIV.

AFFIXATION—NOUNS

I. The prefix " pĕ– "

Par. 132.

The prefix *pĕ–* forms nouns, usually from verbs. Most of the derivatives can be used adjectivally. With occasional exceptions, the prefix *pĕ–* brings about the same consonantal changes as the prefix *mĕ–*. (see par. 117).

The prefix *pĕ–* is used to denote an agent or an instrument (comparable to " sailor " and " ruler " in English.)

Examples.

churi	. to steal	*pĕnchuri*	. thief
borong	. wholesale	*pĕmborong*	. a contractor
putar	. to rotate	*pĕmutar*	. a screwdriver
kapor	. lime	*pĕkapor*	. the lime container in a betel-nut set.
asap	. smoke	*pĕrasap*	. an incense burner
korek	. to dig a hole	*pĕngorek*	. a bradawl

203

gali	. to dig	*pĕnggali*	. a spade
sapu	. to sweep	*pĕnyapu*	. a broom
pĕgang	. to hold	*pĕmĕgang*	. balustrade, handle (note that this is a passive use : " That which is held ".)

chĕlup	. to steep, dye	*pĕnchĕlup* or *ayer pĕnchĕlup* dye
hiris	. to slice	*pisau pĕnghiris* carving knife (an adjectival use)

Note that a noun derived from a transitive verb may retain its power of governing an object.

Examples.

chungkil	. to extract with a pointed instrument	*pĕnchungkil gigi* a tooth pick
tunggu	. to guard	*pĕnunggu pintu* doorkeeper
tunjok	. to point out	*pĕnunjok jalan* a sign-post
kisar	. to revolve	*pĕngisar gandum* a flour mill (*gandum*— wheat)

II. The suffix " –an "

Par. 133.

This suffix forms nouns and adjectives. It is of frequent occurrence, both alone and in conjunction with one of the prefixes *pĕ-*, *kĕ-* or *bĕr*.

Below are set out its uses without these prefixes. Remember, as always, that such a classification does not represent any real cleavage. Many of the derivatives are of dual function, and except for (a), the subdivisions themselves overlap.

Uses of the suffix " –an "

It forms :

(a) Collective nouns expressing extent or variety, the idea of variety being sometimes reinforced by duplication of the root word.

Examples.

buah–buahan	.	fruits of all sorts.
masak–masakan	.	cooked dishes of various sorts.
lautan	.	far-stretching sea, i.e. ocean.
kaparan	.	flotsam (from *kapar*—strew.)
gugusan pulau	.	cluster of islands, archipelago.
gali–galian	.	mineral products (i.e. " things dug up " ; but note that *galian* means a " surface mine ".)
puji–pujian	.	conventional compliments at the beginning of a formal letter. (from *puji*—praise.)

(b) Nouns which denote the result of an action ; or, the action itself (i.e. verbal nouns.)

Examples.

aturan	.	arrangement, *or* act of arranging ; *or* method. (from *atur*—arrange.)
akuan	.	acknowledgement (from *aku*—acknowledge.)

karangan . .	composition (from *karang*– put together.)
ilmu karangan .	the art of composing.
salah ejaan .	a mistake in (or " of ") spelling (from *eja*—spell.)
salah ambilan .	a mis-taking, i.e. a misunderstanding. (from *ambil*—take.)
hubongan huruf .	the joining of letters (from *hubong*—join.)
potongan China .	the " cut " of a garment, Chinese style.
anggaran . .	an estimate (from *anggar*—estimate.)
latehan tuboh .	training of the body (from *lateh*—order), i.e. gymnastic exercises.

(c) Nouns of instrument, which may be compared with nouns formed with the prefix *pĕ-* (par. 132). Some verbs have both derivatives, (e.g. *putar*, *kisar*.)

Note that when the root is a transitive verb, the noun retains the power of governing an object.

Examples.

putaran .	that which rotates .	a windlass
kisaran padi .	that which turns .	a rice mill
ampaian kain .	that which makes to sway .	a clothes line
alangan .	that which bars .	a sand-bar, a difficulty, an obstruction.
apitan .	that which presses .	a copying press

(d) ' Passive nouns ', standing for concrete things on which an action is performed.

Examples.

chetakan .	. that which has been set in a mould	. edition (of book)
gadaian .	. that which has been pledged	. a pledge
muatan .	. that which has been loaded	. cargo
tujuan .	. that which is aimed at	. objective
kĕratan .	. that which has been cut off	. a piece (but usually *kerat*)

N.B. Many of the examples given under (b) might be included also under this heading : e.g.

karangan	. that which has been composed	. a composition
potongan	. that which has been cut	. a slice (but usually *potong*)

(e) Abstract nouns.

Examples.

mashghulan	. sadness (from *mashghul*—sad)
hutangan	. indebtedness (from *hutang* —debt)
kasehan .	. pity (from *kaseh*—pity, love)

(f) Adjectives, which are sometimes purposive, sometimes passive.

Examples.

(purposive)

ayam potongan . a hen for killing . a table bird

sĕkolah latehan	. a school for training	. a practising school
surat kĕnalan	. a letter for making known	. a letter of introduction
kapal tumpangan	a ship for taking passages on	. a passenger vessel

(passive)

harta rampasan	. goods that have been seized	. loot
bunga rampaian	. flowers that have been mixed	. a pot-pourri of petals
anak buangan	. a child that has been abandoned	. a foundling
duit bayaran	. money that is paid	. e.g. entrance money

Note:

1. For the use of the suffix *-an* (adjectival) in conjunction with the prefix *ber-* see par. 123d.

2. There are other *-an* derivatives which do not fit exactly into any of these five subdivisions. e.g.

giliran	.	. one's " turn " (from *gilir*— rotation, successive occurrence)
gĕlaran	.	. a title (from *gĕlar*—to give a title)

III. Prefix and suffix " pĕ . . . an "

Par. 134.

These affixes form nouns, usually from verbal roots.

Examples.

mula	. begin, beginning	*pěrmulaan*[45]	. beginning
habis	. finish, end	*pěnghabisan*	. outcome, end
hingga	. up to, until	*pěrhinggaan* (or *pěrenggan*)	. boundary, limit
pěrang	. war	*pěpěrangan*	. warfare
rasa	. feel, feeling	*pěrasaan*	. feeling
laboh	. to let down (the anchor)	*pělabohan* (or *labohan*)	. anchorage
(*oleh*)	. to get	*pěrolehan*	. that which has been obtained, acquisition
kěrja	. work	*pěkěrjaan*	. work, undertaking

IV. Prefix and suffix " kě . . . an "

Par. 135.

These affixes can be combined with nouns, adjectives, verbs or adverbs.

The derivatives may be :

(a) Nouns denoting state or condition.

Examples.

jahat	. wicked	*kějahatan*	. wickedness
těntu	. certain	*kětěntuan*	. certainty

---

[45] Note that these derivative nouns are sometimes found in composition with other affixes, e.g. *tahu* or *kětahui*—" to know " ; *pěngětahuan*—" knowledge " ; *běrpěngětahuan* (adjectival)—" possessed of knowledge " ; *kuasa*—" power, authority " ; *běrpěnguasaan*—" possessed of authority."

esok	. tomorrow	*kĕesokan* (*hari itu*)	. The 'morrowness' (of that day) i.e. the next day.
sĕmpit	. narrow, cramped	*kĕsĕmpitan*	. scarcity
susah	. trouble-some	*kĕsusahan*	. trouble
mati	. death, die	*kĕmatian*	. bereaved by death; death
raja	. ruler	*kĕrajaan*	. 1. rule 2. the government
ada	. be	*kĕadaan*	. 1. existence 2. state

Note:

1. Some of these derivatives (see the last two examples) may have different meanings according to the context in which they occur.

2. These derivatives usually correspond to English nouns, but they are sometimes used adjectivally as in Exercise 28: *jasa yang jahat lagi kĕbĕngisan* and Exercise 36: *kĕlambu yang kĕĕmasan itu.*

   (b) Nouns and adjectives denoting places.
   Examples.

yang (archaic)	. Divinity, Godhead (cf. *sĕmbahyang*)	*kĕyangan*	. heaven, the Hindu Olympus
diam	. dwell	*kĕdiaman*	. dwelling place

   (c) Adjectives from verbal roots. Such an adjective usually implies that the person (or thing) to which it refers has suffered the action indicated by the verbal root.   Hence it can often be translated by an English passive.

Examples.

1. *Tiba–tiba kĕdĕngaran–lah bunyi suara yang lĕmah lĕmbut.*
   Suddenly a soft voice was heard.

2. *Maseh lagi kĕchil dia kĕhilangan ibu bapa–nya.*
   While he was still a child, he lost his parents.

3. *Puchat muka–nya sapĕrti orang kĕmatian.*
   He looked pale, like a person who has suffered a bereavement.

4. *Kita lambat bertolak jadi kemalaman tengah jalan.*
   We were late setting out, and so we were over-taken by darkness before we reached our destination.

Note: A root word will take either the *pĕ ... an* form for its derivative, or the *kĕ ... an* form. They are not interchangeable. On the whole the *kĕ ... an* form is more often an abstract noun, and the *pĕ ... an* form a concrete noun.

V. The prefix " ke- "

Par. 136.

There are very few derivatives formed with this prefix. The commonest of them are:

(a) substantival:

kĕtua	.	elder (one who is old)
kĕhendak	.	desire (that which is desired)
kĕdua	.	a pair ⎫ (those who are in
kĕtiga	.	a threesome ⎬ a group of 2, 3,
kĕĕmpat, etc.	.	a foursome ⎭ 4, etc.)

(b) verbal:

kĕtahuï	.	to know
kĕhĕndaki	.	to desire

H

Par. 137.

You have now studied all the affixes.

The extract given in paragraph 130 has made it clear that these affixes are used freely in the written language.

You will be able to gauge the extent to which they are used in every-day speech by studying the plays (Texts A and B) in *Sentence Analysis in Modern Malay*. See book-list page x.

Remember that the affixes are not grammatical inflections, subject to fixed rules (as, for example, the rules for the agreement of the participle in French). They are, rather, indications of the speaker's or writer's point of view.

Nor is every verbal root found with every affix. A root will take the affixes which its meaning permits it to take. Later on, if you continue your study of literary Malay, you will waste many a profitable hour browsing in Wilkinson's *Malay–English Dictionary*. In that you will find recorded most of the derivatives that occur in Malay literature. Winstedt's *Malay Grammar* (Chap. VI) affords abundant illustration of their uses.

Below are set out ten root-words with their derivatives, as given by Wilkinson. These will give you some idea of the possibilities of affixation.

But there is no finality about such a list. Certain forms are fixed by usage, as has been explained (see par. 135 *ad fin.*) and a few words have crystallized (see par. 119 note 2, and par. 123 note), but on the whole affixation, especially verbal affixation, is a *live* process which lends to a root-word a temporary particularization of aspect.

For Example:

A writer speaks of "slanders falling-thick-as-leaves-of-the-forest." The expression he uses is: *mĕndaun kayu*, i.e. "behaving as leaves behave."

A suspected poultry-stealer is told that the thief has a

feather sticking to his hair, and his hand at once goes up to his head. The expression used is : *tĕrjabat kapala–nya dĕngan tangan*. The writer shows, by the prefix, that it was an involuntary action. The word *jabat* (to grasp, clasp) would not be shown in any dictionary with a *tĕr–* prefix, but that is exactly what is needed in this sentence.

Such instances show clearly how affixes contribute to the terseness which is a marked characteristic of Malay style.

They show, too, that Malay affixation is an elastic device, not a set of grammatical inflections. Bear this in mind as you study the next paragraph.

Do not use affixes in your conversation except in derivatives which are familiar to your ear, but be prepared to hear them, and to see them, in contexts which may call for translations differing from those given in the dictionaries.

Par. 138.
Ten root–words with derivatives as given in Wilkinson's *Malay–English Dictionary*.

1. Ajar—instruction.

ajarkan	. .	to teach (something)
ajari	. .	to instruct
mĕngajar	. .	to be occupied in teaching
ajaran	}	teaching—the substance
pĕlajaran	}	taught (i.e. what one teaches)
pĕngajaran	. .	teaching—the method (i.e. how one teaches)
pĕngajar	. .	a teacher
bĕlajar	. .	to be instructed, i.e. to learn

2. Alang—position athwart.

alangan	. a bar, obstruction
mĕngalang–ngalang	to obstruct, to worry
mĕngalangkan	. to lay (something) athwart

Cognate words are :

galang . .	. a cross-bar ; rollers for a boat
galangan .	. a slip–way
galang–gĕmalang	. to be constantly in dock (of a ship)
galangkan .	. 1. to lay (a boat) on rollers 2. to ward off (a descending blow)
mĕnggalang .	. to be in the way, to obstruct
tĕrgalang .	. placed in the way, obstructing ; aground
kayu palang .	. cross bar (e.g. on a buffalo's horns)
malang . .	. mischance ; adverse, of fortune
kĕmalangan .	. ill-luck

3. Idar—circling.

mĕngidari .	. to wander around (a place)
mĕngidarkan .	. to hand round (a thing)
bĕridar . .	. revolving
pĕridaran .	. revolution

4. Jadi—come into existence.

mĕnjadi .	. to become
mĕnjadikan .	. to create, to cause to be
kĕjadian .	. creation

5. Jalan—movement in a definite direction.

bĕrjalan (kaki)	. to travel (on foot)
jalani . .	. to travel over
mĕnjalankan .	. to set a thing going
pĕrjalanan .	. a journey

6. Laboh—lowering by means of a rope:

labohan	} a roadstead, an anchorage
pĕlabohan	

labohkan (sauh) . . to let down (the anchor)
bĕrlaboh . . . to lie at anchor

7. Laku—conduct (of person or enterprise).

bĕrlaku . . . to take effect
mĕlakukan . . to put into effect
kĕlakuan . . behaviour

8. Lĕkat—adhering.

lĕkatkan . . to stick a thing (on something else)
mĕlĕkat . . . to adhere
tĕrlĕkat . . . stuck on

9. Muat—loading.

muatkan . . to load with
bĕrmuat. . . laden with
muatan . . cargo

10. Ubah—alteration.

ubahkan . . to change (something)
bĕrubah . . to be different
kĕubahan .
pĕrubahan . } alteration

Par. 139. Examples.

1. *Maksud–nya hĕndak mĕnunjokkan kĕpandaian–nya.*
   He wants to show how clever he is.
   (Lit. His intention is that he shall show his skill.)

2. *Pĕncharian–nya mĕnangkap ikan.*
   He is a fisherman.
   (Lit. His livelihood is catching fish.)

3. *Pada masa sĕkarang dagangan nĕgĕri itu mahal harga–nya.*

At present the goods that come from that country are dear. (Note the idiom " dear price", not " high price".)

4. *Kĕkayaan–nya ta'tĕrkira–kira, tĕtapi haram satu sen pun dia ta'hĕndak bĕrsĕdĕkah.*

His wealth is enormous (Lit. . . beyond counting . .) but not a single cent will he give away.

5. *Pada pikiran (or fikiran) saya, orang itu pĕnipu.*

It is my opinion that the man is a cheat.

6. *Ta'tĕrsĕbut kĕsukaan apabila mĕndĕngar bunyi-bunyian itu.*

I cannot tell you the delight that it gave me to listen to that music. (Lit. . . It is not able to be said. . .)

7. *Tiap–tiap suka itu duka kĕsudahan–nya. (Prov.)*

Every pleasure ends in sorrow. (Lit. . . sorrow is the end of it . .)

8. *Hĕndak masok kĕna minta surat kĕbĕnaran dahulu.*

You must get a pass if you want to go in.

9. *Gĕli hati dia mĕlihat kĕlakuan budak itu.*

He was amused at (Lit. . . seeing . .) the behaviour of the child.

10. *Kĕsusahan itu di–sĕbabkan oleh kĕkurangan wang.*

The trouble was caused by lack of funds.

Par. 140.

Extract from Pa Kadok). This is the first of the stories in *Chĕrita Jĕnaka* (see par. 141).

Ada pun[1] adat Pa Kadok, tĕlah lazim pada–nya sa–tiap pagi mĕmakan[2] nasi dingin yang tĕlah di–rĕndam oleh istĕri–nya pada malam[3] itu : apabila sudah makan nasi yang tĕrsĕbut itu baharu–lah[4] ia pĕrgi barang[5] ka–mana–mana mĕmbuat[6] kĕrja–nya. Hata[1] sa–tĕlah

kĕesokan[7] hari-nya pagi-pagi Pa Kadok pun[8] bangun-
lah bĕrsiap[9] mĕmakai[10] pakaian[7]-nya lalu turun
mĕmikul[11] pĕngayoh[7] bĕrjalan mĕnuju ka-pangkalan[12].
Sĕrta di-lihat oleh istĕri-nya ia pun mĕnyĕru[13] akan
suami-nya, kata-nya, " Hai Pa Siti[14] tidak-kah hĕndak
makan nasi rĕndam ini sĕmĕntangkan[15] 'nak makan
lĕmbu dan kĕrbau, nasi ini di-tinggalkan sahaja ? "
Maka sahut Pa Kadok " Ta'usah-lah, churahkan ka-
tanah[16] : biar di-makan oleh ayam kita." Maka oleh
istĕri-nya dĕngan sa-bĕnar nasi itu di-buangkan-nya
ka-tanah dan Pa Kadok pun turun ka-pĕrahu-nya lalu
bĕrkayoh.

Ada pada masa itu ayer sungai sĕdang surut tĕrlalu
amat dĕras-nya. Maka Pa Kadok bĕrfikir di-dalam
hati-nya, " Ka-mana baik aku pĕrgi ? jika ka-hilir
tiada pĕnat dan tĕrok aku bĕrkayoh hanya mĕnurutkan
ayer hilir sahaja ; tĕtapi kĕrbau sa-ekor ka-mana-lah
pada[17] -nya ? Kalau bagitu baik-lah aku mudek juga.[8]"
Ia pun lalu bĕrkayoh mudek mĕnongkah ayer surut itu.
Apabila pĕnat ia bĕrhĕnti sambil bĕrfikir pula[8], dan
pĕrahu-nya hanyut balek ka-hilir sa-tanjong[18], dua
tanjong jauh-nya ; bĕrkayoh pula ; dĕmikian-lah hal
Pa Kadok kayoh-kayoh bĕrhĕnti dĕngan bĕrfikir juga ;
bĕbĕrapa lama-nya ayer pun tĕnang surut hampir
akan pasang baharu-lah[4] Pa Kadok sampai ka-rumah
jĕmputan[7] itu, tĕtapi apa-lah guna-nya ? Sia-sia
sahaja-lah pĕnat-nya itu karna matahari pun tĕlah
lohor[19], jamuan[7] sudah habis orang turun bĕrkusu-kusu
dari rumah itu pulang ka-kampong masing-masing.

Translation

Now[1] it was Pa Kadok's custom every morning to
eat cold rice, which had been cooked the evening before[3]
by his wife. After that, he would set out to wherever[5]
he was going for his day's work (*or,* He would not
set out . . . until[4] . . .). On the next day, very early,

Pa Kadok got up, dressed, and went down towards the river, carrying his paddle. When his wife saw this, she shouted to her husband, saying, " Hai, Pa Siti, aren't you going to eat the rice that I cooked ? Even though you are going to have beef and buffalo, are you going to leave your rice (because of that)" ? And Pa Kadok answered, " Oh, don't bother about that. Throw it away. Let the fowls eat it." And sure enough his wife threw the rice away, and Pa Kadok got into his boat and began to paddle.

Now at that time the tide was running out very strongly. Pa Kadok pondered, " Where had I better go ? " If I go downstream, I shan't have to wear myself out paddling, I shall simply go with the stream. But one buffalo ! What is that going to be enough for ! So I had better go up–stream after all. Then he paddled up–stream, against the ebbing tide. When he grew weary he would stop and think for a bit, and his boat would drift downstream round a couple of bends[18] ; then he would start rowing again. So he went on, rowing and thinking by turns, and at last the tide was full out. It was not until[4] it was about to turn that he reached the house to which he had been invited. But what was the good ? In vain had he worn himself out, for it was already past noon, the feast was over, and the people were coming out of the house in little groups and returning to their own homes.

Notes

1. Ada pun . } See Chap. XV for punctuation
   Hata   } words.

2. mĕmakan . . *Lazim mĕmakan*—lit. accustomed, eating ; like *hairan mĕlihat*—surprised, seeing. (par. 119(c).)

3. malam itu . . The Muhammadan " day " begins at 6 p.m. on the previous evening. Therefore, the "*malam*" (i.e. the period of darkness) of the day on which Pa Kadok was to eat his rice was already over. (See footnote 77.)

4. baharu–lah . . Be on the watch for this very common idiom.

5. barang . . See Chap. XVII for "indefinite" words.

6. mĕmbuat . . *Pĕrgi mĕmbuat* — went, doing. Participial use of *mĕ*– (par. 119b.)

7. kĕesokan etc. . . Be on the look-out for derivative nouns. They are very easy. All that you have to do is to take off the head and/or tail, and look at the probably familiar disyllable which you have left. The translation of the derivative noun is frequently the same as that of the root.

8. pun, juga, pula . . For balance words see Ch. XVI.

9. bĕrsiap . . . Reflexive : "made himself ready".

10. mĕmakai pakaian . "And put on his clothes". *bĕrpakai* might have been used instead of *bĕrsiap mĕmakai pakaian*.

11. mĕmikul . . . From *pikul*. "went down, carrying". Participial use of *mĕ*–.

12. bĕrjalan mĕnuju ka–pangkalan . . Lit. " walked, making his way towards the place where his boat was tied up." *Pangkalan* is the

usual word for "landing stage". *Měnuju* (from *tuju*) is the usual word for boats making for a port. For the *běrjalan* ("walked"; see par. 123(e)). Compare the common phrase *běrjalan pěrgi* ("went") which to us seems tautologous.

13. měnyěru . From *sěru*. A *mě*- derivative as a finite verb.

14. Pa Siti . Father of Siti (their child). A common form of address between husband and wife. Another instance of the evasion of the use of a person's name. Pa Kadok addresses his wife as *Mak Siti*.

15. sěměntangkan . An uncommon word=*sunggoh pun*.

16. churahkan ka–tanah . "Throw *it* away." Notice again the omission of the pronoun object. *ka–tanah*—the flooring of the cooking-place would be of bamboo slats, and the rubbish would be thrown through the spaces to the ground below, to be washed away by the next tide, or, as here, eaten by the fowls.

17. pada . . " sufficiency." Notice this second meaning of *pada*.

18. sa–tanjong, dua tanjong jauh-nya . lit. " for a distance of one or two headlands."

19. lohor . . . or *dzohor*. See par. 199c.

Exercise 30

Translate the following piece, which is a continuation of the passage given in par. 140. The index figures indicate notes attached to the key, but there is no need to look them up until you have finished your translation.

Maka apabila tĕrlihat[1] oleh tuan rumah akan Pa Kadok datang itu[2], ia pun bĕrkata, " Amboi ! Kasehan-nya di–hati sahaya oleh mĕlihatkan pĕnat sahaja–lah Pa Kadok datang ; suatu pun tiada apa lagi yang ada, sĕmua–nya tĕlah habis, malang sunggoh–lah Pa Kadok ini[3]." Tĕlah di–dĕngar oleh Pa Kadok maka ujar–nya, " Sudah–lah. Apa boleh buat ? Sahajakan[4] nasib sahaya." Maka ia pun bĕrkayoh–lah hilir pula, hasrat-nya hĕndak mĕndapatkan[5] rumah yang mĕmotong kĕrbau itu balek, tĕtapi ayer sudah pasang dĕras. Maka Pa Kadok pun bĕrkayoh–lah bĕrsunggoh–sunggoh hati–nya, mĕnongkah ayer pasang itu di–tĕngah panas tĕrok dĕngan lapar dahaga–nya tĕtapi karna bĕbal–nya itu tiada–lah ia mau singgah ka–rumah–nya langsong sahaja ia ka–hilir hĕndak sĕgĕra mĕnĕrpa kĕrbau yang lagi tinggal itu ; sa–hingga ayer tĕnang pasang hampir surut[6], baharu–lah Pa Kadok sampai ka–sana, pada waktu asar rĕndah[7] dan sakalian orang jĕmputan pun sĕdang hĕndak turun bĕrkayoh pulang oleh sudah sĕlĕsai jamuan itu.

Exercise 31

Translate.

1. Have you always lived in Kuala Lumpor ?—No, I was born in Kuala Lipis.—That's in Pahang, isn't it ?—Yes ; my parents moved when I was quite small, about three years old, I think. Most of my relatives live in Pahang. I often go there for holidays.

2. What a lovely morning ! It's worth while getting up
early, isn't it ? Look at those peaks just coming
through the clouds. How high are we, do you think ?
Just listen to the monkeys ! What a clamour they
are making !

Conversation No. 10

Di–mana–mana pun sa–rupa juga

Ahmad : (sa–orang laki)	Lauk apa kita 'nak makan pĕtang ini ?
Fatimah : (istĕri–nya)	Bĕlum tahu lagi. Si–Hamid 'nak pĕrgi ka–pasar sa–kĕjap lagi.
Ahmad :	Apa dia mahu bĕli ?
Fatimah :	Saya suroh dia bĕli daging lĕmbu dua kati, kobis sa–kati, tĕlor sa–tĕngah dozen. Kalau ada baki duit lagi saya suroh dia bĕli ubi kĕntang sikit.
Ahmad :	Ta–payah bĕli lauk banyak kĕrana saya ta'boleh dudok lama di–rumah pĕtang ini.
Fatimah :	Awak memang bagitu ! Tiap–tiap pĕtang ada hal. Ta' satu satu. Ta'boleh dudok di–rumah macham orang lain.
Ahmad :	Jangan bĕrsungut. Saya ada kĕrja yang mustahak. Kalau tidak, lĕpas kerja di–ofis balek–lah langsong lĕkat di–rumah.
Fatimah :	Ta'apa–lah. Kalau sĕmpat, jangan lupa singgah di–kĕdai Pa' Mahmud, bĕlikan saya jarum sa–kotak. Biar–lah halus, jangan kasar.
Ahmad :	Baik–lah.

Translation.

It's the same everywhere !

Ahmad : (husband)	What are we having for dinner this evening ?
Fatimah : (wife)	I don't know yet. Hamid is going to market presently.
Ahmad :	What is he going to buy ?
Fatimah :	I have told him to buy two *kati* of beef, a *kati* of cabbage and half a dozen eggs. If there is any money over I have told him to buy some potatoes.
Ahmad :	There is no need to buy much, (because) I can't stay in long this evening.
Fatimah :	There you are again ! Every evening there's something. If it isn't one thing, it's another. You can't stay at home as other people do.
Ahmad :	Don't grumble at me. I have some very important work on hand. If I hadn't, I should certainly come home after I had finished at the office, and not go out again.
Fatimah :	All right. If you have time, don't forget to call at Pa' Mahmud's and get me a box of needles. Mind they are fine ones, not coarse.
Ahmad :	Very well.

CHAPTER XV

PUNCTUATION WORDS

Par. 141.

Modern Malays use punctuation marks even when they write in the Arabic character.   This is an innovation. Malay literature, written in Jawi script, uses *words* where we use signs, and these words are retained in the romanized transliteration.   They have meaning, as you will see from the following paragraphs, but they can frequently be omitted in translation.

The extracts in this chapter, with one or two exceptions, are taken from the *Sějarah Mělayu* (*Malay Annals*).

The pieces used in chapters XIII and XIV were from Malay folk-lore. *Hikayat Pělandok Jěnaka* (Stories of the Wily Mousedeer) and *Chěrita Jěnaka* (Farcical Tales) are collections of stories that have lived for generations on the lips of the people.   They were the stock-in-trade of the professional story-teller, the *pěnglipor lara* (soother of cares).   They are written in lively style with the terse idiom of everyday speech, and the vocabulary of everyday life.

The *Sějarah Mělayu* is different, both in origin and in aim.   It is a " history " of the old Kingdom of Malacca, written in the 16th century.   It mingles fact and legend, and freely embroiders both, but the result is a vivid picture of the court life of those days.

Scholars consider it, with the *Hikayat Hang Tuah* (see par. 180), to be the best example of Malay prose style. It is clear, smooth-flowing, leisurely, with constant repetitions which give it an echoing effect. The ear, as one reads, waits pleasurably for the return of remembered phrase or cadence, and the mind is content to follow a narrative that advances with the assured deliberation of a Greek key pattern.

You will find a short account of Malay history and romance, in *Papers on Malay Subjects, Malay Literature*, Part I; and of Malay folk-lore in Part II of the same series.

These *Papers* cover all aspects of Malay life (Amusements, Ceremonies, Industries, Literature, History, Law) and are written in non-technical style. They are of absorbing interest.

For a full account see: *A History of Classical Malay Literature*, by Sir Richard Winstedt. Malayan Branch Royal Asiatic Society. Vol. XXXI. Part 3, June 1958. Luzac and Company.

I. Maka

Par. 142.

Maka is the commonest of the punctuation words. When you are translating a passage, you will find it helpful to think of it as an introductory word marking the opening of a clause, whether main or subordinate. But its real function is rather to join one clause to the next. " This happened, then, that happened." It can sometimes be translated by " and " or " then ", but it is usually better to omit it in translation.

Example 1 is a connected passage, a good example of the " echoing " style referred to in par. 141.

Examples 2 to 8 show a very common type of sentence in which the first half is what would be, in English, an adverbial clause, and the second half, preceded by *maka*, the main clause.

Examples 9 and 10 show sentences in which both clauses are introduced by *maka*.

Note that *maka* is used after any of the introductory and transition words dealt with in pars. 143 and 144.

Examples.

1. " Tĕlah datang ka–Tanjong Bĕmban, maka baginda pun turun bĕrmain ka–pasir ; maka raja pĕrĕmpuan pun turun dĕngan sĕgala bini orang bĕsar–bĕsar dan orang kaya–kaya bĕrmain di–pasir itu mĕngambil[1] karang–karangan. Maka raja pĕrĕmpuan dudok di–bawah pohon pandan di–hadap[2] bini sĕgala orang kaya–kaya[3], maka baginda tĕrlalu suka mĕlihat kĕlakuan dayang–dayang bĕrmain itu, masing masing pada kĕsukaan–nya . . . ada yang mĕngambil kĕtam, ada yang mĕngambil lokan, ada yang mĕngambil daun kayu oleh hulaman, ada yang mĕngambil bunga karang, ada yang mĕngambil agar–agar. Maka tĕrlalu–lah suka chita sĕgala dayang-dayang itu ; ada yang mĕngambil bunga–bungaan di–buat sunting, masing–masing dĕngan tengkah–laku[4]–nya, ada yang bĕrlari bĕrhambat–hambatan[5] tĕrsĕrandong[6] jatoh rĕbah rempah[7] daripada sangat suka–nya itu."

Translation

When the king came to Tanjong Bemban he went down to the beach for a picnic, and the queen went too, with all the wives of chiefs and notables to take their pleasure gathering shellfish on the beach. The queen sat under a *pandan* tree with all the wives of the magnates in attendance. The king took much pleasure in watching the court maidens sporting there, each following her own inclination . . . Some were gathering crabs, and others cockles, and some were gathering leaves to make a salad. Some were gathering coral, and others seaweed. All the maidens were full of gaiety, some of them picking flowers to wear in their hair, each in her own fashion, others racing about chasing each other falling headlong and jumping up again in their merriment.

Notes

1. bĕrmain mĕngambil . Played, gathering. Participial *mĕ-*.

2. di–hadap   .   . *Hadap* is verbal. The phrase might have been *di–hadapi oleh bini* . . . " be–fronted by the wives." i.e. with the wives in attendance. *Mĕngadap*, "presentone-self before," is the usual word for having an audience with a ruler.

3. orang kaya–kaya . A title—lesser chieftains.

4. tengkah–laku . . Or *tingkah–laku*— behaviour.

5. bĕrhambat–hambatan A good example of *ber* . . . *an* for repetition (par. 123(d)).

6. tĕrsĕrandong . . Tripping, stumbling. A good example of " accidental *tĕr-*" (par. 124(b).

7. rĕbah rempah . . A frequentative form, like *lalu lalang*. Note that *rempah* has a full " e ". Do not confuse it with *rĕmpah* "spices", and "ingredients".

2. *Tělah datang ia ka–sabělah Jambu Ayer arah ka–timur, maka di–lihat oleh pawang kěpala manusia lěkat pada kěmudi.* (See par. 189, Note 2.)

When they came towards Jambu Ayer, going eastwards, the shipmaster saw that there was a man's head stuck to the rudder.

3. *Tělah sakalian měněngar kata běndahara itu, maka sakalian orang kaya–kaya itu pun běrdiam diri–nya, masing–masing kěmbali ka–rumah–nya.*

When they heard what the *běndahara* said, all the magnates held their peace, and returned, each to his own home.

4. *Sěbab ia chěrdek, lagi tahu běrkata–kata, maka di–jadikan baginda běntara.*

Because he was clever, and ready with his tongue, the king appointed him a court herald.

5. *Ada běběrapa lama–nya běrpěrang, maka banyak–lah raayat Siam mati, Malaka pun tiada alah.*

The fighting continued for a long time, and large numbers of Siamese fell, but Malaka still held out.

6. *Karna timah hatap istana itu hanchur turun sapěrti hujan yang lěbat, maka sa–orang pun tiada běrani masok měngambil harta raja itu.*

Because the lead on the roof of the palace was melting and pouring down like a torrent of rain nobody would venture to go inside to get the raja's property.

7. *Měngapa–kah maka anak kita hěndak běrmain jauh ?*

Why must our child go so far afield to find amusement ?

8. *Sěbab tuboh dato' itu běrbulu, maka di–sěbut orang Tun Mai Ulat Bulu.*

Because the chieftain's body was covered with hair, men called him *Tun Mai*, the Hairy Caterpillar.

9. *Maka tělah Maharaja Dewa Sura sudah lěpas, maka gajah itu pun dapat–lah di–ambil orang.*

When Maharaja Dewa Sura had been set free, they
succeeded in catching the elephant.

10. *Maka ada bĕrapa hari lama–nya, maka budak itu pun
baik–lah.*
After a certain number of days, the child recovered.

II. Introductory Words

Par. 143.

Kata sahibu'l–hikayat	. the author (lit. the owner of the story) relates.
Alkesah . .	. the story is.
Sa–bĕrmula . .	} the story begins.
Bĕrmula . .	
Sa–kali pĕrsĕtua .	. once upon a time.

Any of these words introduces a new story, or a new
subject, but the story or subject so introduced may be
part of a longer narrative.

Examples.

1. *Kata sahibu'l–hikayat maka pada kĕtika itu juga pĕrgi–
lah nabi Khidzir ka–pada Raja Iskandar.*
The author relates that at that very time the prophet
Khidzir went to Raja Iskandar.

2. *Alkĕsah pĕri mĕngatakan chĕrita raja yang pĕrtama
masok ugama Islam di–Pasai. (Hikayat Raja–raja
Pasai.)*
My story tells of the first Raja of Pasai to become
a Muslim.
(Lit. The story is concerned with telling the tale
of . . .)

3. *Sa–bĕrmula pada suatu hari hanyut bueh dari hulu
Sungai Palembang itu tĕrlalu bĕsar.*
One day there came floating down from the upper
reaches of the Palembang River a great mass of foam.

4. *Bĕrmula di–chĕtĕrakan*[46] *oleh orang yang punya chĕtĕra ini : ada sa–orang hamba Allah di–Pasai, Tun Jana Khatib nama–nya.*

The author of the story states : there was a man of Pasai, called Tun Jana Khatib.

5. *Sa–kali pĕrsĕtua pada suatu hari maka Pateh Aria Gajah Mada mĕmakai sĕrba burok, turun ia bĕrdayong bĕrsama–sama hamba sĕmua–nya, tiada ia di–kĕnal orang·banyak itu.*

One day Pateh Aria Gajah Mada dressed himself in shabby clothes and went down to row with his servants, and he was not recognized by the populace.

III. Transition Words

Par. 144.

Hatta (or *hata*)	.	. next.
Shahadan	.	. furthermore ; the facts are
Arakian	.	. accordingly
Kalakian	.	. lit. thus much time having elapsed, i.e. next, afterwards

These words are used in classical Malay literature to introduce a new topic, or a new aspect of a topic already introduced.

Examples.

1. *Hatta maka kapal itu bĕlayar–lah, lalu ia singgah di–nĕgĕri Mutabar.*

The ship sailed, and after a time it put in at the town of Mutabar.

2. *Shahadan tĕlah di–kĕtahui baginda ĕrti–nya, maka Sang Si–Pĕrba pun mĕshuarat dĕngan sĕgala mĕntĕri, " Baik kita bĕrikan anak kita ini, atau jangan ? "*

When King Sang Si–Perba understood the gist of it, he consulted all his ministers: " Is it well that we should give our child, or not ? "

[46] " Chĕtĕra " is another form of " chĕrita ".

3. *Arakian turun sa–buah kapal dari Jiddah datang ka–Mĕlaka.*

There came a ship from Jiddah to Mĕlaka.

4. *Kalakian maka ada–lah pada suatu pĕtang hari, maka aku pun hĕndak pulang, maka di–panggil oleh Tuan Raffles. (Hikayat Abdullah.)*

One evening I was just about to go home when Mr. Raffles called me.

IV. Bahawa

Par. 145.

Bahawa (Sanskrit—existence).

As with *ada–lah*, and *ada pun* (see next paragraph) the real meaning of *bahawa* is : " the facts are thus " or " the truth is this".

It might have been included with the transition words of the last paragraph but it is found serving as a conjunction more often than as an adverb.

Bahawa introduces a statement, either direct or indirect. When the statement is indirect, *bahawa* can be translated by the conjunction " that".

Examples.

1. *Maka sahut Raja Suran, " Bahawa alam ini tĕrlalu banyak pĕlbagai jĕnis ada di–dalam–nya."*

Raja Suran answered : " Verily in this world there are all sorts of things ".

2. *Kĕtahui oleh–mu bahawa aku mĕmanggil ĕngkau ini*[47] *aku hĕndak bĕrtanyakan bichara kapada–mu*[48]

Know, then, that the reason for my summoning you is that I want to ask your opinion.

---

[47] Note that *ini* qualifies the whole clause *Aku mĕmanggil ĕngkau ini*—" this, the fact that I have summoned you".

[48] Remember this idiom. In Malay, you ask " to " a person, not " from " a person. Cf. French " *demander à quelqu'un* ".

3. *Ada pun sĕkarang di–dĕngar–nya bahawa tuan hamba ada bĕranak pĕrĕmpuan tĕrlalu baik paras–nya.*

He hears now that you have a daughter of great beauty.

V. Ada pun. Ada–lah. Ada–nya

Par. 146.

(a) *Ada pun* introduces a statement. The statement may be explanatory (as in examples 1 and 2), it may denote a return to a subject after a brief digression (example 3), or it may be concerned with a new topic (example 4).

Examples.

1. *Ada pun pĕrigi di–Batu Pahat itu, orang Siam–lah mĕmbuat–nya.*

Now the well at Batu Pahat, it was the Siamese who made it.

2. *Ada pun asal nama–nya Klang Kio, ia–itu bahasa Siam, ĕrti–nya pĕrbĕndaharaan pĕrmata ; oleh kita tiada tahu menyĕbut dia, jadi Ganggayu.*

The name was originally " Klang Kio ", that is to say, a Siamese name meaning " Treasury of Jewels ", but because we could not pronounce it, it became " Ganggayu ".

3. *Maka Raja Suran pun sampai–lah ka–pada sa–buah nĕgĕri Gongga–nĕgara nama–nya, Raja Gongga Shah Johan nama raja–nya. Ada pun nĕgĕri itu di–atas bukit.*

Raja Suran came to a town called Gongga-negara, ruled over by a king whose name was Raja Gongga Shah Johan. Now this town was on a hill.

4. *Ada pun di–chĕtĕrakan oleh orang yang ĕmpunya chĕtĕra ini, bahawa putĕri Shahru'l–Bariyah tĕlah hamil.*

The author of the story (Lit. The person who owns) relates that the princess Shahru'l–Bariyah was with child.

(b) *Ada–lah*, in introducing a statement, stresses the existence of the state of affairs made known by that statement.

Examples.

1. *Maka ada–lah daripada kĕbanyakan raayat bĕrjalan itu sĕgala hutan bĕlantara pun habis–lah mĕnjadi padang.*
   It came about that because of the great multitude of the marching army the spreading jungle was utterly destroyed and became a treeless plain.

2. *Ada–lah bĕsi ini kami bawa dari nĕgĕri China sapĕrti lĕngan bĕsar–nya, sĕkarang habis haus.*
   Now this iron, when we brought it from China, it was of an arm's thickness, and now it has rusted away almost to nothing.

(c) *Ada–nya*—" Such is the truth of it "—is used to mark the end of a narration.

Examples.

1. *Maka tinggal sang bĕruang itu, dĕngan sa–orang diri–nya juga mĕnunggui ikan itu, ada–nya. (Hikayat Pĕlandok Jenaka.)*
   Mr. Bear stayed there, all alone, keeping guard over the fish.

2. *Maka sa–tĕlah itu, naik–lah kĕreta bĕrjalan pulang, ada–nya. (Hikayat Abdullah).*
   After that, he got into his carriage and went home.

Exercise 32

Translate the following passage from the *Sĕjarah Mĕlayu* :

Maka di–lihat oleh Sang Si–Pĕrba sa–buah kuala sungai tĕrlalu bĕsar : maka baginda bĕrtanya kapada pawang[49], " Apa nama sungai ini ? " Maka sĕmbah[50] pawang, " Ini–lah Kuala Kuantan ; tĕrlalu banyak orang dalam–nya". Maka titah[51] baginda, " Mari–lah kita mudek ka–hulu sungai ini". Dan sakalian orang pun kĕkurangan ayer ; tĕmpat mĕngambil ayer pun tiada. Maka di–suroh oleh Sang Si–Pĕrba lengkar rotan, sa–bĕsar pĕrisai yang bĕsar, maka di–lĕtakkan pada laut itu ; maka baginda turun ka–sampan mĕnchĕlupkan kaki baginda pada ayer masin di–dalam rotan itu ; dĕngan takdir Allah taala[52], daripada bĕrkat baginda anak chuchu Raja Iskandar Dhu'l–Karnain[53], maka ayer masin itu pun mĕnjadi ayer tawar. Maka sĕgala bĕkas ayer pun di–isi orang–lah. Maka datang sĕkarang ini pun ayer itu tawar pada ayer masin itu tĕntang Muara[54] Sapat.

Exercise 33

1. When you have used this piece of rag for cleaning the car, wash it and hang it out in the sun.
2. Mat is in funds again. He has redeemed all his gold buttons. But I expect they will be in pawn again

[49] *Pawang*. Originally, as here, navigating officer. See par. 189, Note 2.

[50] *Sĕmbah*—obeisance, gesture of worship or homage ; then, of any speech addressed to a royal person. It may be translated " said " or " answered ".

[51] *titah*—a royal utterance. It may be translated " said ".

[52] *taala* literally " May he be exalted ". Translate " Most High ".

[53] *Raja Iskandar Dhu'l–Karnain* or *Dzu'l–Karnain*, i.e. Alexander the Great, according to Malay legend ancestor of the royal line of Malacca. See *P.M.S. Malay Literature*, Pt. I.

[54] *Muara=kuala*.

before the end of the month. He is an extravagant young man, but I can't help liking him.

Conversation No. 11

Sĕmangat Padi.

Che'Wan: Aminah choba chĕritakan macham mana adat orang[1], 'nak ambil padi dalam jĕlapang.

Aminah: Oi, ta'boleh buat ta'tĕntu, Che'Wan. Kĕna bĕrtabek dahulu.

Che'Wan: Bĕrtabek pada siapa ?

Aminah: Pada sĕmangat[2] padi itu–lah.

Che'Wan: M–m, padi ada sĕmangat, ia ? Jantan, pĕrĕmpuan ?

Aminah: Pĕrĕmpuan–lah. Kita[1] kĕna kata, "Mek,[3] 'Mak 'nak minta padi sadikit. Ĕnche' jangan jauh hati, ia ?"[4]

Che'Wan: Lĕpas itu ?

Aminah: Lĕpas itu kita naik dĕngan lĕmah lĕmbut ka–atas jĕlapang ; kita sukat baik–baik, jangan dĕngan kasar.

Che'Wan: Lagi apa pula ?

Aminah: Kita tengok kalau minyak dĕngan ayer dalam jĕlapang itu 'dah kĕring, kita tambah pula.

Che'Wan: Fasal ?

Aminah: Jadi dia boleh bĕrsikat rambut dan minum ayer.

Che'Wan: 'Minah, 'Minah ! Ta'ada siapa–siapa[5] minum ayer itu atau pakai minyak itu. Kĕdua–dua[6]–nya di–sĕrap udara.

Aminah :   Saya ta'tahu, Che' Wan. 'Tapi 'mak ajaɪ
            macham itu–lah. Saya pun ikut

Translation

The Rice Soul

Che' Wan : Tell me, Aminah, what is the procedure when
            you want to get some padi from the barn ?

Aminah :   Well, you can't do it just anyhow. First
            of all, you must make your apologies.

Che' Wan : To whom ?

Aminah :   To the soul of the rice.

Che' Wan : Oh ! The rice has a soul, has it ? Male oɪ
            female ?

Aminah :   It's a woman. We must say. " Mek, I
            want some rice. You won't be hurt (with
            me, for taking it) will you ? "

Che' Wan : And after that ?

Aminah :   After that you go up gently into the barn,
            and you measure out the rice very carefully,
            taking care not to be rough about it.

Che' Wan : And what then ?

Aminah :   You look to see if the oil and the water in the
            barn has gone (lit. " has become dry "). You
            put some more.

Che' Wan : Why ?

Aminah :   So that she can comb her hair, and drink.

Che' Wan : Oh, 'Minah ! There isn't anybody who
            drinks the water or uses the oil. They are
            dried up by the air.

Aminah :   I don't know about that, Che' Wan. But
            that is what my mother taught me. I just
            follow what she told me.

Notes.

1. adat orang . . Lit. " the custom of people intending to . . ." Note the usual avoidance of the second person pronoun. Malay never uses the " ideal second person " which is so common in English, e.g. " You never can tell." If a pronoun is used it is *kita*.

2. sĕmangat . . For these animistic beliefs which underlie Malay ritual see *Papers on Malay Subjects, Customs and Beliefs.*

3. Mek . . . A common name for girls in the north of the Malay Peninsula.

4. ia ? . . . Lit. " yes ? " A colloquial use.

5. siapa–siapa . . See par. 161.

6. kĕ–dua–nya . . See par. 182.

CHAPTER XVI

" BALANCE " WORDS

Par. 147.

Malay idiom is crisp and concise. It leaves out much
that would be put in in English. The spoken language
employs few conjunctions. By balancing word against
word, and phrase against phrase, it achieves a degree of
brevity that is at times disconcerting to the foreigner.

On the other hand, you will already have become
familiar with several Malay words which are not always
capable of direct translation into English and which
you may have been tempted, for that reason, to consider
redundant.

That is by no means the case. Such words are not out
of harmony with the principle of economy. On the
contrary, they serve it. A *pula*, a *pun*, a *juga* frequently
colours a whole sentence. In one word it can reveal a
judgment which in English might require a phrase, or
even a clause, for its expression. It represents the
speaker's or writer's comment in the shortest possible
form.[55]

---

[55] I am indebted to Mr. J. E. Kempe for the following illuminating
instance of the use of the word *pula* :

" I was standing on a *jamban* (i.e. a floating bath-house) on the Perak
river with an old Malay *pĕnghulu*, watching a lad poling a small dug-out

The term " balance words " is therefore an inadequate description of such words, but since, in the spoken language, it is largely through brevity[56] that Malay achieves its balanced effects, it is clear that these words contribute to such effects.

The enclitic particles *–lah* and *–tah* have the same dual function.

The pronouns *yang* and *–nya* (see chap. XVII), also, though they never completely lose their pronominal significance, are sometimes used primarily for the sake of balance[57].

I. Juga

Par. 148.

Juga (sometimes *jua*)

The following shades of meaning may be distinguished, but the basic function of *juga* is always to set a limit, sometimes grudging, sometimes exacting.

(a) " All the same " (though the contrary might have been expected.)

Examples.

1. *Bapa larangkan, dia buat juga.*
   Though his father forbade him, he did it all the same.

2. *Kain ini murah, tětapi chantek juga.*
   This sarong is cheap, but it is quite pretty.

3. *Dia ta' běrapa rajin, lulus juga pěpěreksaan.*
   He is not very industrious, but he did get through his examination.

---

up-river against heavy flood water. He was trying to get it alongside the raft. As he struggled up, the current caught the bows just as he came close to us, and swung him off and down again. The old man's only comment was a murmured *Pulak.*—" After all that ! "

[56] For balanced effect produced by echoing repetition, see par. 141.
[57] See notes (*passim*) in Keys.

(b) " Just " (meaning " exactly ").

Examples.

1. *Hari ini juga.*
   This very day.

2. *Sapěrti lazim juga.*
   Just as he had been wont to do.

3. *Ta' mahu lain, hěndak sa–rupa juga děngan chontoh.*
   I don't want anything else, it must be exactly like the pattern.

(c) " Fairly " (often in a deprecating tone of admission, as in the first example).

Examples.

1. *Mat pandai běrhitong?—Pandai juga.*
   You are good at Arithmetic ?—Yes, not too bad.

2. *Jadi–lah tali itu; panjang juga.*
   That rope will do; it's a fair length.

(d) Somewhat similar is the use of *juga* in short answers which repeat the verb of the question. It gives balance to the Malay sentence, but also, perhaps, reflects the Malay's dislike of effusiveness.

Examples.

1. *Bakar suka pěrgi běrsama ?—Suka juga.*
   Would you like to go with me Bakar ? Yes, I should.

2. *Boleh–kah tolong bawa surat ini masok post ?— Boleh juga.*
   Will you post this letter for me ?—Yes, I will.

3. *Ěnche' sělalu běrjalan di–kěbun bunga ?— Sělalu juga.*

Do you often walk in the park ?—Yes, quite often.

(e) *pun ... juga* may be translated 'also'. See par. 150.

Examples.

1. *Kalau abang 'nak tinggal, saya pun 'nak tinggal juga.*
   If you are going to stay, I shall stay too.

2. *Kalau di–běli sampul surat, kěrtas pědap pun baik běli juga.*
   If you are buying envelopes you had better get some blotting paper as well.

II. Pula

Par. 149.

This word may mean " also ", " in addition ", " again ", " all the same "[55], but it is frequently best rendered in translation by intonation only. Sometimes it adds a note of surprise, at other times, a note of protest. The underlying idea is sequence, one thing following another, sometimes naturally, sometimes (hence the surprise) unexpectedly.

Examples.

1. *Kěnapa pula běrsungut? Bukan–nya kěrja yang běrat.*
   Why on earth are you grumbling ? It's not a very heavy task.

2. *Pinggan itu rětak 'nak pakai pula.*
   The plate is cracked, and you are going to use it! (implying " surely not! ")

3. *Apa pula guna–nya měnulis sama sahaja?*
   What in the world is the good of just writing your name ?

4. *Sudah měněbang, di–suroh měněbas pula.*
When he had cut down the trees, he was told
to cut down the undergrowth as well.

III. Pun

Par. 150.

The following uses may be distinguished, but there is
very little difference between them. The underlying
principle of balance, word against word, is usually not far
to seek, with the 'new' word spot-lighted by *pun*. See
par. 148 (e).

(a) To balance alternatives.

Examples.

1. *Garam ta'ada lada pun ta'ada.*
There's no salt and there's no pepper.
2. *Ikan pun suka makan, daging pun suka makan.*
I like fish, and I like meat too.

(b) With single words, for emphasis.

Examples.

1. *Hari ini pun kěna běrtolak.*
We shall have to set out this very day.
2. *Bunga apa awak mahu?—Mana–mana pun jadi.*
What flowers do you want?—Any of them
will do.

(c) " Even " (usually with a negative.)

Examples.

1. *Jangankan sa–puloh biji tělor, sa–biji pun
ta' dapat.*
So far from finding ten eggs, I didn't find even
one *or* I didn't find one single egg, let alone ten.

2. *Ĕngkau ini bukan main bodoh. Budak pun
   lĕbeh pandai.*
   You are silly! A child (even) would know
   better.

3. *Malam tadi angin kuat. Pĕrahu sa–buah pun
   tidak kĕluar.*
   There was a high wind last night. Not a
   single boat went out.

(d) In written Malay, *pun*, attached to the subject,
is used as a partner to *–lah*, when that particle,
attached to a verb, indicates past time. Cf. par.
151 (c).

Examples.

1. *Ia pun mati–lah.*
   He died.

2. *Maka pada malam itu Hang Mahmud pun
   tidor–lah.*
   That night, Hang Mahmud slept.

IV. -lah

Par. 151.

(a) This enclitic particle is sometimes used to emphasize one particular word. That word is frequently
brought to the beginning of the clause as a further
means of emphasis.

Examples.

1. *Anjing–lah yang hilang, bukan kuching.*
   It was a dog that I lost, not a cat.

2. *Hilang–lah, bukan–nya mati.*
   Lost, it is, not dead.

3. *Apa–lah kĕsudahan–nya kita bĕrbantah–bantah
   ini?*
   What is to be the outcome of our dispute?

I

(b) It is used in commands and prohibitions, to make the order less peremptory.

Examples.

1. *Jangan–lah marah.*
   Now don't be angry.
2. *Běrhenti–lah.*
   Stop, please.

(c) In written narrative it is of frequent occurrence after a simple verb, giving the effect of an expected result. In such sentences the subject frequently comes after the verb.[58]

Examples.

1. *Pěrgi–lah ia.*
   Off he went.
2. *Lalu–lah kami.*
   And we went on our way.

V. -tah

Par. 152.

This enclitic particle is attached to interrogative words only.   The result is a rhetorical question rather than a real one.

Examples.

1. *Apa–tah lagi?*
   What then ? (i.e. I needn't tell you—you can guess the rest.)
2. *Apa–tah sudah–nya ?*
   What, I ask you, is to be the end of it ?

Par. 153.

The excerpt given in this paragraph is from *Hikayat Awang Sulong Merah Muda*—" The Romance of the First Born, the Red Prince".

Sir Richard Winstedt (*Papers on Malay Subjects,*

[58] But see par. 150d.

Malay Literature, Part II) calls such folk-lore romances
"the cream of Malay literature". The metrical passages,
which are the parts of the story that have been handed
down in set traditional form, are full of lively descriptions
that remind one of the country pictures in *L'Allegro*.
But the vocabulary of such passages is difficult. For
that reason the extracts have been taken from the prose
passages, which are "told by the rhapsodist in the
language of conversation":

Hata, maka pada suatu hari bĕrtitah[1] tuanku dato'
Batin Alam[2] suroh Awang Sulong mĕmukat di–dalam
laut. Maka sĕmbah[3] Awang Sulong Merah Muda :
"Bagaimana, tuanku, patek tahu mĕmukat : mĕlihat
pun[4] tiada pĕrnah". Maka di–kĕrasi[5] oleh tuanku dato'
Batin Alam suroh dia mĕmukat pula[6]. Maka di–bĕri–
nya akan bĕkalan Awang Sulong bĕras bĕrchampor
dĕngan padi, lalu turun–lah Awang Sulong ka–pĕrahu–
nya mĕmukat. Tĕlah tiba di–laut, ia pun bĕrlaboh
mĕmukat lalu tidor. Maka pada kĕesokan hari ia pun
bĕrgĕrak kĕlihatan–nya sisek ikan pun[7] tiada : lalu naik
ka–darat hĕndak mĕnanak[8] nasi lalu mĕnengok bĕras–
nya bĕrchampor dĕngan padi, di–churahkan–nya ka–
dalam laut sĕraya bĕrfikir : "Sampai–lah hati tuanku
aniayakan aku". Maka ia pun kĕmbali ka–istana.

Translation

One day the lord chieftain, Batin Alam[2], told[1] Awang
Sulong to go and fish with a net in the sea. Then Awang
Sulong answered[3] him : "My lord, how should I know
how to fish ? I have never even seen it done[4]". But the
lord chieftain Batin Alam insisted[5] and told him, nevertheless,[6] to go and fish. And he gave him for food, to take
with him, husked rice mixed with unhusked rice. Then
Awang Sulong got into his boat and went fishing.
When he reached the sea he let down his net, and
then fell asleep. Next day when he wakened he saw

that he had not caught a fish, not even a scale.[7] Then
he went ashore to cook[8] his rice, and he saw that it was
mixed with padi, so he threw it into the sea, thinking
to himself " That my lord should have the heart to
persecute me so ! " Then he returned to the palace.

Notes

1. bĕrtitah . . . See footnote 51.
2. Batin Alam . . Lit. "Chief of the World".
3. sĕmbah . . . See footnote 50.
4. mĕlihat pun . . Notice the double emphasis: position at the beginning of the sentence, and the use of *pun*.
5. di–kĕrasi . . . The " i " suffix is often used for such intransitive passives, cf. *di–kuati–nya* he strove, *di–sunggohi–nya* —he tried with all his might.
6. suroh . . . pula . A good example of *pula* meaning " all the same."
7. sisek ikan pun tiada . A good example of *pun* + negative for " not even".
8. mĕnanak . . . *Tanak* is the correct word to use for boiling rice. *Sa–pĕnanak nasi* " one rice-boiling " was an old measurement of time. Not many years ago the answer given by a little girl in Perlis when asked the age of the child she was carrying on her hip was : " *Dua kali padi*". " Two rice harvests".

Exercise 34

Translate the following passage from *Awang Sulong Merah Muda*:

(This time Awang Sulong, with the help of spirits, has accomplished the task which Batin Alam had set him.)

Maka tuanku Batin Alam pun pulang–lah. Maka di–lihat–nya ada sa–orang laki–laki tidor di–hujong sěrambi. Maka běrtanya–lah ia kapada tuan putěri Dayang Nuramah : " Siapa–kah laki–laki yang tidor itu ? " Lalu di–jawab–nya : " Abang Sulong baharu pulang sa–kějap ini". Maka Awang Sulong pun těrkějut dari–pada tidor lalu di–tanya oleh tuanku Batin Alam : " Sudah–kah ěngkau pěrbuat[59] kakap[60] itu ? " Sěmbah Awang Sulong : " Tělah sudah–lah sapěrti titah tuanku itu". Lalu běrtitah tuanku dato' Batin Alam děngan murka–nya : " Sa–patut–nya–lah ěngkau měnunjokkan kětukangan ěngkau kapada aku". Maka běrlari–lah tuanku dato Batin Alam měngambil kapak, lalu ia pěrgi ka–pangkalan měmbělah–bělah kakap yang di–pěrbuat oleh Awang Sulong itu : sa–kali di–takok–nya, dua tiga gambar běrsěnyuman, jangan rosak běrtambah chantek lagi. Maka kapak di–tangan pun lalu patah lalu lari–lah ia kěmbali ka–istana di–ambil pula běliong panjang, běrlari ka–pěrahu lalu di–takok sa–kali lagi dua tiga gambar běrsěnyuman, badan pun lěteh, běliong pun patah jangankan rosak pěrahu itu běrtambah chantek.

Exercise 35

1. Ask him to buy me a torch. It had better be a big one. I want it for the Hill.

---

[59] Verbal derivatives with prefix *pěr-* are usually causative—" to have a thing done," or " to cause a thing to happen " (e.g. at the opening of a letter *Saya pěrmaalumkan* . . . " I cause it to be known to you", i.e. " I inform you".) But in this sentence the *pěr-* indicates completion.

[60] *Pěrahu kakap*—a type of fishing boat.

2. There is not much paint left. I doubt if it will be enough. It's a fairly long fence. Still, we may be able to manage it. I think the paint will stand thinning. Fetch the turpentine, will you ? It is in a vinegar bottle in the corner of the cupboard where the flower pots are.

Conversation No. 12

Bĕrpindah Rumah

Husain : Ĕmpat hari lagi, kita pindah ka–rumah baharu Hari khamis. Bila 'Mah 'nak bĕrkĕmas ?

Hasmah : Pagi–pagi besok kita mula. Risau hati mĕnengok[1] barang–barang kita tĕrlampau banyak hĕndak di–kĕmaskan.

Husain : Jangan–lah risau, 'Mah. Ĕmpat orang kuli P.W.D. datang mĕnolong kita pindah. Kĕrja 'Mah chuma siapkan sĕmua barang–barang yang 'nak di–angkut[2] itu.

Hasmah : Boleh–kah kita pĕrchaya kuli–kuli itu ? Takut kain baju, pinggan mangkok kita habis lĕnyap atau pun habis binasa.

Husain : Jangan–lah bimbang. Orang kuli itu baik sĕmua, kuat juga bĕkĕrja.

Hasmah : Bĕrapa kĕreta lori datang mĕngangkat barang kita ?

Husain : Dua buah. Kĕrja bĕrpindah boleh habis sa–hari sahaja agak–nya. Rumah baharu itu ta'bĕrapa jauh dari sini. Lĕkas dia orang[3] pĕrgi balek.

Hasmah : Barang kita yang mahal–mahal[4] baik kita kunchikan dalam pĕti bĕsi. Di–mana anak kunchi pĕti itu sĕmua ? Baik kita chari.

Husain :   Těntu ada dalam lachi meja di–bilek tidor
           Sa–malam dapat[5] ěmpat pěti kayu yang
           běsar–běsar[4]. Boleh kita muatkan sěgala
           pinggan mangkok, pěriok bělanga kita.

Hasmah :   Kain baju[6] kita sěmua baik kita lipat taroh[7]
           dalam pěti kita sěndiri. Městi kunchikan,
           takut di–churi kuli.

Husain :   'Mah jangan–lah shak hati lagi . .   'Mah
           suka pindah ka–rumah baharu itu ?

Hasmah :   Suka   juga.   Sa–kadar–nya   sayang–lah
           sadikit měninggalkan[1] rumah ini. Sudah lama
           kita diam di–sini.

Husain :   Elok–lah rumah baharu itu.   Jangan–lah
           susah hati.

Translation.

Moving House

Husain :   In four days time we shall be moving to the
           new house. On Thursday. When are you
           going to do the packing, 'Mah ?

Hasmah :   Early tomorrow we'll begin. I am worried
           when I look at all our stuff that will have to
           be packed.

Husain :   There's no need to be worried, 'Mah. Four
           P.W.D. men will come to help us move.
           All that you will have to do is to get ready
           everything that has to be taken away.

Hasmah :   Can we trust the men ?   I am afraid that
           our clothes and our crockery may all
           disappear, or be ruined.

Husain :   Don't worry. The men are all honest, and they are hard workers, too.

Hasmah :   How may trucks will come to take our things ?

Husain :   Two. We shall be able to finish the move in one day, I should think. The new house isn't far from here. It won't take them long to come and go.

Hasmah :   We had better lock up our precious things in the iron boxes. Where are all the keys ? We must look for them.

Husain :   They will be in the drawer of the table in the bed-room. I got four good-sized wooden boxes yesterday. We can pack the crockery and the kitchen stuff in them.

Hasmah :   We had better fold our clothes and put them in our own boxes. We must lock them, for fear the men should steal them.

Husain :   Don't be so suspicious . . . Are you pleased to be moving to the new house?

Hasmah :   Yes, I am pleased. But I am sad at the thought of leaving this house. We have lived here a long time.

Husain :   Our new house is a finer one than this. You mustn't be sad about it.

Notes

1. risau hati měnengok   . Lit. " Worried, seeing ".
   sayang měninggalkan   . " sorry, leaving ".

2. angkut.   .   .   . Notice the form *angkut*.— because furniture is moved piece by piece.

3. dia orang . . . In conversational style the plural is often shown by the addition of *orang* to the third person pronoun. Cf. the dialect forms for " they ": in Perak : *dema* (i.e. *dia sĕmua*) in Kedah *depa* (i.e. *dia apa*.)

4. mahal–mahal $\Big\}$ . . Not intensive. Comparable to *puteh – puteh* — whitish." rather valuable possessions ", " fairly large boxes ".

bĕsar–bĕsar

5. sa–malam dapat . . " Yesterday I got "— notice the omission of the subject pronoun, as often, in conversation when there is no likelihood of misunderstanding.

6. kain baju . . . This is a common expression for " clothes ". Another is *kain pakaian*.

7. lipat taroh . . . Notice the omission of " and ".

CHAPTER XVII

PRONOUNS

1. Relative

II. Indefinite

Note:

Much of the material that is set out in this and the remaining chapters has already been in use in earlier chapters. It is now gathered together, and tabulated, for purposes of reference. Do not forget that tabulations are apt to be misleading. In this book they offer guiding lines for thought, not water-tight compartments for facts.

In studying Malay it is well to have constantly in mind Chesterton's dictum : " All generalizations are false—including this one".

I. The relative pronoun " yang "
Par. 154.

The word *yang* may be considered the Malay equivalent of the English relative pronoun (who, which, that), but it is by no means identical with it.

Yang is not always used where English uses " who " or " which ". On the other hand, it is often used where English does not use " who " or " which ". It is a difficult word to classify. Collect examples of its uses, as you come across them, and try to make your own classification.

Par. 155.

" Yang " is *not* used after a preposition

a. In expressions of time, such as " The day on which," there is no equivalent of the English relative phrase.

Examples.

1. The year in which he sailed from England.
   Tahun dia bělayar dari něgěri Inggěris.

2. The day on which he came was wet[61].
   Hari dia datang hari hujan.

b. In expressions of place, such as " the house in which " the word *těmpat* replaces the English relative.

Example.

1. The house in which I lived was in bad repair.
   Rumah těmpat saya dudok sudah burok.

Par. 156.

Most other preposition *cum* relative phrases (e.g. " under which ", " with whom ") introduce descriptive clauses which are equivalent to attributive adjectives (see par. 158b). They mark out, for distinction, the noun to which they refer.

In such sentences *yang* is used, adjectivally, to mark out the noun, but it does not follow the preposition. Another pronoun, further on in the sentence, follows the preposition and stands for the same noun.

Examples.

1. The box under which the puppy had hidden.

---

[61] This type of sentence would more often be rendered by two simple statements : e.g. " The Monday on which he came was wet "—*Dia datang pada hari Ithnain. Hari itu hujan.* (Lit. " He came on a Monday. It rained on that day ").

Pĕti yang anak anjing bĕrsĕmbunyi di–bawah–nya[62].

(Lit. The box which : the–puppy–had–hidden himself–under–it.)

2. The fisherman with whom the prince was friendly.

Orang pĕngail yang anak raja itu bĕrsahabat dĕngan–nya.

(Lit. The fisherman who : the–prince–was friendly–with–him.)

The whole of the hyphened clause is equivalent to the adjective *hitam* in Example 1, Par. 158b. In the place and time examples given above this distinguishing sense is not so strongly present : *Hari dia bĕlayar*—His "sailing date". *Rumah dia dudok*—"His residence".

On the other hand, such a sentence as " a house in which valuable possessions were kept " (i.e. " that sort of a house ") would usually be rendered by a *yang* followed by a prepositional phrase, as in the examples given above.

Such sentences are very common in written Malay.

Examples.

3. *Sa–orang laki–laki yang tiada di–kĕtahui tĕmpat–nya. (Hikayat Bayan Budiman.)*

A man, whose place of abode was unknown.

(Lit. A man who : the–place–of–him–was–not–known, i.e. an unidentifiable man.)

4. *Sa–orang puteh yang ku–kaseh akan dia. (Hikayat Abdullah).*

An Englishman for whom I felt affection.

(Lit. An Englishman who : I–felt–affection–for–him, i.e. a beloved Englishman.)

---

[62] This is the same idiom as was used in the Cockney song " When walking out with Liza which her other name is Jane " i.e. ". . . with Liza who: the-other-name-of-her-is-Jane".

Par. 157.

" Yang " is *not* used :

To translate an English " who " or " which " that introduces what is really an additional statement, parallel to the main statement[63]. In Malay the statements are set side by side.

> Examples.
>
> The prisoner, who was deaf, could not hear what the judge said.
> *Orang salah itu pěkak. Dia ta' dengar apa tuan hakim itu kata.*[64]

Note : If *yang* were inserted in this sentence it would define the noun (see par. 158(b). The sentence would become :

> *Orang salah yang pěkak itu ta' děngar apa tuan hakim itu kata,*

and the meaning would be :

> " The deaf prisoner (not the other one) could not hear . . ." The fact that the *itu* now follows the *pěkak* shows that the adjective has become attributive. It no longer makes a statement, as in the original sentence.

---

[63] In English this distinction is indicated in writing by the commas which mark off the pseudo-relative clause, and in speech by the corresponding pauses. e.g. The papers, which had been posted in good time, arrived too late.

Beware, also, of the word " where " used in the same way (i.e. as a connecting relative, not a defining relative). e.g. " Then they went to another shop, where they bought some fish" . The " where " = " and there ", and is to be translated by *di–situ*, not by *těmpat* as it would be in : " The shop where I buy fish is closed ". Similarly " when " meaning " and then ", is *lalu*.

[64] Comparable to this example are sentences such as the following, very common in written Malay.

1. *Ada sa-ekor katak dudok di'-bawah batu.* . . .
   There was a frog (who) lived under a stone (i.e. and he lived).
2. *Ada sa-orang budak hěndak mengail ikan.*
   There was a boy (who) wanted to go fishing.

Uses of " yang "

Par. 158.

Yang serves to emphasize, to differentiate. The following examples show different aspects of this function:

(a) It serves to distinguish a class, either with or without an antecedent.

Examples.

1. *Yang bodoh ta'mahu bĕlajar.*
   The foolish do not want to learn.

2. *Yang tĕgak di–sokong, yang rĕbah di–tindeh* (Prov.)
   What (i.e. that which) is upright is propped, what has fallen is pressed down.

3. *Murid rajin yang bĕroleh hadiah.*
   It is the diligent pupils that get the prizes.

4. *Ada bĕrjĕnis–jĕnis bangsa laba–laba ; ada yang mĕmbuat*[65] *sarang–nya pada tembok dan dahan kayu ; ada yang tinggal di–lobang tanah.*
   There are spiders of various sorts ; there are some that make nests for themselves in walls and tree-trunks, and others that live in holes in the ground.

5. *Jauhari juga yang mĕngĕnal manikam* (Prov.)
   It takes a jeweller to know a gem.

[65] This use of *yang* is usually combined with the *mĕ-* form of the verb as shown in par. 119d. In these sentences the *yang* is the subject of the verb that comes after it, and its function is to draw attention to its antecedent (which is implicit in it—" those who ") either as in Example (a) 4, as belonging to a class of doers, or, as in Example (b) 4 as belonging to a particular group of doers.

In such a sentence as the last example in par. 156, the *yang* is not the subject of the succeeding verb. The subject of *kaseh* is *ku-*, proclitic, unobtrusive, and the simple verb is used, as always when the object precedes the subject and is therefore in the position of emphasis and of greater importance than the subject. e.g. *Baik-lah raja itu ku-bunoh juga*—" That raja, it would be better if I killed him".

Jangan-lah kami ĕngkau bunoh—" Let me not be slain by you " Note that of two pronouns in such a position it is always the one next to the verb that is the subject of the verb. (cf. par. 83).

6. *Sa–bĕrapa yang ada dapat kapada hamba boleh–
lah hamba ajari.*   (*Awang Sulong M.M.*)
Such (skill) as I possess, that will I teach him.

(b) It serves to distinguish particular persons and
things, and thus to a certain extent fulfils the
function of the English definite article " the".

Examples.

1. *Baju mana ?*   *Yang hitam–kah ?*
Which coat ?   The black one ?

2. *Yang mana baik ?—Yang bĕsar sa–kali.*
Which are the best ?—The biggest ones.

3. *Orang mana yang kĕna dĕnda ?*
Which is the man who was fined ?

4. *Ada yang mĕnangis*[65], *ada yang tĕrtawa.*
There were some who cried, and some who
laughed.

5. *Mĕlainkan Allah juga yang sunggoh.*
God alone is real.

6. *Ada yang mĕmbawa tĕpong lĕmbek–lĕmbek
di–tĕkan–nya di–batu itu.*   (*Hikayat Abdullah.*)
There were some who brought dough and
pressed it on the stone.

(c) It serves to emphasize an attributive adjective,
particularly when the adjective is strengthened
by an adverb of degree.

Examples.

1. *Bahasa yang halus.*
Fine speech.

2. *Rumah yang elok bĕnar.*
A trully beautiful house.

3. *Di–pangkalan ada jam yang bĕsar sa–kali. Muka*

*jam itu di–tutup děngan kacha supaya jangan
rosak jarum–nya yang halus–halus itu.*

At the jetty there is a large clock. The clock
face is covered with glass so that the delicate
hands may be protected.

4. *Hai unggas yang bijaksana, yang tiada běrbagai
di–dalam dunia ini.* (*Hikayat Bayan Budiman*)
Oh bird of great wisdom, whose like there is
not in this world.

(d) Note the use of *yang,* with an adjective, in
crystallized phrases which serve as titles of address,
e.g. on an envelope, or for the opening of a
memorandum or short letter.

Examples.

1. *Yang mulia*[66] *Tuan J. L. Robinson.*
J. L. Robinson, Esq.

2. *Yang těramat mulia Těngku Aishah binti* . . .[67]
The Honourable Těngku Aishah, daughter
of . . .

A phrase of this sort, used as an honorific, comes
before the noun. But as the opening of a personal
letter in modern style, where the phrase is less
formal, it follows the noun.

Examples.

4. *Anak–ku yang di–kasehi,*
My dear son,

[66] *Mulia*—" distinguished ". For the gradation of such titles, and the
traditional rules of letter-writing see *Winstedt's Malay Grammar,*
Appendix.
[67] *binti*—" daughter of . . ."
bin—" son of " (for reigning princes *ibni*).

5. *Sahabat–ku yang sĕlalu di–ingati,*
   My ever–remembered friend,

Par. 159.

Yang is sometimes used as a conjunction, and may be translated " that[68] ".

Examples.

1. *Maka di–wartakan orang–lah yang baginda itu sudah datang. (Hikayat Indĕra Nata.)*
   People reported that the king had come.

2. *Harap–lah beta yang tuan kadzi boleh hantarkan kapada tuan Malim Kĕchil. (Awang Sulong.)*
   I hope that you will take (him) to Malim Kĕchil.

3. *Maka sĕgala bangsa orang dalam Mĕlaka tiada–lah pĕrchaya yang boleh di–pĕchahkan kota itu. (Hikayat Abdullah).*
   People of all races in Malacca did not believe that the fort could be destroyed.

Note : Do not use *yang,* or any other word, to translate an English " that " (conjunction) in conversation.

[68] Other apparent equivalents of the English conjunction "that", in classical Malay, are *bahawa* (see par. 145, examples 2 and 3) and *akan : Maka Bendahara–pun baharu–lah tahu akan Hang Tuah itu anak Hang Mahmud.* " Then the Bendahara knew for the first time that Hang Tuah was the son of Hang Mahmud ". *Bahawa* is still used, but *akan* (as a conjunction) is now obsolete.

In modern Malay, both written and spoken, the conjunction is frequently omitted, e.g. *Dia mĕngatakan dia 'nak mĕnuai padi–nya dalam tiga minggu*—" He said that he was going to harvest his rice in three weeks' time ". Other apparent equivalents of the English conjunction "that" are : *ia–itu* and *ia–lah, kalau, kalau–kalau* (after words denoting apprehension) and commonest of all, some form of the word *kata* following another " saying " word. Examples : *Di–sangka–nya ia–itu suatu jĕnis makanan.* " He thought that it was some sort of food ". *Pĕrasaan–nya ia–lah hantu.* " He thought that it was a ghost ". *Tĕringin–lah dia kalau dapat bĕrsĕkolah sa–mula.* " He wished that he could go back to school again ". *Dia takut kalau–kalau tĕrlewat sampai.* " He was afraid that he might arrive too late ". *Dia mĕnjawab mĕngatakan bapa–nya sudah lama mĕninggal.* " He replied that his father had died a long time ago ".

II. Indefinite Pronouns

Par. 160.—Barang.

Barang[69], used always in front of the word it qualifies, gives an idea of indefiniteness. It is as much an adverb as a pronoun.

> **Examples.**
>
> | | |
> |---|---|
> | *barang ĕmpat jam* | about four hours. |
> | *barang siapa* | whosoever, anybody who ... anybody. |
> | *barang apa* | anything, anything whatever |
> | *barang di–mana* | wherever. |

Par. 161—Apa[69] and Siapa.

Apa, usually duplicated, gives an impression of indefiniteness, or doubt, or interrogation.

> **Examples.**
>
> 1. *Apa–apa pun jadi* . Anything will do.
> 2. *Ada–kah dia pĕsan apa–apa ?* . Did he give any instructions ?
> 3. *Tidak apa* or *Ta'apa* . Very well! (Lit. It is not anything.)
> 4. *Apa–lah* . Somehow or other, to some degree.
> 5. *Apa–apa yang saya buat sĕlalu sahaja salah* . Whatever I do is wrong.

---

[69] Note the use of *barang* and *apa* as modal words, especially in letters.
e.g. *Barang di-sampaikan*—" May it reach you. . . ."
Barang di-lanjutkan Allah taala umor-nya—" May God Most High prolong his life ".
Apa-lah jua kira-nya—" May it somehow chance. . . ."
In such contexts, their function is to impart an indefiniteness not of fact but of mood. The verb becomes what would, in a Western language, be counted a subjunctive or an optative.

Siapa (*si–apa*) usually duplicated, or else with *pun*, is used in the same way as *apa* as an indefinite pronoun or adjective.

Examples.

1. *Ta'patut–lah siapa–siapa pun mĕmukul talipon pada pukul dua–bĕlas malam.*
   It isn't right that anybody should ring up at midnight.

2. *Siapa pun boleh tunjok jalan.*
   Anybody can show you the way.

3. *Siapa–siapa yang lewat datang di–dĕnda dua puloh sen.*
   Whoever came late was fined twenty cents.

Note that these words, in the negative, are used to express " nothing " and " nobody ".

Examples.

1. *Apa pun dia t'ada kata* (or *Satu*[70] *apa pun*)
   He didn't say anything.

2. *Siapa pun ta'ada di–mahkamah* (or *Sa–orang*[70] *pun ta'ada*).
   There was nobody at the court.

Par. 162.—Mana.

In Malay literature *mana* is commonly used to mean " whatever ". In speech and in modern writing it is common in duplicated form meaning " any ".

Examples.

1. *Mana titah patek junjong.*
   Whatever is the royal command, I will obey it.

---

[70] Note also the following expressions : *Salah sa–orang*—" one or the other " (of persons). *Salah satu*—" one or the other " (of things). *Sĕrba salah*—" wrong in either case ", and therefore " in a dilemma ".

2. *Yang mana kĕhĕndak anak kita itu tiada kita laluï.*
Whatever my child's wish may be, I shall not refuse it.

3. *Yang mana mahu ?—Mana–mana pun jadi.*
Which do you want ?—Any one of them will do.

4. *Pa Kadok hĕndak pindah ka–mana–mana rumah yang lain.*
Pa Kadok wanted to move, to any other house at all.

Par. 163—Orang and Mĕreka.

Besides its specific use as a noun meaning " human beings " and its use as numerical coefficient for human beings, *orang* is used as an indefinite pronoun meaning " anybody ", " people in general ".

Examples.

1. *Kata orang dia yang kaya sa–kali dalam pĕkan ini.*
They say he is the richest man in town.

2. *Itu kĕreta orang.*
That is somebody's car (i.e. somebody else's, not yours).

3. *Jangan di–dĕngar sĕbut–sĕbutan orang.*
Don't listen to gossip.

4. *Ada orang di–rumah ?*
Is there anybody at the house ?

5. *Sĕkarang pun Padang Maya di–sĕbut orang (Sej. Mal.)*
To this day people call it " Padang Maya ".

Mĕreka is sometimes used, in the same way, as an indefinite pronoun.

Example.

Orang yang jahat itu di–bĕnchi oleh sĕgala mĕreka.

Wicked people are hated by everybody.

Note : *Mĕreka* is becoming the commonly accepted pronoun for the third person plural in writing.

Par. 164—Masing–masing and Tiap–tiap.

The word *masing–masing*, meaning " each ", may be used with or without a noun. It is used only of people.

Examples.

1. *Pulang–lah ia masing–masing ka–tĕmpat–nya.*
   And they all returned, each to his own house.
2. *Masing–masing bangsa ada kapitan–nya.*
   Each race had its own captain.

The word *tiap–tiap* meaning " each " may be used of people and things. It is used always with a noun, never alone.

Examples.

1. *Tiap–tiap bulan di–kirim–nya surat.*
   Every month he sent a letter.
2. *Tiap–tiap orang pĕnjual ada bangsal–nya sĕndiri.*
   Every salesman had his own booth.

Note also *sa–suatu*—each, but *satu satu*—" one by one".

Par. 165.

Sĕmua, sakalian and *sĕgala*, meaning " all ", or " the whole ", and *sĕrba* meaning " all," or " all sorts of".

Examples.

1. *Sĕmua orang Mĕlayu suka minum kopi.*
   All Malays like coffee.
2. *Sakalian orang mĕmujikan dia.*
   Everybody praised him.
3. *Sĕgala jĕnis buah–buahan di–jual orang.*
   All sorts of fruit are for sale.

4. *Sĕrba jĕnis minuman dapat di-bĕli.*
 All kinds of drinks could be bought.

Par. 166.

Note that *barang, masing–masing, tiap–tiap, sĕmua, sakalian and sĕgala* all precede the nouns with which they are used. They suggest quantity and may be compared to the numerals.

But *sĕmua* and *sakalian* are used also after the noun, sometimes with a limited, not an indefinite, meaning.

> Examples.
> 1. *Tiba–tiba lĕnyap–lah budak sĕmua itu.*
> Suddenly, all the children vanished.
> 2. *Dĕngar–lah kamu sakalian.*
> Listen all of you. (i.e. all who are here.)

Note also : *kĕsĕmua–nya* (Cf. par. 182.) . all of them.

Par. 167.

The words *banyak* (much, many) and *sadikit* (few) also precede the noun and may be classed as indefinite numerals.

> Note :
> *banyak orang* . many people.
> *kĕbanyakan orang* . most people, the majority.
> but :
> *orang banyak*   } . the ordinary people, the
> *orang kĕbanyakan* } . populace.

It is, however, possible to use *orang banyak* to mean " there were many people " e.g. *Orang banyak di–wayang* —" There were many people at the performance ". The adjective is probably felt to be predicative : " The people were many ". Note, too, Example b.1. in par. 146, where *kĕbanyakan* is used as a pure abstract noun : " because of the multitude (i.e. the many–ness) of the marching army ".

Par. 168.

This extract is taken from the *Hikayat Bayan Budiman* (*Tales of the Wise Parrot*), of which the oldest manuscript dates from about 1600.

Read the piece aloud and you will agree that it has the same clear bell-like resonance as the *Sějarah Mělayu*. The classical texts are easier to understand than most modern Malay prose. The tales in the *Hikayat Bayan Budiman* are in conversational style and afford abundance of useful vocabulary and idiom.

" Hatta běběrapa lama–nya pada suatu hari maka tuan putěri anak baginda itu turun běrmain–main ka–taman[1] bunga. Maka ia běrjalan hampir sa–pohon kayu bunga : tiba–tiba kěluar–lah sa–ekor ular dari bawah pohon bunga itu lalu di–pagut–nya ibu kaki tuan putěri itu. Maka děngan sa–kětika itu juga tuan putěri itu pun rěbah pengsan těrhantar[2] tiada khabarkan diri–nya, sapěrti orang mati laku–nya[3]. Maka sěgěra–lah dayang–dayang pěrgi měnyěmbahkan ka–pada pěrmaisuri[4]. Maka baginda laki istěri pun těrkějut–lah, rioh–lah di–dalam astana itu. Maka baginda kědua pun měněpok dada dan měnampar–nampar kěpala–nya sěrta děngan tangis–nya sěraya měnyuroh měnchari[5] tabib. Tělah běběrapa–lah orang datang, sa–orang pun tiada yang boleh měnawar bisa–nya, mangkin[6] běrtambah–tambah sakit–nya. Maka těrlalu–lah sangat duka chita baginda laki istěri oleh mělihat hal anak–nya. Maka baginda pun měnyuroh měmukul[5] chanang běrkěliling něgěri itu, sěraya měnyuroh měmanggil[5] sěgala anak raja–raja hulubalang sakalian isi něgěri itu. Maka sakalian pun běrkampong–lah. Maka baginda pun měmběri kurnia[7] sěgala fakir dan miskin sěrta měnjamu sěgala anak raja–raja itu makan. Sa–tělah sělěsai–lah dari–pada itu maka titah baginda, " Barang siapa dapat měngubati dan měnawar bisa–nya ular mĕmatok anak beta ini, maka beta bĕrikan anak beta pada–nya sĕrta beta ambil akan mĕnantu beta."

Translation.

Now some time after this, the princess, the king's daughter, went down one day to play in the garden. She was walking near a flowering bush, when suddenly a snake came out from under the bush and bit the princess' big toe. In an instant she swooned, and fell and lay stretched[1] upon the ground, unconscious and like to one dead[2]. Her maidens went at once to tell the queen. The king and queen were horrified, and there was a clamorous uproar in the palace. The royal pair smote their breasts and beat their heads and wept, and ordered doctors to be summoned. Many came, but not one of them could counteract the poison ; its effect grew more and more violent. The king and queen were in great distress at seeing their daughter in this state. Then the king ordered the gongs to be beaten throughout the city, and ordered that all the young men of royal blood should be summoned, and all the officers of the soldiery and all that were in that city. They all assembled. Then the king gave gifts to all the beggars and the poor, and made a feast for all the princelings. When all this was done, the king announced : " Whoever shall find an antidote to counteract the poison of the snake that has bitten my daughter, I will give him my daughter and I will take him for my son-in-law."

Notes

1. taman . Garden, pleasure-ground. A literary word.
2. tĕrhantar . From *hantarkan*—" to lay down ", not the same word as *hantar*—to conduct.
3. sapĕrti . . . Lit. " like a dead person, the behaviour laku–nya   of her".
4. permaisuri. Queen

5. měnyuroh　Note that when an ordering verb has the
   měnchari　*mě-* prefix it demands the *mě-* prefix in
   the verb that follows, even though the
   order is not addressed to a particular
   person. (Contrast par. 114c.)

6. mangkin　. Another form of *makin.*

7. kurnia　. Gift, from a superior to an inferior;
   favour.

Exercise 36

Translate the following passage from the *Hikayat Bayan Budiman.* It is part of the same story.

Maka kata Khalis, "Dahulu Allah, kěmudian Rasul[1]-nya! Yang měnawar bisa-nya ular itu hamba-lah.[2]" Maka anak raja itu běrkata-kata ka-pada Khalis, "Hai saudara-ku! jika děmikian, mari-lah kita měngadap baginda běrtěgohkan janji-nya baginda itu." Maka kětiga pun pěrgi-lah měngadap baginda. Maka sěmbah Khalis "Ya tuanku! Sunggoh sapěrti titah yang maha mulia[3] itu, běrjanji hěndak měmběrikan paduka[4] anakanda[5] akan barang siapa yang boleh měngubati dia?" Maka titah baginda, "Sunggoh-lah, sapěrti titah-ku itu: tiada-lah aku mungkir janji-ku." Maka Khalis itu pun měnyěmbah lalu ia kěluar pěrgi ka-pada anak raja itu. Maka di-khabarkan-nya-lah sapěrti titah baginda itu. Maka apa-bila sudah di-děngar-nya itu, maka anak raja itu pun masok-lah měngadap běrsama-sama děngan Khalis. Maka oleh anak raja itu pun di-bawa-nya masok ka-pada těmpat tuan putěri. Maka oleh Khalis di-suroh-nya labohkan kělambu těmpat tuan putěri itu. Maka Khalis děngan anak raja itu pun masok-lah kapada těmpat tuan putěri itu. Maka di-suroh Khalis sělimuti tuboh tuan putěri itu, hanya ibu kaki-nya itu kěluar. Sa-tělah itu, maka sěgala orang yang měnunggui tuan putěri itu pun di-

suroh–nya kĕluar sĕmua–nya dari dalam kĕlambu yang
kĕĕmasan itu : hanya–lah Khalis dĕngan anak raja itu
juga yang di–dalam kĕlambu itu. Maka Khalis pun
mĕnjadikan diri–nya sa–ekor ular. Maka di–hisap–nya
ibu kaki tuan putĕri itu tiga kali. Maka kĕluar–lah
bisa–nya. Maka di–muntahkan–nya pula tiga kali
bĕrturut–turut. Maka tuan putĕri pun tĕrkĕjut bangun
dudok.

Notes

1. Rasul . . . Lit. "one sent": apostle.
Usually used of Muhammad
only.

2. Yang . . . hamba–lah . Note the accumulation of
emphasis in this sentence,
all drawing attention to
Khalis : first *yang*, then
mĕ–, then *hamba* in a position
of emphasis at the end of
the sentence, and further
strengthened by *–lah*.

3. yang maha mulia . . " Most illustrious " : A
title reserved for reigning
princes and their royal con-
sorts. (See par. 158d.)

4. paduka . Lit. "shoe". May be translated " royal ". A relic of
the days when the subject
dared address only the
footwear of his sovereign.
The word is still used as a
conventional honorific in
letter writing. (Cf. Exercise 40, Note 2.)

5. anakanda   . Honorific form of *anak*.
                             Other such forms are:
                             ayahanda (from *ayah*),
                             kakanda (from *kakak;* used
                             for brother or sister) ; *bonda*
                             (from *ibu*) ; and *adinda*
                             (from *adek;* used for sister,
                             wife, lover.) All these
                             words are still universally
                             used in letter-writing, as
                             terms of respect or endear-
                             ment.

Exercise 37

Translate

How long does the voyage take ?—It all depends. If
we call at two or three ports it will take a month. If we
went direct, we should get there in sixteen or seventeen
days. But I don't think any ships ever do go direct. All
ships have to call at least at Port Said, because the traffic
through the canal is regulated.

Conversation No. 13

Mĕnjĕmput Kawan

Che' Rakiah : Sila–lah masok, Che' Hawa.

Che' Hawa : Baik–lah, Che' Rakiah.

Che' Rakiah : Makan–lah sireh[1].

Che' Hawa : Baik–lah[2] . . . Saya mari ini ada–lah
hajat sadikit[3]. Datang ini[3] hĕndak
jĕmput ĕnche' ka–tĕratak[4] saya pada hari
khamis yang datang, kĕrana ada sadikit
kĕnduri[5] mahu kahwinkan[5] anak laki–laki
saya. Sudi[6]–lah ĕnche' datang.

Che' Rakiah: Kalau ta'ada apa aral[7], sampai–lah saya ka–rumah ĕnche'.

Che' Hawa: Kalau tidak datang, kĕchil hati saya. Sĕkarang saya minta diri[8] dahulu.

Che' Rakiah: Sila[9], Che' Hawa.

Translation.

An Invitation

Che' Rakiah: Come in, Che' Hawa.

Che' Hawa: Thank you, Che' Rakiah.

Che' Rakiah: Help yourself to *sireh*[1].

Che' Hawa: Thank you[2] . . . I have come about a little matter[3]. I have come[3] to invite you to my house on Thursday next. We are going to have a bit of a feast for our son's wedding. Would you care to come ?[6]

Che' Rakiah: If there is nothing to prevent me[7], I will come.

Che' Hawa: If you don't, I shall be hurt. I must say good–bye now[8].

Che' Rakiah: Good–bye[9], Che' Hawa.

Notes

1. Makan–lah sireh . By this time the two women would be seated on the ground, on the creamy–green *mĕngkuang* matting of the inner room. Che' Rakiah pushes the betel-nut box (*bĕkas sireh*) across to Che' Hawa, and

there is a pause while they prepare
their " quids " for chewing. The
ingredients of a quid are : lime,
gambier, tobacco, betel–nut and
sireh leaf.
Malays are never effusive in their
manner of greeting, and their
conversations are usually quiet
and leisurely, with few words and
long pauses.

2. baik–lah   .   .   This expression is often used where
English would use " Thank you ".

3. saya mari . . .   Lit. " This my coming, there is
    Datang ini   something that I wish, this coming,
I wish to invite". The *ini* in each
case belongs to the whole verbal
idea (see footnote 47). Such a
phrase is frequently opened by a
yang which still further singles
out the verbal idea as being the
subject under discussion. *Yang
saya datang ini*.—" This my
coming".

4. tĕratak   .   .   Lit. " hut ". Here—humble home,
in modest depreciation.

5. kĕnduri and   Often spelt *khĕnduri* and *kawin*
    kahwin   respectively

6. sudi–lah   .   .   Lit. " Be pleased to come".

7. aral   .   .   .   Malay women nearly always add
this condition in accepting an
invitation. Similar phrases are
Jikalau tiada udzor (illness), i.e.
" If I am well " and *Insha' Allah*—
" God willing ".

8. minta **diri** . . Lit. " ask for myself ".

9. sila . . . Frequently used as a word of farewell to a parting guest, probably a shortened form of *Sila–lah pula*—" Come again", which is commonly used in the north of the Peninsula.

CHAPTER XVIII

PRONOUNS (continued)

    I.   Interrogative

    II. Possessive

    III. Emphatic and Reflexive.

    IV. Personal

    V. Demonstrative

I. Interrogative Pronouns and Adjectives

Par. 169.

  Apa? – What? What sort of? (referring to things)

    Examples.

      1. *Apa ini ?* . . What is this ?
      2. *Kĕbun apa itu ?* . What sort of an estate is that ?
      3. *Apa hajat ?* . What do you want ?
      4. *Apa–apa kueh yang di–bawa 'tu ?* What cakes are those that you have brought ?

Par. 170. Siapa? – Who?

    Examples.

      1. *Siapa tahu ?* . Who knows ?
      2. *Siapa lagi ?* . Who else ?
      3. *Siapa nama dia ?* . What is his name ?

4. *Siapa–siapa yang* Who were at the tea-party?
   hadzir di–jamuan
   itu?

Par. 171.   Mana? – Which? What?

Examples.

τ. *Jalan mana?*   . Which road?

2. *Yang mana dari-* Which of these rooms?
   pada bilek ini?

II. Possessive Pronouns

Par. 172.

Any pronoun placed after a noun is in the genitive
case, and therefore serves the purpose of an English
possessive adjective or pronoun.

Examples.

Rumah saya   .   . the house of me, i.e. my
house.

Salah siapa? .   . the fault of whom? i.e.
whose fault?

Par. 173.   " –ku " and " –mu ".[71]

As genitives the pronouns *aku* (" I ") and *kamu*
(" you ") are usually found in the enclitic forms *–ku* and
–mu, unless there is need for emphasis on the pronoun
itself.

Examples.

1. *Adek–ku*   .   .   . My sister (or brother.)

2. *Sa–lama hidup–ku* } As long as I live (lit. as
   Sa–umor–ku   } long as the life of me.)

3. *Bětulkan hati–mu*   First of all, straighten
   dahulu   your heart.

[71] Literary form.

Note that, unless there is emphasis on the pronoun itself, *–ku* and *–mu* are the forms that are used after compound prepositions, e.g. *daripada–mu, kapada–ku.*

Par. 174. " –nya "

As genitive, the form of the pronoun *dia* (or *ia*) is *–nya*, unless there is need for emphasis.

Examples.

1. *Nama–nya pun ta'tahu*   I don't even know his name.

2. *Ini kĕreta saya, kĕreta*   This is my car, his is *dia sa–bĕlah sana*   over there.

Par. 175.

The word *–nya* is of frequent occurrence, with apparent variety of function. But it is possible to trace the genitive idea in most of its uses.

Examples.

1. *Apa pula malu–nya bĕkĕrja ?*   What disgrace is there, in working ? (Lit. " What is the shame of it".

2. *Sĕrta di–lihat–nya* . When it was seen by him, when he saw it. (see footnote 36.)

3. *Agak–nya* . . . probably (by the guess of it.)

   Rupa–nya   . apparently (by the appearance of it.)

4. *Kata–nya* . . . he said (the words of him.)

5. *Tujoh kaki panjang–nya*   7 feet long (the length of it.)

K

> *Lima tahun umor–nya* 5 years old (the age of him.)

> *Bukan main bĕrat–nya* Exceedingly heavy (no joke, the weight of it.)

6. *Bukan–nya saya takut .* It isn't that I am afraid.

7. *Chomel–nya kĕreta itu .* What a lovely car !

Par. 176. Punya.

The use of *punya* after a pronoun to express possession[72], when the thing owned is not named, has already been noticed in par. 36.

Examples.

1. *Kasut ini dia punya* (or *Kasut ini kasut dia*) These shoes are his.

2. *Bĕnda tĕrsepah–sepah sahaja di–atas meja. Siapa punya ?* (or *Bĕnda siapa ?*) There are things strewn all over the table. Whose are they ?

III. The Emphatic and Reflexive Pronoun.

Par. 177.

Sĕndiri (a derivative of *diri*—" body ", " self ")— oneself, self.

Note that the word is used, as is its English equivalent, both as emphatic pronoun and as reflexive pronoun.

(a) Emphatic.

It is used in conjunction with any of the personal pronouns. e.g.

---

[72] *Untok* (a share) *hak* (property) and *milek* (ownership) are also used to show possession. e.g. *Untok siapa bilek ini ?*—" Whose room is this ? " (i.e. for whom). *Parang itu hak saya. Jangan angkat.* " That chopper is mine. Don't take it away ". *Tanah ini milek saya*—" I am the owner of this land ".

saya sĕndiri . I myself.

ĕngkau ⎫
awak ⎬*sĕndiri* . you yourself, or yourselves.
kamu ⎭

dia sĕndiri . . he himself, she herself, they themselves.

It can be used alone as an indefinite emphatic pronoun, e.g.

rumah sĕndiri . . one's own house.

(b) Reflexive.

As a reflexive pronoun the form *diri* is used. e.g.

minta ⎫*diri*   to ask leave to go, to take
pohon ⎭   one's departure.

bĕrkata di-dalam to say to oneself.
diri

bunoh diri . . to commit suicide.

Note: The more usual way of expressing the reflexive idea is by the *bĕr-* derivative. e.g.

bĕrmohon . . to take one's leave (to ask for oneself.)

Sometimes both forms are used : e.g.

bĕrsĕmbunyikan
               diri   to hide oneself.

In literary Malay the form *diri* is commonly used with an enclitic genitive pronoun. e.g.

diri–ku . . I (lit. the self of me).
diri–mu . . you
diri–nya . . himself, etc.

Example.

Tiada aku mĕngaku akan diri–ku pandai. (*Hikayat Abdullah.*)

I do not acknowledge myself to be a learned man, i.e. I make no claim to be a scholar.

Note also the phrase *sa–orang diri*—alone.

IV. Personal Pronouns

Par. 178.

The personal pronouns have been discussed in Chapter IX.

Additional points to be noted :

(a) The enclitic forms *–ku*, *–mu*, *–nya* (par. 173–4).

(b) The proclitic forms *ku–* and *kau–* used, before the simple verb, when there is no emphasis on the doer of the action.

Example.

Ku–děngar raja itu pěnyakit sopak. Aku tahu ilmu tabib. Aku–lah měngubati dia. (*Hik. Bay. Bud.*)

It has come to my ears that the Raja has a skin disease. I am skilled in medicine. I will cure him.

Notice the crescendo :

   1. *Ku–* and the root verb . a general report.
   2. *Aku* and the root verb . a factual statement, unemphasized.
   3. *Aku* emphasized by *–lah*. *I* am the one who and *mě–* . . . will effect the cure.

(c) In written Malay, after *děngan*, *akan* and *–kan* :

–daku is used for *aku*.

–dikau is sometimes used for *ěngkau*.

dia is always used for the third person.

(d) A reminder. Avoid using second person pronouns in your conversation as far as possible.

V. Demonstrative Pronouns and Adjectives

Par. 179.

The demonstrative pronouns have been discussed in Chapter IV.

A few reminders :

(a) *Itu* and *ini* may be either adjectival or pronominal. When they are adjectives they follow the noun. e.g.

pĕlandok itu	.	.	that mouse-deer.
pĕrangkap ini	.	.	this trap.

When they are pronouns they precede the noun. e.g.

Itu pĕlandok	.	.	That's a mouse-deer.
Ini pĕrangkap	.	.	This is a trap.

(b) When they are used adjectivally they come after any other attributive adjectives or adjectival phrases which qualify the noun[73]. e.g.

mĕja panjang itu	.	that long table.
mĕja yang baharu di–bĕli itu		the table that I have just bought.

(c) Any adjective which comes after *ini* or *itu* is predicative, i.e. it makes a statement. e.g.

Nasi ini sudah basi	.	This rice is stale.

The three sentences given below summarize what has been stated in (a), (b) and (c) :

(1) *Ini ubi tĕrkupas, bukan–nya buah susu.*
These are peeled potatoes, they are not passion fruit. (*Ini* used as a pronoun.)

---

[73] An adjectival *itu*, therefore, always " looks backward ". If you remember that fact when you are reading, and refuse to let your voice glide upward until you come to the *itu*, you will be less likely to miss the writer's meaning.

(2) *Bawa ubi (yang) tĕrkupas itu.*
Bring me those peeled potatoes. (*tĕrkupas*—
attributive.)

(3) *Ubi ini tĕrkupas.*
These potatoes are peeled.
(*tĕrkupas*—predicative.)

(d) *Ini* is sometimes used as an intensive
adjective. e.g.

aku ini . . I myself.
sa–kĕjap ini ⎱ this very moment.
sĕkarang ini ⎰

(See also conversation 8, note 3.)

(e) *Ini* and *itu* may be used to qualify phrases, or
sentences.

For examples see footnote 47, and conversation
13, note 3.

Par. 180.

The following piece is taken from the 16th century
romance of the hero Hang Tuah, another classical text.
You will recognize the same clear, unhurried style.

Maka ada pun Hang Mahmud itu bĕrkata kapada
istĕri–nya, yang bĕrnama Dang Mĕrdu Wati, "Tuan,
baik–lah kita pĕrgi ka–Bĕntan[1], supaya mudah kita
mĕnchari makanan, lagi pun nĕgĕri besar; baik–lah kita
pindah pĕrgi tiga bĕranak". Maka sahut Dang Mĕrdu
Wati, "Sa–bĕnar–nya–lah sapĕrti kata tuan itu". Maka
pada malam itu Hang Mahmud pun tidor–lah, lalu ia
bĕrmimpi, bulan jatoh dari langit, maka chahaya–nya
pĕnoh di–atas kĕpala anak–nya Hang Tuah. Maka Hang
Mahmud pun tĕrkĕjut dari–pada tidor–nya, lalu bangun,
di–riba anak–nya, di–pĕlok dan di–chium–nya sa–luroh
tuboh anak–nya itu. Maka hari pun siang lah; maka

sĕgala mimpi–nya itu pun sĕmua–nya di–katakan–nya
ka–pada anak–nya dan istĕri–nya.

. . . .

" Ada pun akan anak kita ini hĕndak–lah tuan pĕlihara
baik–baik, jangan di–bĕri bĕrmain jauh–jauh, karna anak
kita ini sangat nakal–nya ; karna aku hĕndak sĕrahkan
ia mĕngaji[2], maalim[3] pun tiada; lagi ia bĕlum tahu bahasa;
sĕkarang baik–lah kita pindah ka–Bĕntan, mari kita
bĕrsimpan pĕrkakas kita". Maka Hang Mahmud pun
bĕrlĕngkap–lah sa–buah pĕrahu ; sa–tĕlah sudah maka
Hang Mahmud pun bĕrpindah ka–Bĕntan, maka ia pun
bĕrbuat suatu rumah hampir kampong Datok Bĕndahara.
Maka Hang Mahmud pun bĕrkĕdai makan–makanan.

Translation.

Then said Hang Mahmud to his wife, whose name was
Dang Merdu Wati, " Lady, it were well that we should go to
Bentan so that we may more easily seek a livelihood.
Moreover, it is a large settlement ; it were well that we
should move thither, we and our child. Dang Merdu
Wati answered, " What you say is true". That night
Hang Mahmud slept ; and he dreamed that the moon
fell from the sky, and the brightness of it was full upon
the head of his son, Hang Tuah. Hang Mahmud started
up from his sleep and arose, and took his child on his lap,
and put his arms round him, and kissed him all over his
body. When dawn came he told the whole of his dream
to his son and to his wife.

. . . . . .

" Now as for this child of ours, you must look after
him carefully. You must not let him wander far away
in his play, for he is very wayward, this child of ours. I
should like him to study the Koran, but there is no
scholar here to whom I can entrust him. Moreover, he

has not yet learned courteous speech. It is well that we should move to Bentan. Let us put together our household goods. Then Hang Mahmud fitted out a boat. When it was ready he moved to Bentan, and (there) he made for himself a house, near the homestead of the Datok Bendahara, and set up a food shop.

Notes

1. Běntan . . An island, south-east of Singapore.
2. měngaji . . From *kaji*, which is seldom used. *Měngaji* usually means to study religion, or to study the Koran, but it is frequently used also with the general meaning of attending school.
3. maalim . . A learned person, particularly of one skilled in navigation.

Exercise 38

Translate the following :

Maka tatkala itu Hang Tuah kělima (*see par.* 182) běrsahabat pun ada běrmain di–kědai–nya, maka di–lihat oleh Hang Tuah akan Batin[1] itu, lalu ia pun měmběri hormat ka–pada Batin itu, serta měngajak singgah ka–rumah–nya. Maka Batin itu singgah–lah sěraya kata-nya, " Di–sini–kah rumah saudara–ku ini ? " sambil měměgang tangan Hang Tuah. Maka sahut Hang Tuah, " Di–sini–lah těmpat sahaya ". Maka Batin itu pun dudok–lah di–kědai itu. Maka Hang Mahmud pun datang–lah měmbawa těmpat sireh, sěraya kata–nya, " Makan–lah sireh[2] Batin ; oleh kaseh Batin akan anak hamba itu tiada–lah těrbalas[3] oleh hamba." Maka Batin itu pun makan–lah sireh, sěraya kata–nya, " Hai

bapa hamba, jangan–lah bapa–ku bĕrkata demikian itu ;
ada pun Hang Tuah kĕlima ini sudah–lah mĕnjadi
saudara pada hamba ". Maka sa–kĕtika dudok bĕrkata–
kata, Batin itu pun bĕrmohon–lah turun ka–pĕrahu–nya.

Exercise 39

Translate.

We had better measure the distance from the garage
to the ditch before we begin digging. I think we shall
be able to put in four rows, if they are not too wide apart.
Where is that rope we had just now ? Oh, here it is.
I'll hold this end. You take the other end and walk
towards the ditch. When it is taut, make a mark.
Don't go crooked. Keep your eye on that fence.

Conversation No. 14

Pĕlayan orang sakit dĕngan orang sakit

Che' Mĕriam : Misi, mari sa–bĕntar !

Pĕlayan : Kĕnapa Che' Mĕriam ?

Che' Mĕriam : Tolong saya sadikit.

Pĕlayan : Boleh. Apa Che' mahu ?

Che' Mĕriam : Tolong bagi saya tilam. Tĕmpat tidor
ini kĕras, bĕrlapekan papan sahaja. Tulang
sĕndi badan saya sakit.

Pĕlayan : Apa 'nak buat ? Tilam ta' chukup.

Che' Mĕriam : Kalau bagitu biar–lah. Tolong gosok
bĕlakang saya. Tĕrsangat lĕngoh rasa–
nya.

Pĕlayan : Nanti saya pĕrgi ambil minyak, boleh
gosok.

. . . . . .

Che' Mĕriam : Misi pandai mĕnggosok. Bĕrasa lĕga
kĕbas–kĕbas dan lĕngoh–lĕngoh.

Pĕlayan :   Barang kali pĕtang ini boleh dapat tilam.
               Orang itu, yang sakit dada nun itu, 'nak
               kĕluar sa–bĕntar lagi.   Dia chuma
               mĕnanti Doktor datang mĕmotong nama
               dia.   Sabar–lah dahulu.

Che' Mĕriam : Baik–lah.

Translation.

Nurse and Patient

Che' Mĕriam : Nurse, come here a moment, will you ?

Nurse :   Why, Che' Mĕriam ?

Che' Mĕriam : Do something for me. (Lit. " Help me
               a little.")

Nurse :   Yes.   What is it that you want ?

Che' Mĕriam : Give me a mattress, will you ?   This bed
               is very hard ; it has only wood underneath
               it. My bones and my joints are aching.

Nurse :   I can't. (lit. What am I to do?)   There are
               not enough mattresses.

Che' Mĕriam : If that's the case, it doesn't matter.   Rub
               my back, will you ?   I feel quite stiff.

Nurse :   I'll go and get some oil to rub it with.

               . . . . . .

Che' Mĕriam : You massage well. Already the numbness
               and the stiffness is getting less.

Nurse :   Perhaps there will be a mattress to be had
               this evening. That patient over there
               the chest case, is going home presently.
               She is only waiting for the doctor to give
               her her discharge.   Be patient.

Che' Mĕriam : Yes, I will.

CHAPTER XIX

I. Ordinal numbers

II. Fractions

III. Measurements

I. Ordinal Numbers

Par. 181.

Ordinal numbers are formed thus :

1st	. . *yang pĕrtama*
2nd	. . *yang kĕdua*
3rd	. . *yang kĕtiga*
4th	. . *yang kĕĕmpat*
678th	. . *yang kĕĕnam ratus tujoh puloh dĕlapan*
592 1st	. . *yang kĕlima ribu sĕmbilan ratus dua poloh satu*

These forms are adjectival and follow the noun ;

Examples.

1. the second time. *kali yang kĕdua*

2. page 6 (i.e. the
   6th page) .   . *muka yang kĕĕnam*

Par. 182.

The words *kĕdua*, *kĕtiga*, etc. when used without *yang* are collective words and precede the noun.

The collective idea is sometimes strengthened by a *bĕr–* derivative.

Note the idiomatic phrases for groups of relatives, friends, etc.

Examples.

1. *kědua tangan*
   or *kědua–dua tangan* } both hands.
   or *kědua–bělah tangan*

2. *kětiga–nya* . . . the three of them, all three.

3. *kědua laki istěri* . . husband and wife.

4. *kědua běranak* . . father and child *or* mother and child.

5. *kětiga běranak* . . father, mother and child
   or father and two children.
   or mother and two children.

6. *kěěmpat běradek* . the four brothers
   or four sisters
   or four brothers and sisters.

7. *kělima sahabat*
   or *kělima běrsahabat* } the five friends.

Par. 183.

When such an expression is used in apposition to a pronoun, or a noun, it is put after it.

Examples.

1. *kami kětiga* . . . all three of us.

2. *kita kělima ini* . . we five.

3. *saya tiga běranak* or
   saya kětiga běranak } I and my wife and child.

4. *saya dua laki–istěri* or
   saya kědua laki–istěri } my wife and I *or* my husband and I.

Note the shade of difference between the following :

1. *saya kĕĕmpat* . . . I and *the* three others, all four of us (i.e. all who were there.)

2. *saya bĕrĕmpat* . . I and three others (i.e. four of us, out of those present.)

Par. 184.

The Hang Tuah quintet supplies numberless examples of this idiom. Here are five sentences :

1. *Maka ada pun suatu hari Hang Tuah dudok bĕrsama–sama dĕngan sahabat–nya kĕĕmpat.*
One day Hang Tuah was sitting with his four friends.

2. *Hang Tuah kĕlima pun mĕngambil orang luka itu, di–bawa–nya turun ka–pĕrahu–nya.*

Hang Tuah and the four others picked up the wounded men and carried them down to the boat.

3. *Nama beta ini Hang Tuah dan yang ĕmpat ini saudara hamba.*
My name is Hang Tuah and these four are my comrades.

4. *Jika ada kaseh pĕnghulu akan kami kĕlima bĕrsaudara ini hamba hĕndak bĕrbalek–lah ka–Bĕntan.*
If you will graciously permit us, we five friends will return to Bentan.

5. *Maka Hang Tuah kĕlima saudara itu pun sama mĕnghunus kĕris–nya.*
Then the five of them with one accord drew their daggers.

Par. 185.

Pĕrtama, kĕdua, kĕtiga, etc. are used to mean " firstly ", " secondly ", " thirdly ", in enumerations.

Examples.

Ada pun pĕrkataan yang hĕndak bĕrhuruf bĕsar, ada–lah sapĕrti tĕrsĕbut di–bawah ini :

Pĕrtama :   *Nama orang.   Mithal–nya : Muhammad, Daud, Puteh dan sa–bagai–nya.*

Kĕdua :   *Gĕlaran orang bĕsĕrta nama–nya. Mithal–nya : Haji Abdullah, Shaikh Salim, Pĕnghulu Abu, d. s. b.* (Note this abbreviation.)

Kĕtiga :   *Nama nĕgĕri dan tĕmpat. Mithal–nya : bĕnua Asia, nĕgĕri Perak, jajahan Larut d. s. b.*

Translation.

Words which should be written with capital letters are the following :

    1st :   Names. e.g. Muhammad, Daud, Puteh, and so on. (*or* etcetera.)

    2nd :   Titles, with the names to which they are attached, e.g. Haji Abdullah, Shaikh Salim, Penghulu Abu, etc.

    3rd :   Names of countries and places. e.g. the continent of Asia, Perak, the district of Larut, etc.

II. Fractions
Par. 186.

Fractions are expressed thus :

    $\frac{1}{4}$:   *satu suku*, or *sa–suku*, or *suku*.

$\frac{1}{2}$: *sa–tĕngah*, or, as an approximate measure, *sa–paroh*.

$\frac{3}{4}$: *tiga suku*.

$\frac{1}{3}$: *sa–pĕrtiga*.

$\frac{2}{3}$: *dua pĕrtiga*.

$\frac{7}{15}$: *tujoh pĕrlima–bĕlas*.

But with the exception of the first three these expressions are anglicisms and should be avoided. Even the first three are much less definite, except in Arithmetic books, than the corresponding expressions in English.

Suku (a section) is used for " a small proportion of ", *sa–tĕngah* and *sa–paroh* are commonly used to mean " some ". e.g.

       Kata sa–tĕngah orang . Some people say.

For " $\frac{3}{4}$ ", *tiga bahagian* (*bagi* or *bahagi*—to allot, divide) is commonly used, just as we say " three parts full " i.e. " out of four".

For " $1\frac{1}{2}$ ", *tĕngah dua* is commonly used, and the "unit" from which the "half" is taken need not be one whole number. It may be a ten, or a hundred, or a thousand. e.g.

      25 : *tĕngah tiga puloh* (i.e. a half–ten from 3 tens *or* a half of the third ten.)

      350 : *tĕngah ĕmpat ratus* (i.e. a half–hundred from 4 hundreds)

      4,500 : *tĕngah lima ribu* (i.e. a half–thousand from 5 thousands.)

Par. 187.

Note the following :

      9% : *sĕmbilan pĕrratus* (or *pĕr sen*) or, commonly, *dalam sa– ratus sĕmbilan*.

      5·7 : *lima pĕrpulohan tujoh*.

      ·77 : *pĕrpulohan tujoh tujoh*.

kĕrat dua . ⎫
potong dua . ⎪
kĕrat sama tĕngah ⎬ to cut in half.
potong sama tĕngah ⎭

bahagi dua . . to share between two.

dua–dua sa-kali . two at a time.

tiga kali ganda . three times as many.

sĕlang satu or . ⎫
lat satu . ⎬ every other one.

ganjil . . ⎫
gasal . . ⎬ odd.

gĕnap . . . even (full, complete).

sa-gĕnap kali . . every single time.

sa-gĕnap dunia ⎫
sa-luroh dunia ⎬ the whole world.

III. Measurements

Par. 188.

(a) Weight.

satu kati, sa–kati . a " catty "—about $1\frac{1}{3}$ lb.
satu tahil, sa–tahil. a tahil, i.e. $\frac{1}{16}$ of a kati—about $1\frac{1}{3}$ ozs.

In the table of weights, 100 kati make 1 pikul, but the " pikul " in practice is not an absolute measurement of weight. It varies according to the commodity.

The three–looped steelyard used by most stall–holders in the market is called a *daching*.

(b) Length.

1 inch . . *satu inchi*
1 foot . . *satu kaki*

1 yard . . *satu ela*

1 mile . . *satu batu* (i.e. 1 milestone) or *satu mail.*

The following Malay measures are also in common use :

sa–jěngkal
(a span) . 9 inches ⎫
sa–hasta .
(a cubit) . 18 inches ⎬ for cloth.
sa–kabong . 2 yards ⎭

satu děpa . 6 foot (span of outstretched arms).

(c) Area.

The English square measures (e.g. *satu batu pěrsěgi*—1 square mile) are commonly used.

The *rělong* (or *orlong*) is a Malay measure for land.

1 *rělong* = about 1⅓ acres.

But the *rělong* is frequently used as a linear measurement of 240 feet.

(d) Capacity.

1 *chupak* . a little more than a quart.

1 *gantang* . about 1¼ gallon.
(4 *chupak*)

(e) Numerical.

sa–pasang . a pair.

satu kudi . a score.

Par. 189.

This is an extract from *Misa Mělayu*, a Perak chronicle of the 18th century.

Titah baginda, " Hai Sang Paya Indĕra dan Sang Paya 'diraja, di-mana sungai yang baik beta hĕndak mĕnuba ? "[1] Maka sĕmbah pawang[2] kĕdua itu, "Tuanku ampun! ka-pada pĕmandangan patek sakalian, sungai yang baik dan ikan-nya banyak Sungai Budiman-lah yang patut tuanku bĕrangkat[3] bĕrmain-main mĕmbawa adinda baginda sakalian ". Maka titah baginda, " Jika dĕmikian, bĕrlĕngkap-lah mika[4] sakalian, kita hĕndak sĕgĕra pĕrgi itu ". Maka bĕrmohon-lah sĕgala pawang itu bĕrlĕngkap akan sĕgala bĕlat pĕngalir bubu[5]. Maka baginda pun bĕrtitah ka-pada Raja Muda dan anak raja-raja dan orang bĕsar-bĕsar hulubalang rayat sakalian-nya mĕnyuroh bĕrlĕngkap sĕgala kĕlĕngkapan mĕnuba dari-pada[6] tuba dan sĕrampang pĕrbuatan Teja dan sauk-sauk[7]. Sa-tĕlah itu, maka di-suroh himpunkan tuba dari-pada sa-gĕnap tĕlok rantau dan anak sungai. Maka sĕgala kĕlĕngkapan itu pun di-pĕrbuat orang-lah bĕrbagai-bagai rupa-nya dan jĕnis-nya. Ada pun pada masa itu ada yang mĕmbuat sauk-sauk ĕmas akan sĕgala anak raja-raja dan ada yang mĕmbuat sauk-sauk suasa[8] akan sĕgala anak orang baik-baik dan anak tuan-tuan dan ada yang bĕrbuat sauk-sauk perak akan sĕgala isi istana dan dayang-dayang baginda, dan ada yang bĕrbuat sauk-sauk tĕmbaga dan bĕsi dan kayu akan sĕgala hamba raja dan sĕgala rayat sakalian . . . Sa-tĕlah sudah sĕgala kĕlĕngkapan itu, maka tuba pun di-himpunkan orang-lah. Maka sĕgala pawang pun datang-lah, masing-masing dĕngan bĕlat-nya. Sa-tĕlah mustaed-lah sakalian-nya, maka baginda pun bĕrangkat-lah dĕngan adinda baginda dan sĕgala isi istana dan dayang-dayang pĕrwira[9] sakalian.

Translation.

The Sultan made enquiry : " Hai, Sang Paya Indĕra and Sang Paya 'diraja, which is the best river for tuba fishing ? " The two *pawang* answered, " Your Highness, in the opinion of all of us, the best river, where there would be most fish, is Sungai Budiman. That is where Your Highness should go for your sport, taking with you all your ladies ". Then the Sultan gave orders, " If that is so, do you, all of you, make ready. We would go thither without delay ". All the *pawang* departed, and made ready all manner of traps and lines, and the Sultan commanded the Raja Muda and all the princes, and the chiefs, and the officers and the ordinary people, and bade them make ready all the equipment for tuba–fishing, that is to say tuba root, and spears, of Teja workmanship, and scoops. After that, he bade them collect tuba root from all the bays and reaches and tributaries. They made ready all the equipment, of all kinds and fashions. At that time there were some making scoops mounted with gold, for all the princes, and some making scoops mounted with alloy of gold for all the people of birth and quality, some made scoops mounted with silver for the inmates of the palace, and the court damsels, and others made scoops mounted with brass and iron and wood for the Sultan's slaves and the ordinary people . . . When all the equipment had been made ready, the tuba root was brought together, to one place. All the *pawang* came, each with his trap. When they were all ready, the Sultan set out, with all his ladies, and all the royal household and all the court damsels, and all the warriors.

Notes

1. hěndak měnuba .   A method of fishing, by using *tuba* (poisonous vegetable extract) to stupefy the fish.

2. pawang   .   .   From Wilkinson's *Malay–English Dictionary:* 1903 Edition. *"Pawang:* a sorcerer, a medicine-man, a

practitioner of the black art. A *pawang* is, however, as a rule, less of a witch–doctor than of a practitioner of some harmless art such as hunting, agriculture or fishing, for the proper success of which ceremonies (relics of an older religion) are deemed necessary". 1932 Edition: "At the present day, in S. Malaya, *pawang* is used specifically of the village medicineman . . . who is supposed to be in touch with the world of spirits, and plays a part in exorcising illnesses . . . choosing lucky times for opening a new mine, or planting a new crop, and performing the customary rites on such occasions". Etym. = Shipmaster, navigating officer.

3. běrangkat   =*běrjalan*. One of the few words which are courtly equivalents for everyday words. You have already met *titah* (command) and *patek* (I). Others are: *běradu=tidor; gěring= sakit ; mangkat=mati ; hulu= kěpala ; santap=makan.*

1. mika   .   . Perak—" you ". Corresponding to *těman*—" I ".

5. bělat   .   . a net formed by tying together lengths of rattan; a fish trap of this type.

pěngalir   .   . = *pěnghilir*, a type of fish trap which points down river.

bubu   .   . a large conical rattan trap.

6. dari pada . . note this use of *dari pada* for
                "comprising", or "including".
                Cf. *dari pada laki–laki pĕrĕmpuan*
                in Exercise 40.

7. sauk   . from Wilkinson's *M.E.D.*: *Sauk*:
                1. lassoing; 2. a pot–lid; 3. scoop-
                ing up with the hands; 4. sighing.
                Here = small landing nets.

8. suasa   .   . gold alloyed with copper.

9. pĕrwira .   . warrior.

Par. 190.

The extract given in this paragraph is taken from
the *Pĕlayaran Abdullah* (from Singapore to Kĕlantan,
in 1838.) Abdullah bin Abdulkadir (1796–1854) was a
Malacca Malay of mixed Arab and Indian descent. His
father was a Malay letter-writer and Abdullah studied
Malay as well as Tamil, Hindustani, English and Arabic.
In his boyhood he was a protégé of Sir Stamford Raffles,
who won his affection and admiration. In later life he
taught Malay to several other Englishmen, and his
autobiography *'Hikayat Abdullah)*, written in 1840,
contains lively portraits of some of them.

Abdullah's style lacks the crystal clarity of the classical
writers. His sentences have not the rhythmic swing of
the old Malay idiom ; they are in easy-going colloquial
style. He is garrulous and sententious, but his subject
matter is of great interest, and his vocabulary is wide.

Maka ada–lah tatkala masok itu, pada sangka hati
sakalian orang, pĕrahu itu pĕchah–lah sĕbab bĕsar sangat
ombak–nya, sapĕrti pohon nyior tinggi–nya. Maka
masing–masing bĕrtĕriak. Kĕmudian, dĕngan tolong
Allah, masok–lah dĕngan sĕlamat–nya dĕngan tiada
sa–suatu mara–bahaya. Ada–nya dua buah sĕkochi[74]

---

[74] *Sĕkochi* (Dutch)—a sailing boat of European type.

itu, maka sĕkochi bĕsar itu tinggal di–kuala. Maka
" Water–witch " di–bawa mudek ka–hulu. Maka ada-
lah sipat–nya sungai itu tĕrlalu–lah lebar, kira–kira
sayup mata mĕmandang, sa–bĕrang–mĕnyĕbĕrang, kiri
kanan–nya pasir puteh dan ayer–nya tawar.

Shahadan, ayer–nya itu sĕntiasa hilir sahaja, tiada
bĕrbalas pasang ; dan kalau kĕtika hujan di–hulu sampai
tĕngah laut–nya ayer tawar. Dan lagi dalam sungai itu
ada bĕbĕrapa buah pulau, ada kĕchil ada bĕsar. Maka
ada kira–kira tĕngah dua jam bĕlayar mudek itu, sampai-
lah di–Kampong China. Maka sahaya lihat ada bĕbĕrapa
ratus orang Mĕlayu dan China tĕlah mĕnanti dĕngan
lĕmbing dan sĕnjata di–darat. Maka naik–lah sahaya
bĕrtiga–tiga. Maka kata–nya, " Pĕrahu dari–mana
ini ? " Maka jawab sahaya, " Pĕrahu ini dari Sĕlat
mĕmbawa surat hĕndak pĕrgi ka–Kĕlantan". Kĕmudian
datang–lah Tĕngku Siak dan Tĕngku Tanjong sĕrta
bĕratus–ratus orang bĕrtanya khabar nĕgĕri Sĕlat dan
harga dagangan. Maka sahaya bĕrkhabar–khabar–lah
dĕngan dia : lalu sahaya bĕrtanya–lah, " Mana Dato'
Bĕndahara ? " Maka jawab–nya " Dato' Bĕndahara
dan Kapitan China sudah mudek ka–Jĕlai, di–tĕmpat
orang mĕnchĕbak mas". Maka kata sahaya, " Lima--
bĕlas hari mudek boleh sampai". Dan lagi kata–nya,
" Sa–panjang sungai kita mudek itu ada kampong orang ;
maka ada buaya tĕrlalu ganas dalam sungai itu". Maka
sahaya lihat hal nĕgĕri Pahang itu sapĕrti dusun ada–nya,
tiada bĕrpasar dan kĕdai, dan tiada lorong yang boleh
bĕrjalan–jalan, mĕlainkan di–Kampong China itu sahaja
yang boleh bĕrjalan, ada kira–kira lima–puloh dĕpa.

Translation.

As we entered, everybody thought that the boat would
be dashed to pieces because the waves were so big, as
high as coconut palms. Every man on board gave a
shout. Then, with the help of Allah, we went safely in,
without a single mishap. Of the two boats, the big one

remained at the mouth, but " Water Witch " was taken
up-river. In appearance the river was very wide, one
could only just see across from bank to bank, on the right
and on the left there was white sand, and the water
was fresh.

Moreover, the water always flowed out to sea, there
was never a returning inward tide, and when there was
rain in the upper reaches, the water was fresh far out to
sea. When we had sailed up-river for about an hour
and a half, we came to Kampong China. I saw that there
were several hundred Malays and Chinese waiting on the
shore with spears and weapons. The three of us landed.
They asked us, " Where is this boat from ? " We
answered, " This boat is from Singapore. We bring
letters and are on our way to Kelantan." Then came
Tengku Siak and Tengku Tanjong with hundreds of
others asking for news of Singapore, and the price of
merchandise. I told them what they wanted to know,
and then I asked, " Where is the Datok Bendahara ? "
They answered, " The Datok Bendahara and the Kapitan
China have gone up-river to Jelai, the place where they
are digging for gold". " That's a fortnight's journey
up-river", I said. And they said, " All along the river,
as we went upstream there were homesteads, and in the
river there were fierce crocodiles ". I saw that in Pahang
there were patches of cultivation, but few market-places
and shops, and no paths where you could walk for
any distance, except at Kampong China where you could
walk for about a hundred yards.

Exercise 40

Translate this extract from *Misa Mělayu*. It is a
continuation of the passage given in paragraph 189.

Maka tĕrlalu–lah ramai sĕgala pĕrahu mĕngiringkan
baginda itu. Maka sĕgala bunyi–bynyian pun di–palu

orang–lah. Maka rioh rĕndah sa–panjang rantau itu
dari–pada sĕgala pĕrahu raja–raja itu. Maka tiada–lah
bĕrapa lama–nya antara di–jalan itu, maka baginda pun
sampai–lah ka–Sungai Budiman tĕmpat yang hĕndak
di–tuba itu. Sa–tĕlah hari malam, maka baginda pun
bĕrhĕnti–lah di–situ. Maka pada malam itu Sungai
Budiman pun di–bĕlat–lah oleh sĕgala pawang. Sa–tĕlah
kĕ–esokan hari–nya, bĕlat pun sudah–lah tĕrlaboh.
Maka tuba pun di–pukul orang–lah. Sa–tĕlah tuba
tĕrpukul, maka di–pukul pula gĕndang pĕrang sĕrta
di–pasangkan sĕmboyan[1] tiga kali. Sa–tĕlah itu, maka
tuba pun di–labohkan orang–lah. Sa–kĕtika lagi, maka
ikan pun timbul–lah tĕrlalu banyak–nya. Maka ramai–
lah sĕgala anak raja–raja yang mĕngiringkan duli[2]
baginda itu mĕnikam ikan. Maka sĕgala anak raja
pĕrĕmpuan pun tĕrlalu–lah ramai–nya dan sĕgala orang
baik–baik mĕnyauk ikan. Maka sĕgala dayang–dayang
dan hamba raja dan rayat sakalian pun tĕrlalu–lah
banyak mĕngambil ikan dari–pada[3] laki–laki pĕrĕmpuan,
ada yang mĕnyauk, ada yang mĕnikam. Maka rioh
rĕndah gĕgak gĕmpita sa–panjang–panjang sungai itu,
sĕrta dĕngan sorak tĕmpek sĕgala hamba raja itu dan
rayat sakalian, tambahan pula jĕrit pĕkek sĕgala
pĕrĕmpuan, karna sĕbab suka–nya mĕngambil ikan itu ;
ada yang rĕbah rempah koyak–koyak dĕngan kain baju
mĕreka itu dan ada yang jatoh ka–dalam sungai ; maka
tĕrbanyak–lah bĕrgomul sama sĕndiri–nya bĕrĕbutkan
ikan itu. Sa–tĕlah itu, maka hari pun pĕtang–lah.
Maka tĕrlalu banyak mati ikan itu. Maka bĕrhenti–lah
orang dari pada mĕnikam dan mĕnyauk ikan itu.

Notes

1. sĕmboyan	. An alarm signal, or a signal of warning.

2. duli   .   . Lit. dust. The dust beneath a ruler's foot to which a subject humbly addressed himself : and so by transference, a title of honour : "Your Highness", "His Highness". (Cf. Exercise 36, Note 4).

3. dari pada .   . See par. 189, Note 6.

Exercise 41

Translate. (This is a modern piece, written by an English–speaking Malay, in colloquial style.)

Kĕdai–kĕdai Makan di–London.

Sa–lama saya bĕrpindah dari Cambridge tinggal di–bandar London ini sĕlalu saya makan malam di–rumah, kadang–kadang kĕluar makan di–kĕdai jikalau di–jĕmput kawan atau pun jikalau saya sĕndiri hĕndak mĕnjamu sahabat–sahabat. Ada pun di–London tĕmpat makan tĕrlalu banyak, hidangan–nya bĕrjĕnis–jĕnis, bĕnda makanan yang sĕdap bĕlaka. Kalau saya sa–orang diri sahaja, biasa–lah saya mĕlawat sa–buah kĕdai makan di–Regent Street, di–dapati lauk–lauk di–situ dĕngan ulaman yang mĕndatangkan sĕlera, kueh–kueh–nya sĕmua sĕdap, kopi–nya pun bĕrasa juga. Tambahan pula bĕrseh tĕmpat–nya sĕrta dĕngan pinggan mangkok–nya, chahaya lampu–lampu–nya pun tĕrang, pĕrĕmpuan pĕlayan–nya sĕmua bĕrbahasa dan manis–manis pula ayer muka masing–masing.

Ada suatu daerah di–London yang tĕrutama kĕdai–kĕdai makan–nya, ia–lah daerah yang bĕrnama Soho, Kĕbanyakan kĕdai makan di–situ kĕdai orang bangsa luar, ada kĕdai Pĕranchis, kĕdai Spanyol, kĕdai China, kĕdai Hindu. Mula–mula–nya mĕlawat daerah Soho itu, saya pĕrgi makan di–kĕdai orang Pĕranchis di–Old Compton Street, kĕchil kĕdai–nya, meja makan chuma

dua–bĕlas buah sahaja. Ada juga sa–buah kĕdai lagi
yang saya suka mĕlawat ia–itu kĕdai Spanyol ; tuan
kĕdai itu sangat bĕrhormat mĕnyilakan mĕreka yang
datang ka–tĕmpat–nya kĕrap kali ia bĕrjabat tangan
dengan orang datang, lagi pun bila hĕndak kĕluar lĕpas
makan dĕngan bĕrchakap–chakap pula sa–dikit. Di–
kĕdai Spanyol itu tĕrdapat makanan masak chara
Spanyol, nasi di–masak sama dĕngan daging ayam dan
daging udang galah sĕrta sayur–sayuran.

Jikalau sĕmpat, wang di–kochek pun chukup, siapa–
siapa sudi mĕrasa makanan bangsa–bangsa lain, pĕrgi–lah
mĕrayau di–daerah Soho itu.

Exercise 42

1. This total isn't right. It doesn't tally with the
   receipts. It is too little by $2.50. I must have
   missed out an item somewhere. I'll go through them
   again. Just tick them off on this list for me, will you ?

2. Bring me the chisel when you come back. You
   needn't make a special journey. Finish whaɩ you are
   doing first of all. It will take me a good five minutes
   to plane this piece for a cover. Have we any hinges
   left ? Have a look in the tool–box, will you ? I
   believe I left it outside the kitchen door.

Conversation No. 15

Pĕgawai Daerah dĕngan Pĕnghulu.

Pĕgawai Daerah : Saya dĕngar kata orang anak to'
pĕnghulu 'nak kahwin bulan dĕpan
ini. Jangan lupa jĕmput saya.

To' Pĕnghulu : Ta'akan saya lupa ĕnche' ! Tĕtapi
saya 'nak buat kĕrja[1] kĕchil sahaja.
Maalum[2]–lah sĕkarang musim susah.

Lagi pun ta'bĕrfaedah mĕmbuang duit pĕrchuma–chuma macham adat kita dahulu.

Pĕgawai Daerah : Bĕnar sangat–lah, datok. Kalau ada duit atau harta bĕnda lĕbeh baik bĕrikan pĕngantin itu kĕdua orang. Sĕnang–lah dia mulaĭ bĕrumah tangga[3].

To' Pĕnghulu : Kalau ĕnche' sudi, sila–lah datang bĕrsama–sama dĕngan istĕri ĕnche'.

Pĕgawai Daerah : Tĕrima kaseh. Jangan lupa bĕri tahu hari–nya yang tĕtap. Saya hĕndak mĕmbawa barang sa–dikit. Datok sampaikan salam saya kapada anak datok.

Translation.

Malay District Officer and Village Headman

District Officer : I hear that your son is to be married next month, Datok. Don't forget to send me an invitation.

Headman : I shouldn't be likely to do that. But it is not to be an elaborate wedding. It has been a poor season, you know. In any case, there is no point in spending money needlessly, as we used to do, in days gone by.

District Officer : That's quite true, Datok. If you have money, or goods, it is better to give them to the bride and bridegroom, so that they can set up house more easily.

Headman : If you would care to, I shall be very pleased if you and your wife will come.

District Officer : Thank you. Don't forget to let me know the date. I am going to bring a few little things. Give my greetings to your son.

Notes

1. kĕrja　　.　　. This word is often used of customary ceremonial.

2. maalum　.　　. The phrase more often used is *lĕbeh maalum* or *tĕrlĕbeh maalum*—" You know well"—" I need not tell you". *Maalum* in its various forms is the conventional opening for letters e.g. *Sahaya bĕrmaalum, Beta maalumkan, Di-maalumkan—* " I have to inform you ". *Maalum-lah* is very common in modern Malay as an introduction to an explanatory phrase, with the force of the parenthetic English expression " you see ".

3. bĕrumah tangga. The phrase *rumah tangga* is used figuratively to mean " household ", " family ".

CHAPTER XX

I. Clock Time

Par. 191.

The Malay method of telling the time is simple.   The examples given below show that there are in Malay, as in English, several ways of making the statements.

But if you are still a beginner (i.e. if you have turned to this chapter for information, before you have studied the intervening chapters) you may find it helpful to fix one method in your mind by memorizing the two following points.

(a) For a time that is " <u>past</u> " the hour, begin with the word *Pukul.*

(b) For a time that is " <u>to</u> " the hour, begin with the word *Kurang.*

Examples.

For the exact hour .	(*jam*) *pukul tiga* .	3 o'clock
,, a quarter past .	*pukul tiga suku* .	3.15.
,, half past . .	*pukul tiga sa–těngah*	3.30.
	or	
	těngah pukul	
	ěmpat cf. par. 186	
	ad fin.	

303

For a quarter to	.	*kurang suku pukul ěmpat*	.	.	.	3.45.
,, 10 minutes past		*pukul tiga sa–puloh minit*	.	.	.	3.10.
,, 10 minutes to	.	*kurang sa–puloh minit pukul ěmpat*	.	3.50.		

a.m. is expressed by *pagi* or *malam*.
p.m. is expressed by *pětang* or *malam*.

Par. 192.   Further examples.

5 p.m.	.	.	*pukul lima pětang.*
6.25 a.m.	.	.	*pukul ěnam dua puloh lima minit pagi*
7.15	.	.	*pukul tujoh suku* or *pukul tujoh lima–bělas minit.*
8.23	.	.	*pukul (dě)lapan dua puloh tiga minit.*
10.20 p.m.	.	.	*pukul sa–puloh dua puloh minit malam.*
3.55	.	.	*kurang lima minit pukul ěmpat.*
		or	*pukul ěmpat kurang lima minit.*
		or	*pukul tiga lima puloh lima minit.*
		or	*lagi lima minit pukul ěmpat.*
9.33	.	.	*kurang dua puloh tujoh minit pukul sa–puloh* or *pukul sěmbilan tiga puloh tiga.*
11.45	.	.	*kurang suku pukul dua–bělas*
		or	*pukul sa–bělas tiga suku*
		or	*pukul sa–bělas ěmpat–puloh lima minit.*
12 noon	.	.	*pukul dua–bělas těngah hari.*
Exactly mid–day	.		*těngah hari těpat.*
12 midnight	.		*pukul dua–bělas těngah malam.*

Par. 193.   Miscellaneous expressions of time.

1. What time is it ?   .   *jam pukul bĕrapa ?*
2. Exactly 5 o'clock   .   *pukul lima bĕtul.*
3. Early in the morning   *pagi–pagi* or *siang–siang.*
4. Every morning   .   *tiap–tiap pagi.*
5. Three days ago   .   *sudah tiga hari,* or *tiga hari sudah,* or *baharu tiga hari,* or *tiga hari dahulu.*
6. In three days' time.   *lĕpas tiga hari,* or *lagi tiga hari,* or *tulat.*
7. Last week   .   .   *minggu lĕpas,* or *minggu sudah,* or *minggu lalu.*
8. Next week   .   .   *minggu dĕpan,* or *minggu yang akan datang,* or *minggu datang.*
9. To–morrow week   .   *lagi (dĕ)lapan hari* or *'lapan hari lagi.*
10. Next time   .   .   *lain kali.*
11. A long time ago   .   *lama sudah.*
12. Within two months   *dalam dua bulan.*
13. Within the next two months   *dalam dua bulan yang akan datang.*
14. Within the last two months   *dalam dua bulan yang lalu.*
15. These last few months   *dua tiga bulan ini.*
16. For seven or eight months   *tujoh 'lapan bulan lama–nya.*
17. How much longer   .   *bĕrapa lama lagi ?*
18. All night long   .   *sa–panjang malam.*
19. Night after night   .   *sa–malam–malaman* or *tiap–tiap malam.*
20. He has been ill for three days   *sudah tiga hari dia sakit.*

21. I have just heard .   *baharu saya děngar.*

22. Last Thursday week   *hari khamis sudah dua minggu.*

23. On Tuesday week .   *hari sělasa lagi dua minggu.*

24. At that time .   .   *pada masa itu*, or *pada waktu itu.*

25. For such and such a time   *sa-kian lama.*

26. After some time .   *lěpas běrapa lama–nya.*

27. Forever   .   .   *sa–lama–lama–nya.*

28. At last   .   .   *lama–lama–nya,* or *lama kělamaan,* or *akhir–nya,* or *kěsudahan–nya.*

29. After that .   .   *lěpas itu, kěmudian dari pada itu.*

30. At the end of the month   *pada akhir bulan.*

31. Daily (i.e. every day)   *sa–hari–hari,* or *tiap–tiap hari.*

32. Twice a week .   *sa–minggu dua kali.*

33. Every other day .   *sělang sa–hari,* or *lat sa–hari.*

34. At any time .   *barang bila* or *bila–bila pun.*

35. Some day (in the future)   *kěmudian hari,* or *bělakang hari,* or *esok* or *esok–esok.*

II. The Calendar

(1) The Western Calendar.

Par. 194.

The months.

In all parts of the Peninsula the Western calendar (January, February, etc.) is known and used.

The days of the month are denoted by cardinal numerals before the word *hari*.

Examples.

On Jan. 1st 1830 . *Pada satu hari bulan*[75] *January tahun sa-ribu dĕlapan ratus tiga puloh.*

What is the date ? . *Bĕrapa hari bulan ?*

October 30th . . *Tiga–puloh hari bulan October,* **or** *Tiga–puloh hari bulan sa–puloh.*

Par. 195.

The days of the week.

The days of the week are denoted by cardinal numerals <u>after</u> the word *hari.* "Sunday" is an exception :

Monday	.	*hari satu*
Tuesday	.	„ *dua*
Wednesday	.	„ *tiga*
Thursday	.	„ *ĕmpat*
Friday .	.	„ *lima*
Saturday	.	„ *ĕnam*
Sunday	.	„ *minggu* (from Latin "dominus"—"lord" via Portuguese "domingo").

A week is *satu minggu.*

Note. Except for the word *minggu,* these terms are used mainly by foreigners.

Par. 196.

Method of dating.

The Malay equivalent of "A.D." is "T.M." standing for *Tahun Masehi*—"The year of the Messiah".

The Malay equivalent of "The Christian Era" is *Tarikh Masehi.*

The Muhammadan Era dates from the *Hijrah* or *Hegira* —the flight from Mecca in A.D. 622, and a year of this era is denoted by the letter "T.H."[76] standing for *Tahun Hijrah.*

---

[75] The phrase *sa-hari bulan* is used also to mean "the new moon".
[76] In Western books by the letters "A.H." i.e. "Anno Hegira".

L

Example.

19 January T.M. 1946 = *16 Safar T.H. 1365.*

(b) The Muhammadan Calendar.

Par. 197.

The months.

On the mainland the Muhammadan calendar is in daily use, usually side by side with the Western calendar.

The Muhammadan year is a lunar year, eleven days shorter than the solar year.

The months are known by their Arabic names. They are of 30 days and 29 days alternately :

1. *Muharram*—30 days.
2. *Safar*—29 days.
3. *Rabi'i'l–awal* (or *Bulan Maulud*—the month of the Prophet's birthday.)
4. *Rabi'i'l–akhir.*
5. *Jamadi'l–awal.*
6. *Jamadi'l–akhir.*
7. *Rějab.*
8. *Shaaban.*
9. *Ramdzan* (or *Bulan Puasa*—the month of the fast.)
10. *Shawal* (or *Bulan Raya*—the month of the great feast, *Hari Raya Běsar.*)
11. *Dzu'l–kaedah.*
12. *Dzu'l–hejah.*

Par. 198.

The days of the week.

The Arabic names for the days of the week are as follows :

Monday	.	*hari ithnain* (usually pronounced *isnin* or *sěnayan*.)
Tuesday	.	*hari thalatha* (usually pronounced *sělasa*.)
Wednesday	.	*hari arbaa*, (usually called *hari rabu*.)
Thursday	.	*hari khamis*.
Friday .	.	*hari jumaat* (i.e. **the** day of assembly.)
Saturday	.	*hari sabtu* (i.e. " the sabbath[77].)
Sunday	.	*hari ahad* (i.e. " the first ", Monday to Thursday being 2nd, 3rd, 4th and 5th respectively.)

A week is *sa–jumaat*, but the expression is seldom heard in modern Malay.

III. Religious Terms

Par. 199.

(a) General terms :

ugama or *agama*		religion
masjid .	.	a mosque.
surau .	.	a small place of worship, chapel.
mimbar	.	the lectern in the mosque.
mihrab .	.	the niche in the mosque, showing the direction in which Mecca lies.
sěmbahyang	.	worship, prayer.
madrasah	.	a school in conection with the mosque.
Kaabah .	.	the Temple at Mecca.

[77] The day, as a unit of time, begins with sunset. The night, therefore, is included with the day which follows it : *Pukul sěmbilan malam khamis* means : " At 9 p.m. on Wednesday " not Thursday. So, also, *sa-malam*, although it usually means yesterday, may sometimes mean " the night before last ", i.e. " one night from now ". Cf. par. 140, Note 3.

sunat (or   .   circumcision.
   khatan)

khutbah nikah.   the formula used at the marriage
   service.

talak   .   .   divorce, deed of separation.

(b) The titles of the mosque officials :

imam   .   .   presiding elder, who leads the
   prayers at the Friday service.

khatib   .   .   second officer, reader, preacher.

bilal   .   .   the muezzin, who calls wor-
   shippers to prayer.

siak   .   .   the caretaker.

(c) The names of the five daily prayers (*lima waktu*).

sĕmbahyang suboh   .   at dawn (about 5.0 a.m.)

sĕmbahyang lohor   .   at noon.
   (or *dzohor*)

sĕmbahyang asar   .   in the afternoon.

sĕmbahyang maghrib   .   at sunset.

sĕmbahyang isha   .   .   in the early evening.

IV. Geographical Terms

Par. 200.

The points of the compass.

north   .   .   *utara.*

south   .   .   *sĕlatan.*

east   .   .   *timor* (also *matahari tĕrbit* and
   matahari naik.)

west   .   .   *barat* (also *matahari turun* and
   matahari jatoh.)

N.E.	.	.	*timor laut.*
N.W.	.	.	*barat laut.*
S.E.	.	.	*tĕnggara.*
S.W.	.	.	*barat daya.*

Par. 201.

Other geographical terms.

Towards the North	.	*sa–bĕlah utara.*
In a southerly direction	.	*arah ka–sĕlatan,* or *hala ka–sĕlatan.*
The compass point from which the wind is blowing		*mata angin*[78].
Due East	. . .	*timor tĕpat.*
The Malay Peninsula	.	*sĕmĕnanjong Tanah Mĕlayu.*
The Malay Archipelago	.	*Gugusan Pulau–pulau Mĕlayu.* (lit. cluster of islands.)
Java . . .	.	*Tanah Jawa.*
Borneo . .	.	*Pulau Bĕrunai.*

Par. 202.

This is a piece from the *Hikayat Abdullah.*

Ada kira–kira panjang sumbu–nya itu lĕbeh–lĕbeh sa–puloh dĕpa, di–pĕrbuat–nya dĕngan kain, di–isi–nya ubat bĕdil; ada–lah kasar–nya sapĕrti ibu kaki, kĕmudian lobang yang tĕrsĕbut itu di–suroh–nya tutup, sĕrta di–tumbok rapat–rapat dĕngan batu dan tanah di–asak. Maka ada pun mĕngĕrjakan lobang sa–buah itu sampai sudah–nya lima ĕnam hari, sa–puloh dua– puloh orang. Sa–tĕlah itu maka di–pukulkan chanang, maka esok–nya pukul dĕlapan pagi sa–orang pun jangan

---

[78] *Mata angin* is also used as a comprehensive term for "the points of the compass". Cf. *utara sa–mata timor* for N.N.E.

běrjalan di–saběrang, dan yang mana rumah děkat–děkat di–situ di–surohkan běrpindah ka–rumah jauh–jauh. Maka sa–tělah kěesokan hari–nya, datang–lah Tuan Farquhar běrkuda, sěrta měměgang murang[1] pada tangan–nya ; maka di–suroh–nya orang naik ka–atas kota[2] itu měnghalaukan orang di–saběrang itu, maka orang pun lari–lah sara–bara. Maka sa–běntar itu juga lalu di–chuchohkan–nya sumbu itu, maka sa–tělah itu lalu di–gěrtakkan[3]–nya kuda–nya. Maka ada–lah kira–kira sa–puloh minit lama–nya, maka mělětup–lah ubat bědil itu sapěrti bunyi pětir ; maka těrbongkar–lah batu kota itu sa–běsar–běsar rumah, dan ada yang sa–běsar gajah, bětěrbangan[4] ka–dalam laut ; maka ada batu yang těrbang sampai ka–saběrang dan měngěnaï rumah–rumah. Maka těrkějut–lah orang sěmua–nya sěbab měněngar (i.e. měnděngar) bunyi–nya itu, sěrta děngan běsar–běsar hairan, sěbab sa–umor hidup měreka itu bělum pěrnah měněngar bunyi yang děmikian, dan sěbab mělihatkan bagaimana běsar kuasa ubat bědil itu, sampai boleh ia měngangkatkan batu sa–běsar–běsar sapěrti rumah.

Translation.

The fuse was about sixty feet long, made of cloth, and filled with gunpowder. It was about the thickness of a big toe. Then they ordered the hole to be filled in. Stones were hammered in, fitting closely together, and the earth was beaten down hard, on top of them. It had taken them five or six days to make the cavity, with ten or twenty men at work on it.

Then a gong was beaten and a notice given out that at 8 o'clock on the next morning nobody was to be on the other side, and all the people who lived near were told to move to houses further off.

On the next day Mr. Farquhar came, on horse-back, with a slow-match in his hand. He sent men up to the fort to chase away anybody who was on that side, and the people raced off, helter-skelter. Then without a moment's pause he lit the fuse and set spurs to his horse. In about ten minutes time the gunpowder exploded, with a noise like a clap of thunder. The masonry of the fort went up, in great masses the size of houses. Some pieces, as big as elephants, were hurled into the sea, others flew across the river and struck some houses on the other side. Everybody was thunderstruck by the noise, and amazed, because in all their lives they had never heard anything like it, and because they saw how great was the power of gunpowder, that it could lift rocks as big as houses.

Notes

1. *murang*	.	Match for cannon ; fuse.
2. *kota*	.	i.e. The fort of Malacca.
3. *gĕrtak*	.	Or *gĕrĕtak*—rapping (an onomatopoeic word.) Here, of clapping the heels against the horse's flanks.
4. *bĕtĕrbangan*	.	The affixes give the idea of frequency —" piece after piece".

Par. 203.

This is a piece from *Hikajat Sinar Bulan* (The Story of Princess Moonlight) published in Java in 1933.

Comparison between the two scripts, (a) and (b), will show examples of most of the following points of difference.

Malay Romanisation	Indonesian Romanisation
" y "	becomes " j " (e.g. *jang* for *yang*)
" j "	„ " dj " (e.g. *djika* for *jika*)

Malay Romanisation	Indonesian Romanisation
" ch "	becomes " tj " (e.g. *mentjari* for *měnchari*)
" kh "	,, " ch " (e.g. *chabar* for *khabar*)
" sh "	,, " sj " (e.g. *sjahdan* for *shahadan*)

Affixes and enclitics are joined to root-words without hyphens, e.g. *dimana, badannja*.

The " indeterminate ě " has no mark over it. e.g. *dengan* for *děngan*.

The " full e " is sometimes marked by an acute accent e.g. *oléh* for *oleh*.

The prefixes *ka–* and *sa–* are written as *ke* and *se*.

(a) Malay Romanisation:

Di-mana ia běrtěmu děngan pohon kayu yang běsar sěrta rendang, běrhěnti-lah kědua-nya di–bawah pohon itu mělěpaskan lělah–nya, dan jika ia běrtěmu děngan sungai yang jěrneh ayer–nya, di–situ–lah kědua–nya běrhěnti mandi, měmběrsehkan badan–nya. Jika ia běrtěmu děngan těmpat yang sěntosa, di–situ–lah kědua–nya běrhěnti, lalu měnchari buah–buahan yang dapat di–makan–nya, měnghilangkan lapar dan dahaga–nya.

(b) Indonesian Romanisation:

Dimana ia bertemu dengan pohon kaju jang besar serta rindang, berhentilah keduanja dibawah pohon itu melepaskan lelahnja, dan djika ia bertemu dengan sungai jang djernih airnja, disitulah keduanja berhenti mandi, membersihkan badannja. Djika ia bertemu dengan tempat jang sentosa, disitulah keduanja berhenti, lalu mentjari buah–buahan jang dapat dimakannja, menghilangkan lapar dan dahaganja.

Translation.

Wherever they came across a large shady tree, they would stop, the two of them, to rest beneath it; and if they came to a river with clear water, there they would stop to bathe, and cleanse their bodies. If they came to a quiet, peaceful spot, there they would stop, and look for fruit to eat, to satisfy their hunger and quench their thirst.

Par. 204.

As a *bonne bouche* here is a *pantun* (No. 36 in *Pantun Mělayu.*) It is one of several verses which the editors have grouped under the heading, "Wilful Youth".

> *Banyak orang běrgělang tangan,*
> *Sahaya sa–orang běrgělang kaki.*
> *Banyak orang larang jangan,*
> *Sahaya sa–orang turut hati.*

> Bangle worn on wrist's the fashion,
> I wear mine another way.
> Others bid me curb my passion.
> What care I what others say ?

A *pantun* is a four-lined verse of which the first couplet is a prelude to the second couplet. It is not merely that it prepares the ear for the end-rhymes that are coming. The whole couplet foretells the sound of the last two lines.

This sound-echo is always clear to the ear. Sometimes, there is also a clear connection between the thought of the two couplets. In this one, for instance, a flouting of fashion in the first two lines prepares us for the young man's flouting of advice in the second couplet. But in many verses this connection of thought is difficult to trace, though scholars are of the opinion that it is probably always there.

The first couplet may be a picture, jumping to the eye in a few bold strokes (see Exercise 45), it may be an historical allusion to which the reader holds no clue, or it may be just a jingle of words, ready to chime with lines 3 and 4 when they strike the ear.

The words of a *pantun* are usually simple, but they are seldom easy to translate because the ' scanty plot of narrow ground ' demands an economy of expression that exceeds even the succinctness of everyday Malay speech.

Most of the quatrains are traditional, with love for their theme, but the *pantun* is much used also for topical verses such as are extemporised at the Boria celebrations in Penang.

For a full discussion of the *pantun* see *Pantun Mĕlayu, Malay Literature Series* No. 12.

Exercise 43.

(This is a study of Sir Stamford Raffles, from the *Hikayat Abdullah*.)

Maka tĕrlalu pandai ia mĕmbĕri hormat akan orang, sĕrta dĕngan manis muka–nya ; bĕrbahasa dĕngan orang, ĕnchek dĕngan ĕnchek, tuan dĕngan tuan. Dan lagi banyak ia mĕnaroh kasehan akan orang maka tangan–nya tĕrbuka ka–pada orang miskin. Dan lagi sĕlalu apabila ia bĕrchakap dĕngan tĕrsĕnyum–sĕnyum, dan lagi tĕrlalu kuasa ia mĕmĕreksa akan sĕgala pĕrkara yang dahulu–dahulu. Dan lagi jikalau barang suatu pĕrkara yang di–dĕngar–nya itu, tiada–lah boleh sudah dĕngan sa–dikit, mĕlainkan sampai kĕsudahan–nya. Dan lagi ada–lah sĕlalu ia suka tinggal di–dalam tĕmpat sunyi, maka tiada apa lain pĕkĕrjaan–nya mĕlainkan mĕnulis dan mĕmbacha kitab–kitab. Dan lagi apabila waktu ia bĕlajar dan bĕrchakap, mĕski pun barang siapa datang ka–rumah–nya, tiada ia mahu bĕrtĕmu, mĕlainkan apabila habis ; dan lagi ku–lihat barang apa pĕrbuatan–

nya masing–masing děngan waktu–nya, tiada běrchampur suatu děngan suatu.

Exercise 44. Translate.

[This is a modern letter, of informal style, opening with a direct address to the recipient, and ending with the writer's signature.

In the traditional style of letter-writing the first paragraph announces, in due order, and with many conventional flourishes, the following facts: the name of the writer, his dwelling place, the name of the recipient, his dwelling place. This style is now obsolete. For examples, see Winstedt's *Malay Grammar*, Appendix.]

Sahabat saya yang sělalu di ingati, Tuan Smith, děngan sělamat.

Kěmbang–lah hati saya běsěrta kawan–kawan di–sini kěrana měněrima khabar daripada Tuan James měngatakan sahabat saya di–dalam sělamat.

Banyak–banyak saya těrima kaseh kěrana sahabat saya mělayangkan surat sa–puchok yang sangat di–kasehi itu. Bagaimana sahabat saya ingatkan saya sakalian di–sini, děmikian juga saya tidak lupakan sahabat saya sakalian di–England.

Pada minggu yang lěpas tělah saya měnyurat kapada tuan tětapi surat itu tidak dapat–lah saya hantar děngan kapal těrbang, sěbab di–něgěri ini tidak ada " Air Mail " lagi. Jikalau nasib baik barang kali ada juga kapal těrbang mel yang akan měngutip surat–surat itu pada salah satu tempat yang di–tanah Mělayu ini. Jikalau tidak, kěna ikut jalan biasa ia–itu děngan kapal api . . . . Pěpěrangan itu sa–bagai satu pěnyakit kudis. Sa–tělah di–ubatkan naik pula anak–anak–nya. Jika di–dapati ubat yang boleh měmbunoh kuman pěnyakit itu, baharu–lah dunia ini těrlěpas daripada kětakutan. Tětapi sa–lagi manusia běrpěrangai bĕngis dan bĕrsikap pahlawan[1], sadikit ada pĕluang kita boleh bĕrbingkas agak–nya . . . . Di–tanah England mĕreka kĕsusahan sĕbab sĕntiasa di–sĕrang dari udara : di–tanah Mĕlayu mĕreka kĕsusahan sĕbab tidak kĕbebasan sapĕrti yang lazim di–rasaï. . . . . Tĕtapi mĕrepet–repet[2] sahaja. Biar saya chĕritakan hal kawan–kawan tuan di–sini. Salim, Man, Minah bĕrkirim tabek bĕlaka sĕrta bĕrtanyakan khabar tuan. Che' Osman, Che' Timah, Che' Arifin, sĕmua–nya bĕrkirim salam di–iringi[3] dĕngan sayang rindu.

(Maafkan kĕrtas yang burok ini. Suka ta'suka di–bĕli juga sĕbab ta'dapat lain. Tĕrok bĕnar saya ini tinggal chuma sa–hĕlai sa–pinggang[4] sa–lama bĕrlaku pĕpĕrangan itu. 'Tapi, ta'apa–lah, asal tinggal nyawa jadi–lah.)

Tĕrtulis 2.11.45.

Notes.

1. *pahlawan*   "Leader in war", "champion". Here " war-like ".

2. *mĕrepet* . Dialect form of *mĕrepek*—to chatter inconsequently.

3. *di–iringi* . Lit. " followed in ceremonial order " —one of the conventional terms of formal letter-writing.

4. *sa–hĕlai sa–pinggang*

    Lit. " one sarong per waist ". A proverbial expression for extreme poverty.

Exercise 45

Translate.

> *Anak bĕrok di–kayu rendang*
>   *Turun mandi di–dalam paya.*
> *Hudoh burok di–mata orang,*
>   *Chantek manis di–mata saya.*

VOCABULARY

Malay—English

Notes

1. With a few exceptions, which have been included as reminders, root forms only are given in this vocabulary. Affixation is discussed in Chapters XII–XIV. Prefixed words which occur in the earlier chapters are explained in notes.

If you fail to find a word which you are looking for, see if it is possible to remove one, or more, of the following prefixes: *mě–*; *bě(r)–*, *tě(r)–*, *pě(r)*.

2. Words which are merely adaptations of English words have, as a rule, been omitted.

A few words of Chinese, Portuguese and Dutch origin have been so marked, as a matter of interest. For other, and much wider, streams of foreign loan words (chiefly Sanskrit and Arabic) see Winstedt's *Malay Grammar* pp. 21–24.

3. Abreviations used:

lit.	. .	literally.
lity.	. .	literary; used in the written language only.
met.	. .	metaphorical.
coll.	. .	colloquial; used in conversational style.
pol.	. .	polite; a more elegant, or more respectful equivalent for a parallel word in everyday use.

(For some of the words used in the strictly limited "court" vocabulary, see par. 189, Note 3.)

baz.	. .	bazaar; used in the debased Malay of the sea-ports which freely adopts foreign words and constructions, with a consequent loss of the clean-cut terseness of Malay idiom.
num. coeff.	.	numeral coefficient.
Ch.	.	Chinese.
Dut.	.	Dutch.
Port.	.	Portuguese.

4. The frequent references given are intended to take the place of a separate index.

5. This is a vocabulary, not a dictionary. If you want to profit by the Malay which you are hearing round about you, get a dictionary and mark in it each new word that you collect. You will find that vocabulary varies slightly according to locality.

A.

abang	. .	elder brother
ada .	. .	exist, be present; have (baz.)
adat	. .	custom, tradition, habit
adek	. .	younger brother or sister
adohi!	. .	Oh! (usually regretfully)
agak	. .	guess, conjecture
agar–agar	.	a kind of sea–weed from which jelly is made
ahli .	. .	lit. versed in; *ahli rumah*—housewife
ahual *or* ahwal .		affairs; usually *hal ahual*
ajak	. .	invite to do, incite

ajar	. . .	teach (see par. 138)
akal.	. . .	intelligence, mind
akan	. .	towards, concerning ; intending to, likely to
akar	. . .	root
akhir	. . .	last, the end
aku	. .	1. I (see pars. 85 and 173). 2. acknowledge
alah.	. .	to be beaten ; to lose (game, battle)
alam	. . .	the world
aleh	. .	change, shift ; *bintang běraleh*— a wandering star
alkesah	. .	see par. 143
alir .	. . .	flow along
almari *or* lěmari (Port.)		cupboard, *almeirah*
amah	. . .	children's nurse (Chinese)
amat	. .	very
ambil	. .	take (for oneself)
ambohi ! . amboi !	.	}My word ! Oh ! (usually gleefully)
ampun	. .	pardon, forgiveness
anak	. .	child ; the young of any creature ; part of a comprehensive whole, e.g. *anak tangga*—rung of a ladder ; *anak kapal*—crew ; *běranak*—1. to bear a child 2. to possess a child *pěranakan*—native born
angin	.	wind ; air
angkat	. .	lift
angkut	. .	lift and take away piecemeal
aniaya	. .	oppression
anjing	. .	dog
antara	. .	space or time between

antok	. .	. *tĕrantok*—collide ; *bĕrantok*—knocking against each other (e.g. knees)
apa ?	.	. what ? (see par. 169)
apa	. .	. anything (see par. 161)
apabila	. .	. when
api .	. .	. fire
ara .	. .	. fig-tree
arah	. .	. direction, in the direction of
arakian	. .	. see par. 144
aral	. .	. hindrance
aruah *or* arwah		. soul, spirits of the dead
asah	. .	. grind, sharpen
asak	. .	. ram down, cram in
asal	. .	. origin ; *asalkan*—provided that
asar	. .	. afternoon ; *sĕmbahyang asar*— afternoon prayer
atas	. .	. position above ; about, in connection with
atau	. .	. or, or else
atur.	. .	. arrange
awak	. .	. you (lit. " body ", see par. 85)
awal	. .	beginning
awat (=apa buat?)		. why ?
ayah	. .	. 1. father. 2. children's nurse (Indian or Javanese)
ayam	. .	. fowl
ayer	. .	. water, liquid, juice

B.

bacha	.	. read
badan	. .	. the body
bagai	. .	. species, sort ; like ; *pĕlbagai*— of all sorts ; *dan sa-bagai-nya*— etcetera
bagai-mana ?	.	. how ?
bagi	. .	. allot, *coll.* give ; for

baginda *or* bĕginda . ruler, king
bagini (bagai ini) . thus, in this way
bagitu (bagai itu) . thus, in that way
bagus . . . fine, excellent
baharu . . . new, newly, just, only then, not until then
bahasa . . . language ; manners, courtesy
bahawa . . . see par. 145
baik . . . good, useful ; well
baji . . . wedge
baju . . . coat
baki . . . balance, surplus
bakul . . . basket
balas . . . pay back ; requite, reply
balek . . . reverse; return, move in reverse direction ; *tĕrbalek*—upset, over-turned
bandar . . . sea-port ; town
bangku . . . bench, stool
bangsa . . . race, family
bangsal . . . shed
bangun . . . rise, get up
bantah . . . dispute
banyak . . . much, many (*not* " very ") ; quantity, number ; *kĕbanyakan* —majority
bapa *or* bapak . . father
barang . . . things; anything, any; ordinary; about. (see par. 160)
baring . . . lying down
basah . . . wet ; *basah kuyup*—soaking wet
basi . . . musty, stale " gone off " (of food)
basoh . . . wash
batang . . . tree-trunk, rod (see par. 48)
batok . . . cough
batu . . . stone, rock ; mile

bawa	. . .	convey, bring, conduct; *bawa naik*—take upstairs. *Bawa* has many idiomatic uses
bawah	. . .	underneath
bawal	. . .	pomfret
bayan	. . .	parroquet
bayar	. . .	pay
bĕbal	. . .	stupid
bebas	. . .	free
bĕdal	. . .	swish, beat
bĕdil	. . .	*ubat bĕdil*—gunpowder
bĕkal	. . .	provisions for a journey
bĕkas	. . .	trace; wrapper, receptacle
bĕku	. . .	coagulated
bĕla	. . .	to bring up, rear; attend to
bĕlah	. . .	split, cleave; one of two sections, side; *sa–bĕlah*—one of a pair. e.g. *buta mata sa–bĕlah*—blind in one eye; *sa–bĕlah mĕnyabĕlah*—on both sides
bĕlajar	. . .	learn (see footnote 43 and par. 138)
bĕlaka	. . .	altogether, without exception; quite
bĕlakang	. . .	back; *bĕlakang hari* (coll.)—later on; some day
bĕlayar	. . .	sail
bĕli	. . .	buy
bĕliong	. . .	hatchet, adze
bĕlum	. . .	not yet (see par. 77)
bĕnang	. . .	thread
bĕnar	. . .	true, correct; *bĕnarkan*—authorize
bĕnchi	. . .	hate
bĕnda	. . .	thing, article
bĕndahara	. . .	(in Malay literature) Treasurer Mayor of the Palace
bĕndang	. . .	wet rice-field
bĕngis	. . .	cruel

bĕngkak	. .	swollen, inflamed
bengkok	. .	bent
bĕntar	. .	*sa–bĕntar*—a moment
bĕntok	. .	curve (see par. 49)
bĕnua	. .	continent
bĕrani	. .	brave
bĕrapa ?	. .	how much ? *bĕrapa banyak ?* how many ?
bĕrapa	. .	some ; to a certain extent
bĕras	. .	husked (uncooked) rice
bĕrat	. .	heavy
bĕrĕnang	. .	swim
bĕrhĕnti	. .	(from *hĕnti* or *rĕnti*) stop
bĕri	. .	give
bĕrkat	. .	blessing, favour
bĕrkek	. .	*burong bĕrkek*—snipe
bĕrok	. .	the " coconut " monkey
bĕrseh	. .	clean
bĕsar	. .	big
bĕsi	. .	iron
beta	. .	I, me (see footnote 24)
bĕtapa ?	. .	how ? why ?
bĕtina	. .	female (see footnote 6)
bĕtul	. .	straight, correct
biar	. .	allow, let
biasa	. .	accustomed
bibir	. .	lip, edge
bichara	. .	court case ; opinion
bidan	. .	midwife
bijaksana	. .	prudent ; discretion
biji .	. .	seed, grain (see par. 48)
bila	. .	when. (For relative " when " use *masa* or *waktu*.)
bilah	. .	lath ; coeff. for knives etc. (see par. 48)
bilang	. .	to count ; recount ; tell (baz.)
bilek	. .	room

bimbang . . . anxious

binasa . . . ruined

bingkas . . . rebound, recover

bini . . . wife ; *anak bini*—family

biru . . . blue

bisa . . . blood-poison, venom

bising . . . noisy, talkative

bisu . . . dumb

bodoh . . . stupid, foolish

bohong . . . lie ; untrue

boleh . . . can, be able ; used colloquially before another verb as a polite form of command

bomoh *or* bomor . Malay doctor

bonda (pol.) . . mother

bongkar . . . heave up

buah . . . fruit (see par. 48)

bual . . . bubble up ; *bĕrbual*—gossip, chatter

buang . . . throw away

buat . . . do, make ; *colloquially*, serve as, *hence*, for

buaya . . . crocodile

buboh . . . put

budak . . . child, young person

budi . . . disposition, understanding, kindness

budiman . . . wise, prudent

bueh . . . froth, foam

bujor . . . longer than wide ; *bulat bujor*—oval

buka . . . open ; take off (clothes)

bukan . . . not, no (see par. 75)

bukit . . . hill

buku . . . 1. joint, knot, node ; 2. book (English)

bulan . . . moon, month

bulat	. .	round
bulor	. .	starving ; hunger
bulu	. .	nap, fur, feathers
bumbong	. .	roof
bunga	. .	1. flower. 2. interest, on money
bunoh	. .	slay
bunyi	. .	noise ; *bunyi–bunyian*—music
burok	. .	worn out, shabby ; rotten (of wood) ; ugly
burong	. .	bird
busok	. .	rotten, decayed (of animal matter)
busut	. .	ant-hill

Ch.

chabai	. .	long pepper, chillies
chabut	. .	pluck out
chahaya	. .	brilliance, glow
chakap	. .	*bĕrchakap*—talk, speak
chamchah	. .	spoon
champor	. .	mix
chanang	. .	gong
chantek	. .	pretty
chap	. .	seal ; " brand " ; print
chapai	. .	reach for, grasp
chara	. .	style, fashion, manner
chari	. .	seek
chawan	. .	tea-cup
chayer	. .	watery, " thin " (of liquids)
chĕbak	. .	dig out by side-long blows
chĕlaka	. .	cursed, " wretched "
chĕlup	. .	dip, dye
chĕpat	. .	speed ; quick, nimble
chĕrai	. .	separate ; *bĕrchĕrai*—divorced
chĕrdek	. .	cunning, quick-witted
chĕrita	. .	story
chĕrmat	. .	neat, careful

chita	. .	feeling, thought; *suka chita*—happy; *duka chita*—sad
chium	. .	smell; kiss (Malay fashion)
choba	. .	try; " please ", " just "
chobak-chabek	.	tattered and torn
chomel	. .	pretty
chontoh	. .	pattern, model
chuchi	. .	cleanse
chuchoh	. .	set alight
chuchok	. .	pierce, drive a point into
chuchu	. .	grandchild
chukai	. .	tax, dues
chukup	. .	enough
chuma	. .	vain, useless; gratis; as adverb of degree " only " (usually in combination with *sahaja*); *chuma-chuma*—in vain
churah	. .	empty out
churi	. .	steal
chuti	. .	leave of absence

D.

dada	. .	chest
daerah	. .	district
daging	. .	flesh, meat
dahaga	. .	thirst, thirsty
dahan	. .	bough, branch
dahi	. .	brow
dahulu	. .	before, in front
daki	. .	filth, dirt
dalam	. .	inside, in; during; deep
dan	. .	and; *ta' dan*—no time to
dapat	. .	get; manage to; find
darah	. .	blood
darat	. .	dry land; interior

dari	. . .	from; *dari pada*—from, out of; concerning; than (see p. 295, n. 6)
datang	. . .	come
datok *or* dato'	.	grandfather; chief; Sir
daun	. . .	leaf
dawat	. . .	ink
daya	. .	stratagem; *daya upaya*—resource, means
dayang	. .	damsel; *dayang-dayang*—attendants in a court
dayong	. .	oar
děkat	. .	near
dělapan	. .	eight (see Ch. V and Ch. XIX)
děmam	. .	fever; *ubat děmam*—quinine
děmi (lity.)	.	at the same time as, when, by
děmikian	.	thus
děnda	. .	a fine
děngan	. . .	with, etc. (see par. 63c. and 70)
děngar	. .	hear
děngu	. .	dull, stupid
děpa	. .	Malay fathom (i.e. width of outstretched arms)—6 ft.
děpan	. .	i.e. *di–hadapan*—in front
děras	. .	rapid (of movement)
di- .	. .	at, in, on (see par. 57)
dia .	. .	he, him, she, her, it; they, them
diam	. .	1. be silent, quiet. 2. dwell
dinding	. .	screen, wall
dingin	. .	cold
diri .	. .	self (see par. 177)
dua	. .	two (see Ch. V and Ch. XIX)
dudok	. .	1. sit. 2. dwell
duit (Dut.)	.	money, cent
dunia	. .	the world
duri	. .	thorn
dusun	. .	settlement; orchard

E.

eja	.	.	.	spell
ekor	.	.	.	tail
elok	.	.	.	beautiful, excellent
ĕmak *or* mak	.	.	.	mother
ĕmas *or* mas	.	.	.	gold
ĕmbun	.	.	.	dew, haze
ĕmpat	.	.	.	four (see Ch. V and Ch. XIX)
ĕnam	.	.	.	six (see Ch. V and Ch. XIX)
ĕnche' *or* ĕnchek	.	.	.	see par. 86
ĕngkau	.	.	.	you (see par. 85)
ĕntah	.	.	.	perhaps ? I don't know (see par. 91)
esok *or* besok	.	.	.	tomorrow

F.

faedah	.	.	.	gain, advantage
fakir	.	.	.	religious beggar
fasal *or* pasal	.	.	.	section, paragraph ; concerning; *apa fasal*—why ?
fikir *or* pikir	.	.	.	think

G.

gajah	.	.	.	elephant
gali	.	.	.	ḍig
gambar	.	.	.	picture, representation
ganas	.	.	.	fierce, daring (of animals)
ganti	.	.	.	substitute
garam	.	.	.	salt
gĕgak	.	.	.	noise, uproar, din of battle (usually *gĕgak gĕmpita*—an intensive)
gĕlang	.	.	.	bracelet or anklet
gĕlap	.	.	.	dark
gĕlinchir *or* gĕlingsir				slip away, to the side

gĕlĕtar	. .	*mĕnggĕlĕtar*—quiver, shake
gĕlut	. .	*bĕrgĕlut*—strive, compete
gĕmok	. .	plump, fat
gĕndang	.	drum
gĕrak	. .	*bĕrgĕrak*—move, stir
gĕtah	. .	tree-sap, rubber
gigi .	. .	tooth
gigit	. .	bite
gila .	. .	mad
gomol	. .	*bĕrgomol*—wrestle
goreng	. .	fry
gosok	. .	scrub, rub
gugor	. .	fall prematurely or unnaturally ; *bintang gugor*—shooting star
gula.	. .	sugar
gulai	. .	curry
guna	. .	use
gunong	. .	mountain
gunting	. .	scissors, shears
guru	.	teacher

H.

habis	. .	done, finished, used up ; utterly
hadap	. .	position in front (see p. 142 n. 2)
hadiah	. .	present
hajat	. .	desire, intention
haji	. .	see par. 86
hakim	. .	a judge (supreme court)
hal .	. .	affair ; condition, case
halaman	.	court-yard, open space
halau	. .	drive away
halus	. .	fine, delicate
hamba	. .	1. slave. 2. I (see par. 85)
hambat	.	chase
hamil (pol.)	.	pregnant
hampir	. .	near, nearly

hanchor . . . melted, crushed ; *hanchor luloh*—crushed to powder

hangat . . . hot

hantar . . . escort, send

hanya . . . except ; only

hanyut . . . drift, float

haram . . . forbidden by religion. Used colloquially, with *ta'*, as a very strong negative

harap . . . hope, expect ; confidence

harga . . . price

hari . . . day (24 hours ; also, of daylight hours only) ; *malam hari*—night time

harimau . . . tiger

harta . . . property, wealth

harus . . . 1. current, stream. 2. fitting, desirable ; probable, likely

hasil . . . rent, revenue

hasrat . . . longing, desire

hatap (usu. atap) . roofing ; thatch of palm leaves

hati . . . heart, liver ; core ; *pĕrhatikan*—realize ; bear in mind, take note of

hatta *or* hata . . see par. 144

haus . . . 1. thirst. 2. worn away, consumed

hawa . . . breath, air ; climate

hela . . . drag, haul

hĕlai . . . see par. 48

hĕmbus *or* ĕmbus . blow (of wind, breath)

hĕndak . . . wish, intention ; as future auxiliary " will " (see par. 112 and footnote 38)

hĕrti *or* ĕrti . . understand ; *hĕrti-nya*—meaning

hidang . . . serve on a dsih

hidong	. . .	nose
hidup	. .	alive
hijau	. .	green, blue
hikayat	. .	story, tale
hilang	. .	be lost, disappear
hilir	. .	flow down ; go down stream ; lower waters of a river
himpun	. .	gather together
Hindu	. .	non-Moslem Indian
hingga	. .	up to, as far as ; until
hiris	. .	slice, cut fine, shred, slit
hisap *or* isap	.	suck ; smoke (of cigarettes)
hitam	. .	dark-coloured, black
hitong	. .	reckon, calculate
hormat	. .	respect, honour, reverence
hudoh	. .	ugly
hujan	. .	rain
hulam *or* ulam	.	uncooked vegetable food, eaten with rice
hulu	. .	upper portion ; upper waters of a river
hulubalang (lity.)	.	leader in war
hunus	. .	draw off; unsheath
huruf	. .	letter of the alphabet
hutan	. .	forest, jungle. *Hutan bĕlantara—* the wilds of the forest
hutang	. .	debt

I.

ia (written)	.	he, she, it, they ; him, her, them
ibu	. . .	mother
ikan	. .	fish
ikut	. .	follow (in space) ; *mĕngikut—*in accordance with
ilmu	. .	knowledge, art of . . ; science of . .

ingat	. . .	remember
Inggĕrís	. . .	English
ini	. . .	this, these
iring	. .	in single file; follow in due order (of royal suite). (See Ex. 44. Note 3.)
isi	. . .	contents; " flesh " of fruit; fill, put (something) in
istana *or* astana		palace
ɪstĕri (pol.)	.	wife
istimewa (lity.)	.	especially
itek	. .	duck
itu	. .	that, those; *ia–itu*—" that is to say, " i.e."
izin *or* idzin	.	permission

J.

jabat	. .	grasp, clasp
jadi	. .	come into existence; be born; become; act as; happen; be satisfactory. (see par. 82 and par. 138)
jaga	. .	be awake, watch
jahat	. .	wicked, evil
jahit	. .	sew
jajahan	. .	district
jalan	. .	road, way; method; movement; *bĕrjalan kaki*—walk, *bĕrjalan kĕreta*, or *bĕrjalan naik kĕreta*—go by car. (see par. 138)
jam	. .	watch, clock; hour
jambatan	.	bridge
jamu	, .	entertain guests
jangan	. .	don't, lest, in order that . . . not (see par. 78); *jangankan*—so far from; to say nothing of

janggut . . . beard
janji . . . *bĕrjanji*—promise, agree
jantan . . . male (see footnote 6)
jarang . . . at wide intervals ; seldom, scarce
jari . . . . finger, toe
jarum . . . needle
jasa . . . meritorious service, loyalty
jatoh . . . fall ; occur
jauh . . . far, distant
jauhari . . . jeweller
jawab . . . answer
jĕlapang . . . a padi-barn
jĕmput . . . pinch, press ; *sa-jĕmput*—a pinch
of ; *jĕmputkan*—to press the hand
of a guest in greeting, hence " to
invite ", e.g. to a feast ;
entertain
jĕmu . . . sick of, sated
jĕnaka . . . of the nature of a practical joke ;
wily ; farcical
jĕnis . . . kind, sort
jĕrat . . . snare, noose–trap
jĕrit . . . shriek. *jĕrit pĕkek*—shrieking and
screaming
jĕrneh . . . clear (of water)
jika *or* jikalau . if
jimat . . . careful, economical
jinak . . . tame
jual . . . sell
juga . . . fairly, just, also, all the same,
and yet ; (see par. 148)
jumpa . . . meet, encounter, come across
junjong . . . carry on the head ; figuratively,
obey (the command of a ruler)
juru . . . a skilled worker (not of
handicrafts)

K.

ka–.	to, towards (see par. 57)
kabut	hazy ; mist
kacha	glass (material)
kachang	beans
kadang–kadang	sometimes
kadar	power; more or less, roughly (coll.)
–kah ?	(an interrogative particle)
kahwin *or* kawin	marry ; marriage
kail	*měngail*—fishing with hook and line
kain	cloth ; " sarong "
kajang	angular palm-leaf awning for bullock-cart or boat; hence used as numeral coefficient for doubled sheets of notepaper
kakak	elder sister
kaki	foot, leg ; pedestal
kalakian	see par. 144
kalau	if
kali	time, occasion ; *sa–kali*—once, altogether ; very ; *barang kali*—perhaps
kalmarin *or* kělmarin	yesterday ; the day before ; a few days ago
kambing	goat
kami	we (see par. 85)
kampong	assembling ; a house with its enclosure ; a small village
kamu	you (see par. 85 and 173)
kanak–kanak	child, children
kanan	right (of direction)
ka–pada	to, up to, (see par. 57)
kapak	axe
kapal	ship (decked)
karam	founder

karang   .   .   . 1. arrange, set in order, compose
                    2. coral reef. 3. *coll.* presently
                    (see Conv. 6.   Note 4.)

karat   .   .   . rust

karna *or* kĕrana   . because

karong   .   .   . bag, made of coarse matting

kasar   .   .   . coarse, rough (of texture, or
                    manner)

kaseh   .   .   . affection, liking, **love**.   *tĕrima
                    kaseh*—thank you

kasehan .   .   . kindness, pity. *Kasehan!*—"Poor
                    thing ! "

kasi (baz.) .   . give

kasut   .   .   . shoes

kata   .   .   . say

katak   .   .   . frog, toad

kathi *or* kadzi . judge, in Muslim law

kati   .   .   . a catty—1⅓ lb.

katup   .   .   . shut

kawan   .   .   . group, herd ; **friend**

kaya   .   .   . rich

kayoh   .   .   . a paddle

kayu   .   .   . wood

kĕbajikan   .   . virtue, merit, good deeds ; profit

kĕbas   .   .   . numb

kĕbun   .   .   . garden, plantation, " estate "

kĕchil (usually pro- small ; younger
nounced " kĕchik ")

kĕdai   .   .   . shop

kĕjap   .   .   . wink ; *sa–kejap*—**a** moment

kĕjar   .   .   . pursue

kĕjut   .   .   . *tĕrkĕjut*—startled

kĕlahi   .   .   . *bĕrkĕlahi*—quarrel

kĕlak   .   .   . may ; perhaps ; will. An adverb
                    used at the end of a sentence
                    to   show   future   possibility

kĕlam	. . .	dark, obscure, gloomy
kĕlambu	. . .	mosquito-curtain
kĕlapa	. . .	coconut
kĕliling	. . .	around
kĕluar	. . .	go out
kĕmas	. . .	pack, put together tidily
kĕmbali	. . .	return to a place
kĕmbang	. . .	opening, expanding (of a flower, a heart)
kĕmbong	. . .	swollen, inflated
kĕmudi	. . .	rudder
kĕmudian (usually pronounced " kĕmdian ")		then, afterwards ; *kĕmudian hari* —later on, subsequently
kĕna	. . .	come up against, incur, experience. (See par. 82 and footnote 34).
kĕnal	. . .	recognize, by sight ; be acquainted with
kĕnang	. . .	recollect with loving regret
kĕnapa ?	.	why ?
kĕnduri *or* khĕnduri	.	a feast
kĕntang	. . .	*ubi kĕntang*—potatoes
kĕpala	. . .	head
kĕping	. . .	piece, fragment. Num. coeff. (see par. 48)
kĕra	. . .	monkey
kĕrani	. . .	clerk
kĕrap	. . .	at frequent intervals (of time and space). *kĕrap kali*—frequently
kĕras	. . .	hard
kĕrat	. . .	to sever, cut through
kĕrbau	. . .	buffalo
kĕreta	. . .	cart, car ; *kĕreta api*—train
kĕring	. . .	dry
kĕris	. . .	Malay dagger
kĕrja	. . .	work ; carry through, undertake
kĕroh	. . .	muddy (of water), turbid

kĕrtas	. . .	paper
kĕrusi	. . .	chair
kĕsan	. . .	trace, foot-mark
kĕtam	. .	1. crab. 2. plane (tool)
kĕtika	. .	time, season, period
khabar	. .	news. *Apa khabar ?*—" How do you do ? " *tiada khabarkan diri-nya*—was unconscious
kira	. .	reckon, estimate. *kira-kira* 1. about (i.e. roughly) 2. accounts
kiri .	. . .	left (of direction)
kirim	. . .	send (things)
kita	. .	we (see par. 85) ; you (equiv. to Fr. " on ")
kitab	. .	a writing ; book (especially of religious books)
kobis	. . .	cabbage
kochek	. . .	pocket
kolam	. . .	pond, tank
konyong	. .	*sa-konyong-konyong*—suddenly
kopi	. . .	coffee
kosong	. .	empty
kota	. . .	fort
kotak	. .	small box, case, chest
kotor	. . .	dirty
koyak	. . .	torn
kuah	. . .	sauce, gravy
kuala	. . .	river-mouth
kuasa	. .	power, strength ; authorization
kuat	. . .	strong
kuching	. . .	cat
kudis	. .	a skin-disease ; scabies ; mange
kueh	. . .	cake
kuku	. . .	nail, claw
kuli	. . .	unskilled labourer
kulit	. .	skin, hide, rind, leather
kuman	. .	parasite, germ

M

kunchi	.	.	. lock ; *anak kunchi*—key
kuning	.	.	. yellow
kupas	.	.	. to skin, peel, husk
kurang	.	.	. less; *kĕkurangan*—scarcity, dearth
kurus	.	.	. thin, emaciated
kusu	.	.	. a small group ; *bĕrkusu-kusu*—in groups
kutip	.	.	. pick up, gather, collect

L.

laba	.	.	. 1. profits. 2. *laba-laba*—spider
laboh	.	.	. let down (e.g. anchor, curtains) (see par. 138)
lachi (Dut.)	.	.	. drawer
lada	.	.	. pepper
lagi .	.	.	. more, moreover, still, also ; while still ; *sa-lagi*—as long as ; while
–lah	.	.	. (emphatic particle. See par. 151)
lain	.	.	. different, other
laki	.	.	. husband ; *laki-laki*—male, masculine
laku	.	.	. manner ; act or behave ; pass current ; *bĕrlaku*—take place (see par. 138)
lalu		.	. move past ; afterwards ; past ; (see par. 97 (b)) *sa-lalu*—always, constantly ; *tĕrlalu*—very ; *lalui* —disobey ; override ; *ta' lalu*— unable to
lama	.	.	. long (of time) ; former, ancient ; old (of things)
lambat	.	.	. slow, behind time
lampu (Port.)	.	.	. lamp
langit	.	.	. sky
langsong .	.	.	. forthwith, straightway ; going on to . . .

lanjut	. . .	lengthy, protracted ; lengthen
lantai	. . .	floor
lapar	. . .	hungry (often *lapar pĕrut*)
lapek	. . .	base, lining, any thin layer that is placed under something else (as a mat is placed under a plate)
larang	. . .	forbid ; prohibited ; *hutan larangan*—forest reserve
larat	. . .	dragging on, protracted ; *ta'larat*—unable to . . ., not strong enough to . . .
lari .	. . .	run, run away ; *bĕrlari*—run
lat .	. . .	alternate
lauk	. . .	food, to be eaten with rice (e.g. fish, chicken, meat)
laut	. . .	sea
lawat	. . .	*mĕlawat*—to visit
layan	. . .	wait on, attend on
layang	. . .	soaring through the air (used conventionally of letters) ; *layang-layang*—1 kite (toy), 2. swallow (bird.)
layar	. . .	a sail ; *pĕlayaran*—a voyage
layu	. . .	faded, e.g. of flowers ; met. pining, wan
lazim	. . .	customary, usual
lĕbai	. . .	" Levite ", pious person
lebar	. . .	broad, wide
lĕbat	. . .	heavy, dense (e.g. rain, foliage)
lĕbeh	. . .	more ; *tĕrlĕbeh*—most, more
lechet	. . .	*mĕlechet*—having the skin rubbed off ; grazed ; chafed
lĕga	. . .	comfortable ; " better ", improving after illness.
leher	. . .	neck
lĕkas	. . .	quickly, speedily
lĕkat	. . .	adhering (see par. 138)

lĕlah . . . exhausted ; *bĕrhĕntikan lĕlah*—to take a rest

lĕmbek . . . pulpy, soft

lĕmbing . . . a spear

lĕmbu . . . ox

lĕmbut . . . soft, flexible, weak *lĕmah-lĕmbut*—gentle

lena . . . sound, of sleep

lengah *or* lenga . . dawdling, loitering

lĕngan . . . arm ; sleeve

lenggang . . . swaying from side to side

lĕngkap . . . complete, equipped, supplied

lĕngoh . . . weak, aching

lĕnyap . . . vanish, disappear

lĕpas . . . loosed, freed ; after (of time)

lĕtak . . . lay down, put

lĕteh . . . tired. *lĕteh lĕsu*—utterly worn out

lĕtup . . . *mĕlĕtup*—explode

lewat . . . past, after, behind time

liat . . . tough, supple, leathery ; *tanah liat*—clay

lidah . . . tongue

lihat . . . see, descry

lima . . . five (see Ch. V and Ch. XIX)

limau . . . citrus fruits. *limau manis*—orange. *limau nipis*—lime

lingkar (or lengkar) . a coil

lintang . . . crosswise, athwart

lipas . . . cockroach

lipat . . . fold

lobang . . . hole

lokan . . . cockle

lokek . . . mean, miserly

lompat . . . jump, spring, leap

lorong . . . pathway, lane

luar . . . outer part ; *di-luar*—outside

luas		spacious, wide
ludah	. .	spit
luka	. .	wound
lulus	. .	just slipping through ; *lulus–kan* —to put through, accomplish, e.g. a project
lupa	. .	forget
luroh	. .	drop, be shed (of leaves, fruit) ; *sa-luroh dunia*—all over the world
lusa	. .	the day after tomorrow
lutut	. .	knee

M.

maaf	. .	pardon
macham	. .	sort, kind ; *macham mana ?*—how
maha	. .	great (used only in compound words)
mahal	. .	scarce, uncommon, precious ; hence costly ; *harga mahal*—a high price
mahkamah	.	Court of Law
mahu *or* mau	.	wish, will, intention ; much used in bazaar Malay as a future auxiliary—" I shall . . ." The better word to use is *hĕndak*, or its abbreviation *'nak*
main	. .	play ; *bukan main*—in no small measure, very
maju	. .	advance, progress
maka	. .	see par. 142
makan	. .	eat, consume
makin . . . makin	.	the more . . . the more
malam	. .	night, the hours of darkness ; eve of . . (see par. 140, Note 3)
malang	. .	mischance ; adverse (see par. 138) ; *malang-nya* (mod.)—unfortunately

malas . . . lazy
malu . . . shy, reluctant, ashamed. *putĕri malu*— " the shy princess "—a name for the sensitive plant that grows on most golf-courses in Malaya
mana ? . . . where ? which ? what ? *Di-mana* or *'tang* (i.e. *tĕntang*) *mana ?* —where ? *ka-mana ?*—whither ? *dari mana ?*—whence ? (par. 171)
mana . . . any ; whatever (par. 162)
mandi . . . bathe
manggis . . . mangosteen
mangkok . . . bowl, cup (without handle)
mangsa . . . food (of animals), prey
manikam . . . gem, jewel ; germ of life
manis . . . sweet
manusia . . . mankind ; human being
mara–bahaya . . dangers, perils
marah . . . angry
mari . . . hither ; hence, as a command, " Come here "
masa . . . time, epoch
masak . . . ripe, cooked ; to cook. *Masak nasi*—to cook a meal
masam . . . acid, sour. *Muka masam*— scowling
maseh . . . while still, while as yet
masin . . . brackish, salt (of water)
masing . . . separate, singly ; *masing–masing* —each (see par. 164)
masjid . . . mosque
masok . . . enter
mata . . . eye ; centre, e.g. *mata luka*— the open part of a wound, *mata kayu*—a knot in wood, *mata kaki* —ankle-bone. Much used in

		figurative and descriptive expressions, e.g. *mata mata*—policeman, *matahari*—sun, *mata pisau*—the cutting edge of a knife
mati	. . .	dead, stopped (of a watch), fixed (of price)
meja (Port.)	. .	table
mělainkan	. .	but ; excepting (after a negative)
memang	. .	naturally, as a matter of course
měnantu	. .	son- or daughter-in-law
měngantok	.	sleepy, drowsy
měngapa ?	.	why? *tidak měngapa*—it's nothing
měntah	. .	raw, uncooked
měntega *or* mantega (Port.)		butter
měntěri	. .	minister of state
merah	. .	red
měreka	. .	they, them. See par. 163 Also *měreka itu*
měshuarat	.	take counsel together; conference, council
měski (Port.)	.	although, even though
městi	. .	must, needs must
mika	. .	you (in Perak) see footnote 25
mimpi	. .	dream
minggu (Port.)	.	week
minta *or* pinta		ask for
minum	. .	drink
minyak	. .	oil, grease. (Used colloquially for petrol.) *minyak tanah* or *minyak gas*—kerosene
miskin	. .	poor
mithal *or* misal		example; *mithal-nya*—for example
mohon	. .	*běrmohon*—ask permission, usually to depart, i.e. a polite form of leave-taking
muat	. .	load with cargo (see par. 138)

muda . . . young; unripe; pale (of colour)

mudah . . . easy, light. *mudah–mudahan—* would that . . .

mudek . . . to go up-stream

mujor . . . lucky, luckily

muka . . . face; front; page

mula . . . beginning, source. *mula–mula—* at the beginning, first of all; *sa–mula*—over again

mulut . . . mouth

mungkir . . break one's word, or promise, or allegiance

muntah . . . vomit

murah . . . bounteous, liberal; cheap

murid . . . pupil, disciple

murka . . . wrath

musim . . . season

mustaed . . ready, in working order

mustahak . . important

N.

nabi . . . prophet

nah! . . . There you are! Take it!

naik . . . go up; *naik ka–darat*—to go ashore; *naik kĕreta*—to get into a car

nakal . . . perverse, naughty

nama . . . name

nampak . . be visible, be seen [not " to look *or* tampak at ", which is *tengok* or *lihat*, e.g. *Sa–malam saya pĕrgi tengok wayang. Di–situ nampak kawan dudok di–atas.* I went to see a show last night, and I saw (lit. " there came into my field of vision ") a friend sitting upstairs]

nanas	. .	pineapple
nanti	. .	wait ; colloquially, auxiliary indicating future time, " shall ", " will ". *měnantikan*—to await
nasi	. .	cooked rice ; food, e.g. *makan nasi*—to have a meal
nasib	. .	fate
něgěri	. .	settlement ; city–state ; town ; state
nenek	. .	grandmother, grandparents
něschaya (lity.)		certainly, inevitably
nipis	. .	thin (i.e. not thick)
nun	. .	yonder
–nya	. .	of him, of her, of it, of them (see par. 174)
nyamok	. .	mosquito
nyaris *or* nyaris ta'		all but, nearly
nyata	. .	clear, obvious, plain
nyawa	. .	life, soul
nyior	. .	coconut

O.

olah	. .	manner, *sa–olah–olah*—as if
oleh (lity.)	.	by, by reason of, by means of ; because ; *běroleh*—to obtain ; *pěrolehan*—acquisition
ombak	. .	wave (of the sea)
orang	. .	person, people ; *sa–orang*—alone

P.

pada	. .	1. at, in ; according to ; than (see par. 57) 2. sufficient
padam	. .	be extinguished
padang	. .	treeless waste land ; open space ; popularly, playing field in village or town

padi	.	.	. rice, as a plant, in the ear, and as unhusked grain
pagar	.	.	. fence
pagi.	.	.	. morning ; early
pagut	.	.	. peck (of birds), bite (of snakes)
pajak	.	.	. monopoly, farm ; *pajak gadai*—pawnbroker's shop (*gadai*—pledge)
pakai	.	.	. use, wear ; observe (e.g. a rule)
paku	.	.	. nail, spike
pala	.	.	. *buah pala*—nutmeg
palu	.	.	. to strike with a rigid instrument (e.g. a snake with a stick)
panas	.	.	. heat ; hot
pandai	.	.	. expert ; clever
pandan	.	.	. smaller screw–pine
pandang	.	.	. gaze at, observe, look at
panggang	.	.	. toast, roast on a spit
panggil	.	.	. call, summon
panggong	.	.	. platform, stage
pangkal	.	.	. beginning ; *pangkalan*—landing-stage, jetty
panjang	.	.	. long
panjat	.	.	. climb (e.g. a rope)
pantai	.	.	. shore, beach
papan	.	.	. plank, board
parang	.	.	. Malay chopper
paras (lity.)	.	.	. appearance (of people)
parit	.	.	. groove, trench, ditch
paroh	.	.	. 1. *sa–paroh*—half. 2. beak (of bird)
pasang	.	.	. 1. to set going (e.g. to light a lamp) ; 2. tidal–flow ; *ayer pasang*—incoming tide ; 3. *sa–pasang*—a pair
pasar	.	.	. bazaar, market
pasir	.	.	. sand

pasu	.	.	bowl, tub
patah	.	.	broken, snapped (e.g. a bone); *patah ka-kanan* to turn off sharply to the right; num. coeff. for words and sayings.
patek	.	.	I, me; a Malay to a member of the ruling house. (see footnote 24)
patok	.	.	peck (of bird)
patut	.	.	seemly, fitting, advisable
pawang	.	.	see par. 189, Note 2
paya	.	.	swamp
payah	.	.	difficult; serious (of illness)
payong	.	.	umbrella
pĕchah	.	.	broken into pieces, e.g. of a cup
pĕdang	.	.	sword, scythe
pĕdap	.	.	absorb
pĕdas	.	.	hot (of taste, e.g. curry)
pĕgang	.	.	hold
pĕgawai	.	.	officer, government agent
pĕjabat	.	.	(from *jabat* to hold) office
pĕkak	.	.	deaf, hard of hearing
pĕkan	.	.	village, market, shopping centre
pĕlandok	.	.	mouse–deer (see par. 130)
pĕlanting	.	.	falling and rebounding
pĕlĕpah	.	.	frond, palm-leaf
pĕlihara	.	.	cherish, rear
pĕlita	.	.	lamp
pĕlok	.	.	put one's arms round, embrace
pĕluang	.	.	lull (in the wind); favourable opportunity, chance
pĕnat	.	.	tired
pendek	.	.	short
pĕngantin	.	.	bride or bridegroom
pĕnghulu	.	.	headman
pengsan *or* pĕngsan	.	fainting, loss of conciousness
pĕnjara	.	.	prison
pĕnoh	.	.	full

pĕrahu	.	.	boat, ship (undecked)
perak	.	.	silver
Pĕranchis	.	.	French
pĕrang	.	.	war
pĕrangai	.	.	disposition, nature
pĕrangkap	.	.	a cage-trap
pĕranjat	.	.	*tĕrperanjat*—startled, alarmed
pĕrchaya	.	.	trust, believe
pĕreksa	.	.	look into ; enquiry, examination
pĕrĕmpuan	.	.	feminine ; woman
pĕrentah	.	.	rule, sway
pĕrgi	.	.	to go
pĕri (lity.)	.	.	matter, concern ; concerned with
pĕrigi	.	.	a well, a spring
pĕrisai	.	.	a round shield
pĕrkakas	.	.	apparatus, tools
pĕrkara	.	.	affair, matter
pĕrmata	.	.	gem, jewel
pĕrnah	.	.	ever ; usually negative *ta'pĕrnah* or *bĕlum pĕrnah*—never
pĕrsĕtua (lity.)	.		*sa–kali pĕrsĕtua*—once upon a time
pĕrtama	.	.	first (see par. 181 and 185)
pĕrut	.	.	stomach, abdomen, womb
pĕsam–pĕsam	.	.	tepid
pĕsan	.	.	order, instruct, commission
pĕtang	.	.	afternoon, evening
pĕti	.	.	box
pĕtir	.	.	thunder
pikul	.	.	to carry a heavy burden on the shoulders ; a measure of weight = 100 kati.
pileh	.	.	choose
pinang	.	.	areca nut
pindah	.	.	move from one place to another
pinggan	.	.	plate

pinggang	. .	waist
pinjam	. .	borrowing ; *běri pinjam*—lend ; *minta pinjam*—borrow
pintu	. .	door, gate
pipi	. .	cheeks
piring	. .	saucer, platter
pisang	. .	banana
pisau	. .	knife
pohon	. .	1. tree ; 2. to request (see *mohon*)
pokok	. .	stem, trunk, beginning ; *pokok kayu*—tree ; *pokok nyiur*—coconut palm
potong	. .	cut off
puas	. .	satisfied, sated (see Conversation 7, note 3)
puchok	. .	shoot, leaf bud ; num. coeff. for letters, and guns
puji	. .	praise
pukat	. .	drift-net
pukul	. .	strike, hit. (used colloquially in many ways, e.g. *pukul chap*—to print ; *pukul talipon*—to telephone)
pula	. .	again, nevertheless, (see par. 149)
pulang	. .	return to one's base. *pulangkan*—to return a thing to its owner
pulau	. .	island
puleh	. .	revive, be renewed
puloh	. .	ten (see Ch. V and Ch. XIX)
pun	. .	even, also, too. (see par. 150)
pungut	. .	pick up, gather
puntong	.	stump, fag-end
punya	. .	possession (see par. 36 and 176) ; *ěmpunya* and *měmpunyaï*—possess
puteh	. .	white ; *orang puteh*—European

putĕri . . . princess
putus . . . severed, breaking away (e.g. of a rope) ; end, settlement (of a dispute, a law–case)

R.

rajin . . . diligent
ramai . . . crowded, populous
rambut . . . hair
rampas . . . loot, take by force
rantai . . . chain
rantau . . . reach of river
rapat . . . close up to, touching
rasa . . . taste, feeling
rata . . . level. *sa–rata*—all over ; *rata–rata*—everywhere
ratus . . . hundred
raya . . . great. *hari raya*—holiday ; *bunga raya*—hibiscus ; *jalan raya*—main road
rayap . . . crawl, creep
rayat *or* raayat . populace ; subjects
rayau . . . *mĕrayau*—to prowl about, wander about
rĕbah . . . fall to the ground, e.g. *rĕbah pengsan*—to faint
rĕbut . . . snatch
rehat . . . interval, pause
rĕndah . . . low
rĕndam . . . immerse
rendang . . . leafy
rĕput . . . rotten, crumbling to decay (e.g. of wood)
rĕtak . . . crack (in crockery), markings
riba . . . lap ; take on the lap
ribu . . . thousand
ribut . . . storm

rindu	.	.	. pining for one who is absent
ringan	.	.	. light (of weight)
ringgit	.	.	. dollar
roda	.	.	. wheel
rioh	.	.	. usually *rioh rĕndah*—clamour, uproar
risau	.	.	. feel disturbed, uneasy, worried
rokok	.	.	. cigarette
rosak	.	.	. spoilt, ruined
rotan	.	.	. rattan
roti .	.	.	. bread
ru .	.	.	. *kayu ru*—the casuarina tree
ruas	.	.	. space between two joints, e.g. of finger, bamboo
rumah	.	.	. house
rumput	.	.	. grass
rupa	.	.	. form, appearance; *sa–rupa*—alike

S.

sa *or* satu, *or* suatu	. one (see Ch. V and footnote 13)
saat	. moment
sabar	. patient. *Sabar dahulu*—just wait a bit, have patience
sa–bĕrang.	. on the opposite side, or bank
sadikit (*coll*. pron. " sikit ")	. a little, a few
sahabat	. friend
sahaja	. only, simply ; intentionally, purposely ; just, exactly
sahaya *or* saya	. originally, household slave ; hence humble servant ; I, me, we, us (see par. 85)
	Note. In this book the shortened form *saya* (the usual pronunciation) is used when the word is a pronoun, except where it occurs in passages taken from books.

sahut	.	.	.	answer
sais .	.	.	.	groom, driver
sakalian	.	.	.	all
sakit	.	.	.	sick, sickness
saku	.	.	.	bag, pocket
salah	.	.	.	mistake, fault ; *salah satu*—one or the other
salak	.	.	.	to bark
salam	.	.	.	peace. *měmběri salam*—to give the Moslem greeting
salin	.	.	.	change of form, of dress ; translate ; *běrsalin*—to give birth to a child
sama	.	.	.	same ; *běrsama děngan*—along with, together
sambil	.	.	.	simultaneously, with (= *sa* + *ambil*) (see par. 97 (d))
sambut	.	.	.	receive (e.g. as a guest)
sampah	.	.	.	rubbish
sampai	.	.	.	arrive ; *sampaikan*—convey
sampan	.	.	.	small boat
sampul	.	.	.	wrapper
sana	.	.	.	over there
sandar	.	.	.	lean. *běrsandar kapada*—leaning (oneself) against ; *těrsandar kapada* resting against (e.g. of a ladder against a wall) ; *sandarkan*—to rest something against
sangat	.	.	.	very
sangka	.	.	.	suspect, be of the opinion, think
sangkut	.	.	.	be held up, be caught in or by something
sapěrti	.	.	.	as if, like
saput	.	.	.	covering lightly, as with a film
sara–bara	.	.	.	helter–skelter, in confusion
sarang	.	.	.	nest

sarong . . . sheath, wrapper, covering, e.g. *sarong surat*—envelope ; *sarong kaki*—stockings ; *kain sarong*— the Malay *sarong*—tubular cotton skirt worn by men and women (see footnote 10)

saudagar . . . merchant, trader

saudara . . . close relative ; intimate friend ; *anak saudara*—niece or nephew ; *bapa saudara*—uncle

sawah . . . rice–field (either swamp land, or irrigated land)

saya . . . see *sahaya*

sayang . . . longing, love, affection, pity, *Sayang !*—" Dear ! dear ! "

sayup . . . only just in sight

sayur . . . vegetables

sĕbab . . . reason, cause ; because ; *apa sĕbab ?*—" why ? " *sĕbab* or (lity.) *oleh sĕbab*—because

sĕbut . . . say, mention

sĕdang . . . medium ; while, during ; *sĕdangkan*—although

sĕdap . . . pleasant, agreeable ; tasty (of food); *ta'sĕdap badan*—not feeling very well

sĕdar . . . conscious, aware of, alive to

sĕdeh . . . sobbing ; *sĕdeh hati*—grief

sĕdĕkah . . . alms

sĕdia . . . ready

sĕgala . . . all

sĕgar . . . fit and well

sĕgĕra . . . quickly, forthwith

sĕjuk . . . cool, cold

sĕkarang . . . now ; *sĕkarang ini*—at this very moment

sĕkolah . . . school

sĕlamat	.	.	.	peace, safety *Sĕlamat jalan*— " Good-bye " (to one going) *Sĕlamat tinggal*—" Good-bye " (to one staying) *Sĕlamat datang*— " Welcome ! "
sĕlang	.	.		alternate
sĕlat	.	.		strait ; *Sĕlat*—Singapore
sĕlera	.	.		zest, appetite
sĕlĕsai	.	.		settled ; *sĕlĕsaikan*—to bring to a conclusion
sĕlimut	.	.		coverlet, rug, wrap
sĕmangat	.	.		spirit of life, soul
sĕmbah	.	.		see footnote 50
sĕmbilan	.	.		nine. (See Ch. V and Ch. XIX)
sĕmbunyi	.	.		hide ; *bĕrsĕmbunyi*—hide oneself; *sĕmbunyikan*—hide something ; *tĕrsĕmbunyi*—hidden
sĕmĕnjak	.	.		since (of time)
sĕmĕntara	.	.		while ; temporary
sĕmpat	.	.		*ta' sĕmpat*—not able to, no time to
sĕmua	.	.	.	all
sĕnang	.	.		comfortable, easy ; *ta' sĕnang*— busy, having no free time
sĕnapang	.	.		gun, rifle
sĕndi	.	.		joint, sinew
sĕndiri	.	.		oneself (see par. 177)
sĕngaja	.	.		purposely
senget	.	.		heeling over
sĕnjata	.	.		weapon
sĕntosa	.	.		peace, tranquillity
sĕnyum	.	.		smile, smiling
sepah	.	.		*bĕrsepah–sepah* or *tĕrsepah*— littered about
sepak	.	.		kick with the side of the foot
sĕpit	.	.		nip
sĕrah	.	.		surrender, hand over

sĕrambi	. . .	closed verandah of a Malay house
sĕrampang	. .	fish–spear
sĕrang	. . .	onslaught, attack
sĕrap	. . .	absorption. *di–sĕrap udara*— evaporated
sĕraya	. .	along with (see par. 97 (d))
sĕrba	. . .	of all sorts
sĕrta	. . .	along with (see par. 97 (c))
sĕru	. . .	call out, shout
sĕsak	. . .	packed close together ; crammed full
sĕsat	. . .	astray
shabash	. .	excellent ! capital !
shak	. . .	suspicion. *shak hati*—suspicious
si–	. . .	see par. 88
siapa	. .	who ? (see par. 169), whoever (see par. 161)
sia–sia	. .	in vain
siang	. .	daylight
sikap	. .	bearing, mien
sikat	. .	comb ; bunch (of bananas)
siku	. .	elbow, sharp bend
sila .	. .	" please." (see par. 92)
simpan	. .	keep, put by
simpang *or* sempang	.	cross–roads
singgah	. .	call in at, break a journey
sini .	. .	here
sipat *or* sifat	.	appearance
siput	. .	shell, shell–fish
sireh	. .	betel–vine ; betel leaf prepared for chewing
sisek	. .	scales (of fish)
situ	. .	there
sokong	. .	prop up
sopak	. .	a skin disease (white patches on hands and feet)
sorok	. .	draw back, into concealment

sorong	. .	push along; *kěreta sorong*—a hand-cart
suam	. .	luke-warm
suami (pol.)	. .	husband
suara	. .	voice
subor	. .	healthy (of plants)
sudah	. .	done, over, past; has, had
sudi	. .	willing
suka	. .	pleasure. *suka hati, suka chita*—glad
sukat	. .	measure out (of capacity)
suku	. .	quarter, section
sulong	. .	eldest
sumbu	. .	wick, fuse
sumpah	. .	swear; *běrsumpah*—take an oath
sungai	. .	river
sunggoh	. .	true, genuine; *sunggoh pun*—although
sungut	. .	*běrsungut*—to mutter, grumble, scold
sunting	. .	wearing flowers in the hair
sunyi	. .	lonely
supaya	. .	in order that
surat	. .	letter, document
suroh	. .	tell to do a thing, instruct, order; send on an errand
surut	. .	*ayer surut*—ebb-tide
susah	. .	troublesome
susu	. .	breast; milk
susup	. .	crawl under; *susupkan*—insert (something) under
sutěra	. .	silk

T.

tabek	. .	greeting; *minta tabek*—ask pardon for a possible breach of etiquette. Cf. *běrtabek* in Conv. II.

tabib	. .	doctor
tadi	. .	just now; *baharu tadi*—a moment ago
-tah	. .	interrogative particle—see par. 152
tahan	. .	bear, sustain; restrain; "last" (e.g. of materials)
tahi	. .	dregs, refuse, excrement. (Many compound nouns, e.g. *tahi kĕtam*—wood shavings)
tahu	. .	know
tahun	. .	year
tajam	. .	sharp
takdir	. .	decree of providence
takok	. .	notch
takut	. .	fear; afraid; for fear that
tali	. .	rope, line
tambah	. .	adding on; *tambahan pula*—the more so
tampar	. .	slap
tampi	. .	winnow, by up and down movement
tanah	. .	land, soil, country
tanam	. .	plant; bury
tandok	. .	horn
tangan	. .	hand
tangga	. .	house–ladder; stair–case
tangis	. .	*mĕnangis*—weep
tangkap	. .	catch, capture
tanggoh	. .	put off, postpone
tanjong	. .	promontory; *Tanjong* (locally)— Penang
tanya	. .	ask, enquire
tarek	. .	draw, pull
tari	. .	*mĕnari*—dance
taroh	. .	put, deposit. *bĕrtaroh*—stake, *mĕnaroh*—have, possess, feel,

e.g. *měnaroh kasehan*—to feel pity

tatkala . . .	at the time when
tawar . . .	1. without flavour, insipid; harmless; fresh, not salt, of water; *měnawarkan*—to counteract, act as an antidote. 2. offer; bargain
těbal . . .	thick
těbang . . .	to fell (big trees)
těbas . . .	to cut down bushes, undergrowth
těgah . . .	prohibit
těgak . . .	erect, upright
těgap . . .	sturdy, well-knit
těgoh . . .	firm, strong
teh	tea
těkan . . .	press down, on a flat surface
tělaga . . .	a well, small lake
tělah (lity.) .	has, had, did; a word used to indicate past tense. *sa–tělah*—when; *sa–tělah itu*—after that
tělinga . . .	ear
tělok . . .	bay
tělor . . .	egg
těman . . .	companion; *těmankan* to accompany. (See footnote 24)
tembak . . .	to shoot
těmbaga . . .	brass
tembok . . .	wall; embankment, *hence*—a made road
těmpat . . .	place
těmpek . . .	cheering; *těmpek sorak*—cheering and shouting
tempoh . . .	time allowed; extension of time
těmu . . .	*běrtěmu*—to meet, come together
těnang . . .	still (of water), calm
těngadah . . .	looking upwards

těngah	. .	middle ; while
těnggělam	.	sink, be submerged
těnggiri	. .	*ikan těnggiri*—Spanish-mackerel
tengok	. .	to look at, distinguish by sight (see *nampak*)
těntang	. .	facing ; concerning ; *běrtěntang* —opposite
těntu	. .	certainly
těpi	. .	edge
těpok	. .	beat, clap (with flat of hand)
těpong	. .	flour
těrang	. .	clear, obvious
těrbang	. .	to fly
těriak	. .	cry out
těrima	. .	receive
těrlampau	.	very, too, exceedingly
těrok	. .	severe (of illness, etc.)
těrpa	. .	*měněrpa*—leap forward, spring at
těrtawa	. .	laugh
těrus	. .	right through in a straight line
tětap	. .	constant, fixed
tětapi *coll.* 'tapi	.	but
tiap-tiap	. .	each, every
tiarap	. .	face downwards
tiba	. .	to arrive at ; *tiba–tiba* suddenly
tidak	. .	not, no. (see par. 74)
tidor	. .	sleep
tiga	. .	three (see Ch. V and Ch. XIX)
tikam	. .	stab, spear
tikus	. .	rat, mouse
tilam	. .	mattress
timah	. .	tin ; *timah hitam*—lead
timbul	. .	come to the surface, appear from below
timbun	. .	heap up
timor	. .	east
timpa	. .	dropping down on, falling on

tindeh	. . .	lying one on another ; press down
tinggal	. . .	left over, remaining ; leave ; dwell ; *měninggal* (sc. *dunia*) to die ; *sa–pěninggalan* (lit. during the absence of)—while
tinggi	. . .	high, tall
tingkah	. . .	*tingkah laku*—behaviour
tingkap	. . .	window (of Malay house)
tipu	. . .	deceive
titah	. . .	see footnote 51
tolak	. . .	push away ; *běrtolak*—set out
toleh	. . .	turn the head to look
tolong	. . .	help ; " please " (see par. 92)
tong	. . .	tub, cask, bin
tongkah (měnongkah)		to travel against the current
topi	. . .	hat
tua	. . .	old, senior ; deep of colour. *kětua*—headman, elder
tuan	. . .	master, lord ; owner. (See par. 85 and footnote 28)
tuboh	. . .	body
tujoh	. . .	seven (see Ch. V and Ch. XIX)
tuju	. . .	making for, aiming at ; *běrsa-tuju*—to be in agreement with
tukang	. . .	workman, craftsman
tukar	. . .	exchange (see " change " in Eng.-Malay vocab.)
tulang	. . .	bone
tulis	. . .	write
tumbang	. . .	fall heavily (e.g. a tree)
tumboh	. . .	sprout, spring up
tumbok	. . .	thump, punch, pound
tumpah	. . .	spill
tumpul	. . .	blunt
tunggu	. . .	watching, guarding ; *tunggui*—to watch over

tunjok	.	.	. show, point out
turun	.	.	. go down, descend; fade, (of colour)
turut	.	.	. follow (instructions, advice)
tutup	.	.	. shut

U.

ubah	.	.	. alter, change. (See par. 138)
ubat *or* obat	.		. drug, medicine, cure
ubi .	.	.	. tuberous plant
udang	.	.	. prawn; *udang galah*—crawfish
udara	.	.	. atmosphere
ujar	.	.	. utter, say
ukor	.	.	. measure length
ular	.	.	. snake
umor	.	.	. age
umpama .	.		. instance, example; *pĕrumpamaan* —proverb
umpan	.	.	. bait
undang–undang		.	. statute law, ordinance
unggas	.	.	. bird
untong	.	.	. fate, destiny, luck; profit
upah	.	.	. payment for service rendered
urat	.	.	. nerve, vein, sinew, strand
usah	.	،	. need, *ta'usah*—there is no need, i.e. don't
usaha	.	.	. industry, persistence
utama	.	.	. excellence. *Tuan yang tĕrutama* —His Excellency

W.

wajib	.	.	. obligatory, necessary
waktu	.	.	، appointed time; time, period
walau	.	.	، although; *walau pun*—even if
wang	.	.	. money
warna	.	.	. colour

warta	.	.	news
wayang	.	.	theatrical performance

Y.

ya *or* ia	.	.	1. Yes ; it is so.
			2. O ! (interjection of address)
yang	.	.	who, which, (see pars. 157–159)

English—Malay

This vocabulary does not include words which are to be found in collected lists in the chapters.   e.g. prepositions; conjunctions ; adverbs of time, place, degree; pronouns ; expressions of time.

For page references to such words, see Table of Contents.

A.

abate (of rain, etc.)	.		rĕda
about (more or less)	.		lĕbeh kurang
accompany	.		ikut
accumulate	.		kumpulkan
acknowledge	.		aku, mĕngaku
across (water)	.		di–sabĕrang
afraid	.	.	takut
age .	.	.	umor
aircraft	.	.	kapal tĕrbang
alarmed .	.		takut
allow	.		bĕnarkan
angry	.	.	marah
another .	.		lain
ant (white)	.		anai–anai
apart	.	.	*wide apart*—jarang
appointed to	.		yang bĕrkuasa (*i.e. having power*)
arm	.	.	lĕngan

arrange	. .	atur ; *make an agreement with*— běrsatuju, běrjanji, běrmuafakat
arrive	. .	sampai ; tiba
ask a question	.	tanya
ask for	. .	minta
axe	. .	kapak

B.

bait	. .	umpan
basket	. .	bakul, raga
beard	. .	janggut
begin	. .	mulaï
belt	. .	tali pinggang
bench	. .	bangku
better (recovering from illness)	lěga ; bětah
big	. .	běsar
black	. .	hitam
blue	. .	biru
blunt	. .	tumpul
boat	. .	pěrahu
body	. .	badan, tuboh ; *carcase*—bangkai
book	. .	kitab ; buku
born	. .	*be born* : jadi ; lahir ; di-pěranakkan
borrow	. .	pinjam
bowl	. .	mangkok, pasu
box	. .	pěti, kotak
bread	. .	roti
bring, fetch	.	ambil, bawa
broken	. .	pěchah, patah, putus
brother	. .	*elder* : abang ; *younger* : adek
bullock cart	.	kěreta lěmbu
burn	. .	bakar
busy, hard-pressed	.	sibok běkěrja ; ta' sěnang
butter	. .	měntega *or* mantega

button	.	.	. butang
buy	.	.	. bĕli

C.

call .	.	.	. *summon*—panggil
			call at—singgah
can, be able	.	.	boleh
capsized	.	.	tĕrbalek
captain (of Arab ship)			nakhoda
capture	.	.	tangkap
car .	.	.	kĕreta
careful (economical)	.		jimat
carpenter	.		tukang kayu
case (in court)	.		bichara
casuarina tree	.		pokok ru
cat .	.	.	kuching
certainly .	.		tĕntu
chain	.	.	rantai
chair	.	.	kĕrusi
chance, opportunity	.		pĕluang
change	.	.	1. *exchange*—tukar
			2. *become different*—ubah
			3. *change position, etc.*—aleh
			4. *replace*—ganti
chat	.	.	bĕrbual *or* bĕrbual–bual
cheeks	.	.	pipi
child	.	.	*son or daughter of :* anak ; *young person :* budak ; *little child :* kanak–kanak
chisel	.	.	pahat
cigarettes	.		rokok
clamour	.	.	hingar
clean (cleanse)	.		chuchi
cleft	.	.	chĕlah
clerk	.	.	kĕrani
climate	.	.	hawa

close against . .	rapat
cloth . .	kain
cloud . .	awan
coconut . .	nyior ; kělapa
coffee . .	kopi
cold, cool .	sějuk
come . .	*come in*—masok
	come back—balek
	come out—kěluar
	come to surface—timbul
complain . .	adu
comply with, follow .	turut
concerning, in connection with	. bĕrkĕnaan dengan
condition, clause	. sharat
cord . .	tali
corner . .	pĕnjuru
correct . .	bĕtul
country . .	nĕgĕri
court (of justice)	. mahkamah, kot
courtyard .	halaman
cover . .	tudong
cow . .	lĕmbu bĕtina
cracked . .	rĕtak
crocodile . .	buaya
crooked (askew)	. serong
cup . .	chawan
cut . . .	potong

D.

dance . .	tari, mĕnari
daring . .	bĕrani
daughter . .	anak pĕrĕmpuan
day . .	hari
delighted . .	suka hati

dentist . . .	tukang gigi
difficult . . .	susah, payah
dig	gali
direct (right through, without stopping)	tĕrus
direction . .	arah, hala. *in the direction of*— hala ka–
dirty . . .	kotor
district officer .	pĕgawai daerah
ditch, trench .	parit
do . . .	buat ; *act as*—jadi ; *do well*— maju
dog . . .	anjing
dollar . . .	ringgit
don't (a command) .	jangan ; ta' usah
door . . .	pintu
drink . . .	minum
dry . . .	kĕring ; (*in the sun*) jĕmor

E.

ear . . .	tĕlinga
easy . . .	sĕnang, mudah
eat . . .	makan
edge . . .	tĕpi
egg . . .	tĕlor
elephant . .	gajah
embassy . .	utusan
empty . .	kosong
end . .	*of rope :* hujong ; *cigarette :* puntong
enforce (a regulation) .	hasilkan maksud (lit. *bring to pass the aim of . . .*)
English . .	Inggĕris
erect, put up .	dirikan
exception, make an exception of .	kĕchualikan

| extravagant | . | . | boros |
| eye . | . | . | mata |

F.

face	.	.	muka
fall .	.	.	jatoh; *of leaves:* luroh; *untimely:* gugor
fat, plump	.	.	gěmok
father	.	.	bapa, ayah
feel .	.	.	rasa
fence	.	.	pagar
fetch	.	.	ambil
fever	.	.	děmam
fierce	.	.	ganas
fine .	.	.	elok
finish	.	.	habiskan
fire .	.	.	api
fish .	.	.	ikan
fish hook .	.	.	kail
fit (healthy)	.	.	sěgar
floor	.	.	lantai
flour	.	.	těpong
flower	.	.	bunga
follow	.	.	ikut
food	.	.	makan
forget	.	.	lupa
friend	.	.	kawan
frond	.	.	pělěpah
fruit	.	.	buah
full .	.	.	pěnoh

G.

garden, estate	.	.	kěbun
gather	.	.	pungut, kutib, ambil
get, obtain	.	.	dapat; *get up*, bangun; *hit*, kěna

girl . . . . budak pĕrĕmpuan
give . . . bĕri, bagi
go . . . . pĕrgi ; *go back*—balek, kĕmbali, pulang ; *go out*—kĕluar ; *go by*—lalu
goat . . . kambing
good . . . baik ; bagus ; *good at*—pandai
grandchild . . chuchu
grass . . . rumput
green . . . hijau
grow (of plants, hair etc.) . . . tumboh
grumble . . bĕrsungut
gun . . . sĕnapang

H.

hand . . . tangan
hang . . . gantong ; *on a line*—sidai ; *trailing* umbai–umbai
hard . . . kĕras
head . . . kĕpala
hear . . . dĕngar
heavy (of rain) . lĕbat
hen . . . . ayam (bĕtina)
hide . . . sĕmbunyi
high . . . tinggi
hill . . . bukit
hinge . . . engsel (*Dut.*)
hire . . . sewa
hold . . . pĕgang
holidays . . *leave* — chuti ; *outing* — makan angin
hope . . . harap
hot . . . . panas, hangat ; *peppery*—pĕdas
house . . . rumah
hurry . . gopoh

I.

Indian (non-Moslem) . Hindu
indolent . . . chulas
island . . . pulau

J.

joints (of limbs) . sĕndi, anggota

K.

keep . . . simpan
king . . . baginda
kitchen . . . dapor
knife . . . pisau
know . . . tahu

L.

ladder . . . tangga
land . . . tanah; *land office*—pĕjabat tanah;
      dry land—darat
large . . . bĕsar
lash, switch . sĕbat
late . . . *behind time*—lewat, lambat
lazy . . . malas
leaf . . . daun
leafy . . . rendang
lean (against) . sandar (kapada)
learn . . . bĕlajar
leave . . . tinggal
lend . . . bĕri pinjam
letter (epistle) . surat
light (not heavy) . ringan
like . . . *(verb)* suka
lime (fruit) . buah limau
line (floating line tali alir
  used for catching
  crocodiles)

N

list . . .	.	daftar
live (dwell)	.	tinggal, dudok
living (alive)	.	hidup
long . . .	.	panjang ; *at long last*—lambat laun
look (appearance)	.	rupa
look after	.	měnjaga, běla
look for . .	.	chari
low . . .	.	rěndah
luck, fate	.	untong, nasib
luckily . .	.	mujor

M.

make . .	.	buat
mark, sign	.	tanda
market . .	.	pasar
measure . .	.	(*linear*) ukor ; (*capacity*) sukat
meat . .	.	daging
meet . .	.	běrjumpa, běrtěmu
mend . .	.	měmbaiki
merchant .	.	saudagar
middle . .	.	těngah
mile . . .	.	batu
milk . .	.	susu
mill . .	.	kelang
mistake . .	.	salah
moment . .	.	saat, sa–běntar
money . .	.	wang, duit (*Dut.*)
monkey .	.	kěra, monyet ; *the gibbon*—wak-wak
moon, month .	.	bulan
mosque . .	.	masjid *or* měsjid
mother . .	.	ěmak, ibu
mouth . .	.	mulut
move (from one place to another)		pindah, běrpindah

ail	. . .	(*of finger*) kuku ; (*spike*) paku
name	. . .	nama
necessary, imperative.		wajib
neck	. . .	leher
needle	. . .	jarum
news	. . .	khabar
noisy	. . .	bising, hingar
notice (public) .		kĕnyataan

O.

obstruct, hinder	.	galang
old		tua ; (*long standing*) lama
open	. . .	buka
opinion . . .		fikiran, sangka
order (a thing to be		pĕsan
made, or sent)		

P.

pack	. . .	kĕmas
packet, parcel .		bung**kus**
page	. . .	muka
paint	. . .	chat
paper	. . .	kĕrtas
parents	. . .	ibu bapa
pawn, pledge .		bĕrgadai ; *pawnshop*—pajak gadai
pay, wages .		gaji
peak	. . .	kĕmonchak
penalty . .		hukuman (from " hukum— " *decree*)
permission .		izin, kĕbĕnaran
persuade, coax .		pujok
picture . . .		gambar
piece . . .		kĕping
pinch (press between		pichit
finger and thumb)		

pineapple	.	nanas
place	. .	těmpat
plain, clear	.	nyata
plane (wood)	.	kětam
plank, board	.	papan
plant	. .	(verb) tanam
plate	. .	pinggan
play	. .	main
pleasant	. .	sědap
pole (for a boat)	.	galah
policeman	.	mata–mata
porch (jutting out)	.	anjong
pot (for flowers)	.	pasu
present, be present	.	hadzir
pretending	.	pura–pura
pretty	. .	chantek, molek
prison	. .	pěnjara, jěl
procession	.	march in procession—běrarak
promise	. .	janji
protest against, oppose	berbantah
pull	. .	tarek
put away	.	simpan

R.

raft	. .	rakit
rag	. . .	pěrcha kain
rain	. .	hujan
rapids	. .	jěram
rat	. . .	tikus
reach (of river)	.	rantau ; upper reaches—hulu
read	. .	bacha
ready	. .	siap, sědia ; (preparations complete) mustaed (lity.)
red	. . .	merah
redeem	. .	těbus
relatives	. .	kaum kěluarga ; sanak saudara

remember.	.	. ingat
revive	.	. puleh
rice .	.	. padi ; běras ; nasi
rice–fields	.	. sawah, běndang
river	.	. sungai ; *go up river*—mudek ; *go down river*—hilir
road	.	. jalan
roof	.	. bumbong
room	.	. bilek
rope	.	. tali
round	.	. bulat
row, line	.	. baris, banjar
run .	.	. lari, běrlari

S.

sail .	.	. (*verb*) bělayar
salt (of water)	.	. masin
same	.	. sama
say .	.	. kata, sěbut ; *inform* běri tahu, khabarkan
schedule .	.	. jadual
scent, smell	.	. bau ; *scented, fragant* wangi
search, (i.e. examine)	.	pěreksa
see .	.	. *look at*—tengok, lihat ; *notice* —nampak (*See Malay-Eng. vocab.*)
seeds	.	. běneh
sell .	.	. jual
sew .	.	. jahit
share	.	. bahagi ; *share umbrella*—tumpang payong
sharp	.	. tajam
shed, lean–to	.	. pondok
shell (of egg)	.	. kulit
sheltered, take shelter		běrtědoh
ship		. kapal

shoes	.	.	.	kasut
shoot	.	.	.	(verb) tembak
shop	.	.	.	kědai
shore	.	.	.	pantai
short	.	.	.	pendek
shortage	.	.	.	kěkurangan
show	.	.	.	(verb) tunjok
sick	.	.	.	sakit; sick of—jěmu, puas
silver	.	.	.	perak
sink	.	.	.	beneath surface těnggělam; founder karam
sister	.	.	.	elder kakak; younger adek or adek pěrěmpuan
sit	.	.	.	dudok
sleep	.	.	.	tidor
slow	.	.	.	lambat
small	.	.	.	kěchil
soft	.	.	.	lěmbut
sorry	.	.	.	I am sorry minta maaf
split	.	.	.	bělah
spoon	.	.	.	sěndok, chamchah
spring, fountain		.	.	mata ayer
stiff, aching		.	.	lěngoh
stone, rock		.	.	batu
storm	.	.	.	ribut
stupid	.	.	.	bodoh, děngu
sugar	.	.	.	gula
sun oneself		.	.	běrjěmor
surface	.	.	.	see come
surprising		.	.	hairan
sweep	.	.	.	sapu
sweet	.	.	.	manis

T.

| table | . | . | . | meja. (Port.); dressing table— meja chěrmin (i.e. with mirror) |

tail . . .	ekor
talk . .	chakap, bĕrchakap
taut. . .	tĕgang, chĕkang
tell . . .	*inform*—bĕri tahu ; *order, instruct* —suroh
thin . .	*lean* kurus ; *of liquids* chayer
thing . .	*article* bĕnda ; *matter*—pĕrkara ; hal
tiger . .	harimau
time . .	*(occasion)* kali ; *no time to* . . . —ta' sĕmpat
tool . .	pĕrkakas
torch (electric) .	lampu pichit
total, addition .	jumlah
tow . .	*(verb)* tunda
trade . .	*(verb)* bĕrniaga
translate . .	tĕrjĕmah, salin
tree . .	pokok kayu ; pohon kayu
trellis . .	jala–jala
trial. . .	*be tried*—kĕna dawa (dawa—*a lawsuit*)
try . . .	choba
turtle . .	pĕnyu, tuntong

U.

understand .	hĕrti

V.

valiant . .	gagah
vinegar . .	chuka
voyage . .	pĕlayaran

W.

wait . . .	nanti

wall	. .	(*masonry*) tembok; (*partition*) dinding
want	. .	mahu, hĕndak
warrior	. .	hulubalang
wash	. .	basoh
watch (wrist)	.	jam tangan
water	. .	ayer
weak (lacking firm- ness)		lĕmah
wear	. .	pakai
weather (season)	.	musim
wedge	. .	baji
well (feeling fit)	.	badan sĕdap, sĕgar
wet .	. .	basah
white	. .	puteh
wife	. .	bini, istĕri
window	. .	(*glass*) jĕndela (*Malay*) tingkap
witness	. .	saksi
wood	.	kayu
work	. .	kĕrja
workman .	.	*skilled* tukang; *unskilled* kuli *workers;* pĕkĕrja–pĕkĕrja
write	. .	tulis
wrong	. .	salah

Y.

year	. .	tahun
yellow	.	kuning

PART II

PASSAGES FOR TRANSLATION

Numbers 1 and 2 are from the *Hikyat Hang Tuah*. Number 3 is from the *Sejarah Melayu*. You will probably not find much difficulty in imitating the clear straightforward style of the originals if you re-read paragraphs 142 and 180 before you begin translating.

Numbers 4 to 8 are for colloquial style.

Numbers 9 to 12 are passages chosen from examination papers. They are more difficult. To translate adequately such a passage as No. 12 you need a deeper knowledge of the structure and the shape of the language than this book has provided. You will find all that you want in Sir Richard Winstedt's *Malay Grammar*.

A note on the English–Malay Vocabulary (pp. 364–378)

No attempt has been made to include in this vocabulary all the words that occur in these passages. Many of them will not be needed for the Malay versions, since Malay idiom will demand much re-casting of phrase and sentence. Forget the words, when you are translating ; think only of the ideas, and try to clothe them in Malay dress. The " keys " are intended as suggested versions only.

1. The Boyhood of Hang Tuah

Now Hang Mahmud's occupation was the gathering and sale of fire-wood. And Hang Tuah, as soon as his father had brought in some wood, would take an axe and split it. He would stay in front of his father's shop, splitting wood ; that was his task.

2. Four Princes

The four princes, when they saw that the captain had gone back to his boat, came out from the cleft of the rock and went back to Bukit Seguntang.   The king asked his four sons, " Where did the four of you go, that I did not see you ? "   And Sang Maniaka told him of the time when they had gone to the island and had come across a boat that had put in to take on water, and how they had not had time to run away and had hidden themselves in a certain place :   " When the captain went back, the four of us came out ".

3. A Malay Ulysses

When all was ready, Awi Dichu sailed to Semudra. As long as they were at sea, they pretended that they were traders, but when they had all arrived, they said that they were an embassy from Raja Shahru'n–nuwi.

As soon as they had landed, Awi Dichu took four valiant warriors and put them into four boxes.   And he said to the four warriors, " When you come into the presence of the Prince of Semudra, open the boxes from the inside and come out, and capture the prince ".

The boxes were locked from the inside, and then they carried them in procession, and announced that they were presents from Raja Shahru'n–nuwi.   When they came before the Prince of Semudra, the letter was read out, and very fine it sounded.   Then the boxes were sent in to him, and the four warriors who were inside them opened the boxes, came out, and seized the prince.

4. Where's Che' Hamid?

Mr. White :   Have you seen Che' Hamid ?   He promised
            to meet me here at 4 o'clock sharp.   I
            wonder where he is.

Che' Daud : I saw him half an hour ago. He was leaning against that fence there, and chatting with Tengku Ismail.

Mr. White : Where can they be, the pair of them ? I want to see Tengku Ismail, too. He promised to give me some turtles' eggs.

Che' Daud : Do you like turtles' eggs ?

Mr. White : I don't know. I've never tasted one. I haven't even seen one. That's why I asked him to bring some for me to see. He said his sisters were going out gathering them last night. They are bigger than hens' eggs, aren't they ?

Che' Daud : Yes, and they have soft shells that you can pinch.

Mr. White : Ah ! Here they come, tearing along at full speed.

Che' Daud : I expect they have been watching them play *sepak raga* on the *padang*.

5. Back at Work

Wan Chik : Hullo ! You're back again I see. Did you have a good holiday ?

Mr. Black : Fine, thank you.

Wan Chik : What did you think of Cameron Highlands ?

Mr. Black : Something like a hill-station ! There's room to walk about on it.

Wan Chik : You will be feeling the better for the rest, I am sure. You were looking pretty run down before you went.

Mr. Black : Yes, I was. I felt washed-out. Now I am quite fit and ready for work again. It's wonderful what a difference a week of cool nights has made.

Wan Chik : It certainly has been stiflingly hot here these last few months. But it ought to begin to cool down a bit now that the rainy weather has come.

Mr. Black : I hope you haven't been working yourself to death while I have been away. You know I told you to leave anything that could be left.

Wan Chik : Oh, we've managed all right. Che' Hashim has been very good, putting in extra time. So have all the clerks indeed. Even so, you will find your minute-baskets pretty full.

Mr. Black : Yes, I expect so. Well, I had better begin work on them.

6. Seeds to Plant

Mrs. Brown : I've just received the parcel of seeds that I ordered last week.

Gardener : Are they ones that will do well in this country, ma'am ? Some plants don't like this hot climate.

Mrs. Brown : These are not from England. They are from Ipoh ; and they are all prize varieties so you will be particularly careful with them, won't you ?

Gardener : Yes, I will. Where do you want them put, ma'am ?

Mrs. Brown : Well, I thought it would be rather nice if we had red balsams along both sides of the drive this time, for a change. We have had xinnias for several months now.

Gardener : Which packet is that ?

Mrs. Brown : This green packet. I'll write it on the outside. Can you read romanised Malay ? No ? I'll try to write it in Jawi then, but it won't be very beautiful writing, I'm afraid. I am only just learning . . . Can you read that, Omar ?

Gardener : " Red flowers, along the drive ". Yes, I can read that. What is in the yellow packet ?

Mrs. Brown : Those are petunias.

Gardener : We have those already.

Mrs. Brown : Yes, I know. But these are particularly fine ones. I want these for the porch.

Gardener : Do you want them in pots, ma'am ?

Mrs. Brown : No, not in pots. I want you to make some long boxes as you did once before. Do you remember ?

Gardener : With stands underneath them, you mean ?

Mrs. Brown : Yes, about three feet high. Then the flowers trail over like a curtain.

Gardener : I shall want some money to buy the wood.

Mrs. Brown : Isn't there any left over from that potting shed that you built the other day ?

Gardener : Yes, there is some. But I doubt if it will be enough.

Mrs. Brown : You had better get some more, in any case. I want you to put up a trellis outside the windows, for moon flowers. Their scent in the evening is a delight.

Gardener : Very well, ma'am. I'll take these seeds now and put them in boxes, as soon as I have got the soil ready.

7. The Malay Lesson

Mr. McNeil : Come in, enche'. How are you this evening ?

Che' Abdul Rahman : I'm all right, thank you. I am sorry I am a bit late. It came on to rain very heavily as I was coming along.

Mr. McNeil : Your coat doesn't seem to be wet. You managed to shelter somewhere, by the roadside ?

Che' Abdul Rahman : Yes ; luckily there was a thick leafy tree about a quarter of a mile from here. Otherwise I should surely have been soaked through. When the rain had eased off a little, a friend of mine happened to pass, with an umbrella, and I shared it.

Mr. McNeil : Do sit down. I have an apology to offer, too. I haven't managed to find time to do that piece of translation into Malay.

Che' Abdul Rahman : They tell me there is an important case on at the Court. I expect you have been very busy ?

Mr. McNeil : Yes, I have been busy at Court, but at home, too, I have had an extra bit of work. The P.W.D. workmen are going to renew the floor-boards in my bedroom, and just now I had to remove all the books on the shelves.

Che' Abdul Rahman : White ants, I suppose ?

Mr. McNeil :　No. Fire. Didn't you hear ? Last week, half the house caught fire. I must have left a cigarette end on the dressing table I think.

Che' Abdul Rahman :　I didn't hear anything about it. On what day was it ?

Mr. McNeil :　On Wednesday evening, at ten o'clock.

Che' Abdul Rahman :　Ah ! That's how I didn't hear about it. I had fever on that day. I was aching in every joint.

Mr. McNeil :　Are you all right now ?

Che' Abdul Rahman :　A little better, thank you. But I am still stiff.

Mr. McNeil :　We had better make it a short lesson then.

Che' Abdul Rahman :　Oh, it doesn't matter. Let's de a bit of reading. What is it you are reading ? *Hang Tuah* isn't it ?

8. Crocodile Shooting.

Che' Saleh :　If you are free on Friday, come up river crocodile–shooting, will you ?

Mr. Smith :　H'm. Don't forget what you Malays say. At long last the cleverest hunter finds himself in the crocodile's mouth.

Che' Saleh :　Oh, that was in the old days. When they used a floating line. Nowadays we use guns. I have arranged to go up–river with Wan Mahmud, this Friday. They say there is a fierce crocodile near Tanjong Ru.

Mr. Smith : All right. Though, as a matter of fact, I have promised my wife that I'll go to Singapore with her. I don't know what she wants to do there. You had better ask her, and persuade her to come (say " go "). She is always saying that she would like to go on a crocodile expedition. Here's her chance.

Che' Saleh : Very well. But if Mrs. Smith is coming with us, we had better hire Haji Ibrahim's motor–boat. We can tow Wan Mahmud's boat. They say that the fierce brute often suns himself near Tanjong Ru. If we are lucky, we'll get a shot at him while he is basking. If we shoot when he comes up in mid–stream, even if we get him, it will be four or five days before the body floats up, and we know that he is dead.

Mr. Smith : Is it a big one?

Che' Saleh : It is ! And a daring one, too, according to report. Sometimes he surfaces close to a boat. Don't be alarmed ! Haji Ibrahim's motor–boat is a fair size. Even if it gets a lash from the tail, it won't capsize.

Mr. Smith : Right you are then, Saleh. I'll be seeing you tomorrow.

9. (*A note from a P.W.D. official to a Malay overseer.*)

Your workmen, Mat, are often late assembling. Perhaps you do not go yourself and take the names before work begins. You should always be present in the early morning and report those workmen who come late. I will find others to take their place. I see, too, that there are three or four men on the check roll who are frequently absent on account of sickness. You had better get rid of them. I want the work done before the end of the year. At present it looks as if it will be six months before it is finished.

10. (*Extract from a letter written by a District Officer to a Major Chief, with reference to a petition received by the latter from the inhabitants of a village.*)

Their complaints, therefore, are only half true. The land was given out originally—some ten years back—for rice cultivation only, and the titles bear this condition plainly stated. The owners know this perfectly well. They are not stupid. Yet you can see for yourself that coconuts and other fruit trees have been planted all along the road, two or three chains deep, and in one or two places, houses have been erected in the middle of the rice fields. I hope you will help me by telling the villagers that they must plant rice, or their lands will be resumed by Government.

11. Notice concerning foodstuffs

In consequence of reports received by the District Officer that many persons are hoarding food far in excess of their needs, and because of the shortness of such foodstuffs, it is found necessary to lay down the following regulations to ensure that all shall receive enough food to maintain health.

1. No one is allowed to keep in his house more rice (sugar, flour, etc.) than is sufficient for 3 days consumption.

2. The amounts considered sufficient for 3 days consumption are laid down in the schedule below.

3. Anyone having in his possession more than the amounts laid down must at once inform the officer

appointed to supervise, who is :—Wan Suleiman bin Wan Harun.

4. The officer in question has power to enter and search any house to enforce this regulation.

5. The officer is also empowered to seize any excess foodstuffs which he may find.

Penalty

An person failing to comply with the above order, or who obstructs the officer appointed to carry it out, shall be liable to summary arrest and trial.

Exceptions

The following are exempted from the operation of the above order.

1. Persons who, by reason of their occupation, accumulate stocks of foodstuffs, e.g. wholesale merchants, rice–millers, etc.

2. Persons who are engaged in growing rice, and store it normally.

12.

The Malays, in my opinion, are deserving of more credit than any other members of the expedition. They were not in receipt of pay and merely accompanied me at my request, leaving their wives and children, their homes, and all the things which a Malay values ; and yet, not only did I never hear a grumble or a protest, but both the Chiefs and people were ever ready to perform even more than was asked of them.   Wet, or dry, hot or cold, weary for want of sleep and tired by prolonged exertion, they were still ever ready to answer to my call urging them to fresh exertions.   To those who regard the Malays as an indolent and lazy people, the manner in which they worked would come as a revelation.

PART III

KEYS FOR EXERCISES

Keys for Chapter III

Exercise 4.

1. Long bones, *or* The long bones, *or* A long bone, *or* The long bone. 2. High chairs *or* The high chairs etc. (n.b. Where the sense permits, any of these phrases may be translated in any of the four ways shown. From this point onwards one rendering only will be given.) 3. White cups. 4. A dirty room. 5. A large courtyard. 6. Clean saucers. 7. A small school. 8 A long nose. 9. A soft voice. 10. Black hair. 11. Red lips. 12. Sour fruit. 13. A high roof. 14. A low wall. 15. Green leaves. 16. Blue flowers. 17. A fine picture. 18. A long neck. 19. A pretty face. 20. A high forehead. 21. Dirty hands. 22. A black board. 23. Small bowls. 24. Short nails. 25. A full basket. 26. Black wood. 27. White plates. 28. A long beard. 29. A green floor. 30. Red cups. 31. These books. 32. An empty house. 33. This table. 34. That leather (*or* skin). 35. Those planks.

Exercise 5.

1. Papan puteh. 2. Mangkok kosong. 3. Tangan puteh. 4. Kuku bĕrseh. 5. Tali pendek. 6. Bakul bĕsar. 7. Kayu kĕras. 8. Gambar kĕchil. 9. Daun bĕsar. 10. Sĕkolah bĕrseh. 11. Buku bĕsar. 12. Pinggan biru. 13. Janggut pendek. 14. Buah hijau. 15. Lantai bĕrseh. 16. Tembok (*or* dinding) tinggi. 17. Bumbong panjang. 18. Papan puteh. 19. Rumah tinggi. 20. Batu bĕsar. 21. Buah manis. 22. Bunga chantek. 23. Lĕngan kurus. 24. Bangku rĕndah

25. Pipi gĕmok. 26. Bilek kĕchil. 27. Bakul kosong. 28. Lantai kotor. 29. Mulut kĕchil. 30. Mangkok merah. 31. Muka ini. 32. Muka itu. 33. Kĕpala itu. 34. Meja ini. 35. Mata itu.

Exercise 6.

1. A high bench (high benches etc.) 2. The wall is low. (Note that this cannot be translated " a low wall "). 3. The room is dirty. 4. A large school *or* The school is large. 5. A small house *or* The house is small. 6. The house is clean. 7. This rope is long *or* This is a long rope. 8. Pretty flowers. 9. A large mouth. 10. The plates are dirty. 11. The fruit is sour. 12. A low roof.

Exercise 7.

1. Bunga puteh. 2. Buah masam *or* Buah–itu masam *or* Masam buah itu *or* Masam–lah buah itu. 3. Bumbong itu tinggi, etc. 4. Rumah elok. 5. Gambar itu bĕsar, etc. 6. Tangan kotor. 7. Buku itu biru, etc. 8. Lantai bĕrseh. 9. Bakul itu kosong, etc. 10. Lĕngan panjang. 11. Kĕrusi itu rĕndah, etc. 12. Buah merah.

Exercise 8.

1. The white wall is low *or* The white walls are low *or* The white wall was low *or* The white walls were low. 2. The long table is low, *etc.* 3. That room is small. 4. This house is high. 5. The green basket is empty. 6. The red fruit is sweet. 7. That's a long cord, *or* That cord is long. 8. The black book is large. 9. The small leaves are green. 10. This cup is empty. 11. A fine large basket. 12. The big basket is a fine one.

Exercise 9.

1. Rumah tinggi bĕsar *or* Rumah tinggi itu bĕsar *or* Bĕsar rumah tinggi itu. 2. Buah hijau masam *or* **Masam**

buah hijau *or* Masam–lah buah hijau. 3. Daun hijau lagi kĕchil. 4. Buku hitam itu kĕchil *or* Kĕchil buku hitam itu. 5. Halaman bĕsar lagi bĕrseh. 6. Bunga biru itu chantek *or* Chantek bunga biru itu *or* Chantek-lah bunga biru itu. 7. Tali panjang itu puteh *or* Puteh tali panjang itu. 8. Mangkok puteh itu kĕchil *or* Kĕchil mangkok puteh itu. 9. Rumah itu kĕchil lagi rĕndah. 10. Rumah yang kĕchil lagi rĕndah. 11. Tangan panjang lagi kurus *or* Tangan yang panjang lagi kurus. 12. Tali ini biru *or* Biru tali ini.

Keys for Chapter IV

Exercise 10.

1. My (elder) brother is ill. [Note : A Malay cannot help specifying " elder " or " younger ", unless he uses the more general term *saudara* (relative)].

2. Elephants' ears are big *or* An elephant's ears are big, (Note : " The elephant's ears are big" would usually be " *Tĕlinga gajah itu bĕsar* ".

3. The (or that) dog's skin is dirty.

4. This bird's head is small.

5. Don't eat that bread.

6. Ahmad's father is tall, with a long neck.

7. This is the carpenter's house.

8. That broken chair is mine.

9. Husain's dog is small, but his monkey is big.

10. Meriam's child is fat, her mother is thin.

11. Fatimah is Hasan's (elder) sister.

12. River water is fresh.

13. Mat has stomach ache.

14. The child fell and broke his tooth (lit. his tooth broke).

15. There are baskets on the bench. (Note : A possible translation would be " There is a basket . .", but for this a Malay would usually say " *sa–biji bakul* " or " *sa–buah bakul.*"   See par. 48.)

16. There are some books in the box.

17. That sick child is Zainab's little brother (or sister.)

18. That blue bowl is large.

19. Those yellow coffee cups are mine.

20. This bread is very hard. (Note. The " very " of the English is used as an equivalent for the emphatic position of the adjective, which is further emphasized by the particle *–lah*.)

Exercise 11.

1. Bumbong rumah itu tinggi.

2. Anjing kěchil itu hitam.

3. Ada lěmbu bětina di–dalam kěbun itu.

4. Anak kuching Ahmad gěmok.   Dia suka minum susu.

5. Jangan minum ayer sungai.

6. Budak pěrěmpuan itu sakit kěpala.

7. Chawan kopi yang hijau itu sudah pěchah (Note. In this sentence the balance is better if " yang " is used.   If the words had been " chawan hijau ' instead of "chawan kopi", the shorter form "Chawan hijau itu sudah pěchah " would have sufficed.

8. Tělinga anjing itu panjang, ekor–nya pendek.

9. Mangkok gula itu rětak.

10. Leher gajah pendek.

11. Rumput itu hijau.

12. Tali pinggan sahaya sudah putus.

13. Itu anak (pěrěmpuan) tukang kěbun.

14. Meja panjang yang puteh ini tidak (*or* ta') běrseh.

15. Bulan itu bulat.

Keys for Chapter V

Exercise 12.

1. 32.
2. 18.
3. 45.
4. 2,691.
5. 10,000,000.
6. 30,000.
7. 700,000.
8. There are three birds on the roof.
9. In the box there are two green bowls.
10. That Chinese bought a row of ten (concrete) houses.
11. The gardener is lighting a cigarette.
12. I bought twenty cigarettes just now.
13. Husain's father wants to sell his car.
14. There are two cars under the house.
15. Is the baker there ?—Yes (lit. He is present)—Buy two loaves.
16. My brother bought a knife, three rulers and two long needles.
17. There are some fine pineapples at that shop. How many do you want to buy ?
18. Just now there came a Malay, wanting to sell two sarongs.
19. I have a large house in Burma.
20. Are there any rifles ?—Yes. (lit. " There are.")—How many ?—Twelve.
21. In the garden there is a (certain) coconut palm.
22. I want a slice of bread.
23. How many eggs are there in the basket ?—Fifteen.
24. My (younger) sister (or brother) is going to write a letter.

25. There are two or three sheets of paper on the round table.
26. Fatimah is sewing a jacket, Sharifah is reading. (Note that Malays usually say " reading a book ").
27. My father wants to buy a coat.
28. There is a black cat on top of the steps of that wooden house.
29. My (elder) sister wants three sheets of writing paper.
30. Hashim is looking for a banana leaf to use as an umbrella. (Note this conversational use of " buat ").

Exercise 13.

1. Sa–bĕlas. 2. Ĕmpat puloh lima. 3. Tiga ratus satu. 4. Lima ribu tujoh ratus. 5. Dĕlapan ribu dua ratus ĕmpat–belas. 6. Dua puchok jarum. 7. Sa-orang Mĕlayu. 8. Gajah lima–bĕlas ekor *or* Lima–bĕlas ekor gajah. 9. Tukang kĕbun. 10. Sa–orang tukang kayu. 11. Tukang sa–orang. 12. Sĕnapang tujoh-bĕlas puchok. 13. Tujoh buah kĕreta lĕmbu. 14. Ada rokok ?—Ada sĕmbilan batang. 15. Budak itu ada batu dua biji. 16. Ada sa–lai kĕrtas di–atas meja (yang) rĕndah itu. 17. Bapa saya 'nak mĕnjual sa–kĕping tanah. 18. Abang Aminah ada sa–buah kĕdai di–Singapura. 19. Saya hĕndak jarum dua tiga puchok. 20. Bĕli baju puteh dua hĕlai. 21. Ada budak ĕnam orang di–bawah rumah. 22. Bapa–nya kĕrja tukang gigi. 23. Ada pokok kĕlapa tiga–puloh batang di–kĕbun itu. 24. Jangan jual kĕreta. 25. Bĕrapa sen sa–biji buah nanas itu ? 26. Tikus makan roti.

Keys for Chapter VI
Exercise 14.

1. At the edge of the river there is a fine house.
2. Push the long chair behind the table.

3. Once there were three mice who lived in a large box.
4. Where is your father ?   He went out just now, he was going to the market.
5. After his meal he went to bed.
6. There is a large court–yard in front of the house.
7. The water in the tub is dirty.   Throw it away.
8. Before that, I lived at Raub.   (A commoner form of the Malay sentence would be " Dahulu, saya tinggal di–Raub ".)
9. Pull the table to the side of the bed.
10. Good morning.   How are you ?—All right (thank you.)—Where are you going ?—I'm going to town.

Exercise 15.

1. Anjing itu lari ka–bĕlakang bangsal (*or* ka–balek bangsal).
2. Di–tĕngah bilek ada sa–buah meja yang rĕndah.
3. Rumah itu dĕkat dĕngan sungai.
4. Saya nanti sampai pukul tujoh.
5. Dia suka makan pisang.
6. Sĕkolah itu bĕrtĕntang dĕngan Pĕjabat Tanah.
7. Kasut dia (lĕbeh) bĕsar daripada kasut saya.
8. Ada dua–puloh lima buah rumah di–pulau itu.
9. Di–mana bukul ?—Di–atas kĕrusi.
10. Bangku itu di–antara pintu dĕngan dinding.

Keys for Chapter VII

Exercise 16.

1. Aishah's three children have fever.
2. Yesterday I received two letters.
3. Wait.   In a minute or two I am going to town.
4. He is walking very slowly.   Perhaps he has a sore foot.

5. He often comes to my house.

6. By the side of the road there is an empty house. On each side of it there is a concrete ditch.

7. Fold those sarongs carefully, and put them away in the box (*or* Fold . . . before you put them away).

8. I haven't any paper. How am I to write a letter ?

9. This thread isn't very strong. It keeps breaking.

10. My needle's broken. How am I going to sew?

Exercise 17.

1. Sĕkarang ini dia dudok di–bangku di–tĕpi sungai.

2. Jarang saya pĕrgi ka–Pulau Pinang.

3. Jangan jalan tĕrlampau dĕras. Ada parit sa–bĕlah mĕnyabĕlah jalan.

4. Baharu sahaja dia pulang.

5. Ini–lah kĕdai tĕmpat saya bĕli ikan.

6. Kĕnapa meja ini rapat dĕngan dinding ? Tarek ka–tĕngah sikit.

7. Bĕlah kayu sa–kĕping ini buat baji dua biji.

8. Jangan bising. Saya mahu tidor.

9. Saya ta' tahu tĕmpat dia tinggal.

10. Kalmarin saya bĕri dia kain sa–panjang ini. Hari ini dia minta lagi pula (see par. 149).

Keys for Chapter VIII
Exercise 18.

1. That pineapple isn't ripe. You had better not eat it.

2. This cupboard is very rickety. Don't move it in case the legs are rotten.

3. The penghulu's house is not far from here.

4. Don't use hot water, or the colour will fade.—It isn't hot, it's only luke–warm.

5. Don't let the child play with the scissors ; he'll cut himself.

6. This morning I got up at six o'clock, before the dew had disappeared.

7. Halijah was caught in the rain. Her *baju* is soaking wet.

8. I have never been up in an aircraft.

9. This lamp is broken. We shall have to get another.

10. Is this a coconut palm ?—No it's a betel–nut. The fronds of a coconut palm are longer.

11. Put the box away in the cupboard. There's no need to open it.

12. Is this Indian dumb ?—It isn't that he's dumb, but he can't speak Malay.

13. Where's your brother ? I want him to go and get some fish. Give him this fifty–cents. Tell him not to loiter. (Note that Malay can use " jangan " of a third person.)

14. Don't be late in the morning. There's a lot of work to do. The head clerk is ill.

15. It's wet. We shan't be able to play football.

16. He hasn't come. Had we better wait for him, or not ?

17. 'Long's mother told him not to bathe in the river. The river water near the village is not clean.

18. It's getting dark. We had better go home.

Exercise 19.

1. Saya ta' suka makan buah yang masam.

2. Ta'ada buaya di–dalam sungai ini.

3. Ta'payah basoh baju itu. Bukan–nya kotor. Sa–jam dua sahaja saya pakai.

4. Dia bodoh běnar—Bukan bodoh, dia malas.

5. Dia minta duit. Baik saya běri–kah tidak ?

6. Meja ini ta'jadi. Rěndah sangat (*or* Těrlampau rěndah) Kěna chari lain.

7. Sudah dia datang ?—Saya bĕlum tahu. Nanti saya pĕrgi tanya kĕrani.

8. Saya hĕndak buat bangku. Ada kayu ? (*or* Ada-kah kayu ?)—Ta' ada.

9. Saya baharu datang ka–pĕkan ini. Jadi bĕlum tahu nama orang kĕdai.

10. Jam tangan saya rosak. Ta' apa. Saya bĕri pinjam jam saya. Ada satu lagi.

Keys for Chapter IX

Exercise 20.

1. Good morning Haji.—Good morning. I haven't seen you for a long time. (lit. What news ?—Good news. For a long time we have not met.)

2. Put out the light, will you, ayah. I'm drowsy, I want to go to sleep (*padam* used colloquially for *padamkan*).

3. (Speaking to Omar). Throw away those plants that are dead, and put others in their place.

4. ('Ngah to his father). Don't be angry (with me.) I didn't hear you call.

5. (A chauffeur speaking). Are you going to call at Mr. Smith's?—No. I haven't time today. You can take a note to him tomorrow.

6. (To a Malay). Have you brought the clay?—Yes.

7. (To the tailor). Have you cut that yellow material, derzi ?—Yes, madam.

8. (To a Chinese). Can you meet me at the edge of the *padang* at 3 o'clock this afternoon. Yes, I can.

9. Put the bath ready, amah. Don't make it very hot.

10. We had better go home quickly. Mother told us not to be late.

11. (To a kathi). Will you wait for me, please, at the judge's house.

12. (To Mahmud). When did you first know ?—I've only just heard about it.

13. (To a Chinese). Is it a coconut estate that you are going to buy or a rubber estate ?

14. (To a haji). Do you know Tuan Sayid Shaikh's brother? No, I don't.

15. These flowers are faded. You had better throw them away. Are there any others?—Yes, there are.

16. You must go down to the village, Hasan, and get some kerosene.—Very well, madam. (A request or order is often acknowledged in this way. Cf. Ex 21.9.)

17. Hai there ! Did you see an Indian go by just now, on a bicycle ?—No, I haven't noticed one.

Exercise 21.

1. Apa khabar tuan haji ? Tuan datang pagi–pagi bĕnar.

2. Panggil orang salah—Dia ada di–sini—Awak dudok di–mana ? — Saya dudok di–sabĕrang. — Bĕrapa umor awak ?—'Lapan–bĕlas tahun—Bapa awak ada lagi ?—Ada.

3. Suroh kuki masok—Tabek, mem—Tabek kuki. Kuki sudah dapat ikan di–pasar ?—Tidak. Mem suroh bĕli daging.

4. Boleh–kah ĕnche' tolong bĕri tahu di–mana rumah tuan hakim ?

5. Timah mahu minum ?—Mahu—Timah suka minum ayer limau ?—Suka. (*Timah* is an abbreviation of *Fatimah*. Nearly all girls' names end in " ah ", and they are frequently shortened to the last syllable only, e.g. " Che' Jah " for " Halijah ").

6. Rumah elok.   Těntu taukeh dudok lama di–někěri Mělayu?   Sělalu taukeh pulang někěri China ?

7. Mat jangan chakap děras.   Těrlampau payah hěrti*.   Saya baharu datang ka–někěri ini.

8. Di–mana Che' Jid?—Dia bělum bangun lagi.

9. Hasan boleh simpan kěreta sěkarang.—Tuan.

10. Apa khabar datok?   Datok ka–mana ?—Saya hěndak ka–rumah chuchu—Jauh–kah,   rumah–nya?—Ta' běrapa jauh.   Běrtěntang bětul děngan masjid.

Keys for Chapter X
Exercise 22.

1. Although you are thirsty, you had better not drink that muddy river water.   Wait a bit, perhaps we shall come to a spring.

2. The mangosteen has a delicious taste.   (Note that *rasa–nya* is not used impersonally here).

3. I feel I am in for a bout of fever.   I had better go home at once.

4. Poor child!   His parents died before he was a year old.

5. How many hours would it take to go upstream from here to Pantai Janggus?—About an hour and a half, I should think. (see par. 186).

6. After going downstream for a whole day, he came to a large and populous village.

7. Isahak likes to sit by the door.   When a car passes he hurriedly writes down its number.   Then in the evening, before he goes to bed, he counts the number of the cars that have passed.

8. The fish wasn't very tasty, Ah Heng.   Next time, put a little mace in; that will improve it.

---

* Better: *payah měnghěrti*. See par 119c.

9. Rattan is pliable. It is easy to bend it, difficult to cut it, and impossible to snap it.

10. May I borrow a few chairs, please? It doesn't matter whether they are big or little.

11. The cat is chasing a mouse. When it has caught it, it will eat it.

12. Last night there was a storm. I am told that two sampans went down, behind Pulau Bintang.

13. The old man has stopped near the door of the mosque. He is going inside, I expect.

14. He lit a cigarette and then (at once) threw it away.

15. He is walking slowly. There is something wrong with his foot, by the look of it (*or*, It looks as if . . .)

16. The *chiku* fruit looks like a potato. (Note that *rupa–nya* is not used impersonally here.)

Exercise 23.

1. Běrapa jauh dari masjid sampai ka–pantai ?— Agak–nya lima batu pěrgi balek.

2. Khabar–nya ada banyak buaya di–hulu sungai itu.

3. Esok jikalau tidak hujan kita mudek sa–batu dua.

4. Běrěnang di–dalam ayer masin, ringan badan rasa–nya.

5. Kata–nya (lit. " the saying of him ") dia ta' hěndak nanti lagi, takut bapa–nya marah.

6. Saya mahu pinjam dua tiga ringgit—'Nak buat apa ?—'Nak běli papan, 'nak měmbaiki sampan. Jikalau tidak, karam–lah.

7. Awak děngar bunyi itu tadi ?—Bunyi apa ?— Sapěrti bunyi kapal těrbang—Ta' děngar.

8. Pada suatu hari sa–ekor harimau minum ayer daripada mata ayer itu, langsong mati.

9. Ribut sa-malam, agak-nya. Ada tiga ĕmpat-puloh batang pĕlĕpah nyior 'dah gugor.

10. Ini rumah tĕmpat saya tinggal masa (see ftn. 18) saya kĕrja mata-mata.

Keys for Chapter XI

Exercise 24.

1. Mangosteens taste better than chikus.

2. Don't be frightened. I was only pretending.

3. In Che 'Nah's uncle's garden there are many sorts of fruit trees. She loves collecting the windfalls.

4. Of the elephant, the tiger, and the monkey, the elephant is the biggest.

5. In days gone by it was only those of princely rank who used yellow umbrellas.

6. You must finish this job within two months at the very latest.

7. The threads of a spider's web are exceedingly fine.

8. At Cheng Huat Hin's shop there are tins of cigarettes of various brands.

9. His shop is the largest in that town (or village).

10. Lift this basket carefully. There are all sorts of fragile glass things in it that would easily get broken.

11. If you have a cough you had better take some medicine.—It isn't a cough that I have. It's only a bit of a temperature.

12. Last night the waves were mountains high. The boats didn't go out.

13. Have you ever seen such a long gold chain ? (Note that in Malay you must say "a chain as long as this," i.e. the second term of comparison must be expressed. An alternative construction would be " . . . *rantai yang bagini panjang* ".)

14. It feels cold. The coconut fronds are quivering. I think there is going to be a storm.

Exercise 25.

1. Ada dua ekor kambing di–padang. Kambing Pa 'Man agak–nya.

2. Rumah Che' Su elok dari pada rumah saya (or lĕbeh elok . . .)

3. Jimat–lah sikit. Kĕrtas ini tĕrlampau nipis.

4. Sorong kĕreta rapat dĕngan tembok.

5. Ada–kah pĕrnah tengok pisang (or buah pisang) sa–bĕsar ini ? (or sama bĕsar dĕngan ini).

6. Ada bĕrjĕnis–jĕnis bunga di–kĕbun.

7. Jikalau budak lapar, bĕri dia sa–dikit roti dĕngan mĕntega.

8. Jikalau mahu chuti besok, kĕrani hĕndak tulis nama (or " sain ") di–dalam buku di–ofis bĕsar.

9. Sudah angkat pinggan kotor, baharu–lah bawa kopi.

10. Papan ini tĕrlampau nipis.—Yang ini jadi–kah ?— Tidak, hĕndak yang lĕbeh tĕbal lagi. Kĕna chari dalam bangsal.

Keys for Chapter XII

Exercise 26.

1. Every day Ali goes fishing.

2. I was surprised to hear about it.

3. Seedlings that are not doing well should be thrown out.

4. One day a dog was wandering about, now here, now there, when suddenly he saw a piece of meat.

5. The medicine that they gave tasted bitter.

6. The goat ate every single one of the flowering plants.

7. In England, the ponds are frozen in the winter time.

8. All children are pleased to get presents.

9. Where can one buy cigarettes? [Notice the difference between this sentence *dapat běli* or *dapat di-běli*—simple verb, no stress on the doer, and Example 5 in par. 120.]

10. In this bag there are two hundred and thirty-four monkey-nuts. If I take away a hundred and seventy-six, how many will be left ?

Exercise 27.

1. Dia pandai měnari.

2. Saya jěmu měnyurat.

3. Suka hati ěmak mělihat anak-nya.

4. Budak itu tahu měnjahit.

5. Dia pěrgi ka-pasar hěndak měmběli ikan.

6. Kalmarin datang sa-orang Hindu minta kěrja. (Note that in the word *minta* the *mě-* is already present in the " m ". The literary form of the simple verb is *pinta*, but the form *měminta* is also commonly used).

7. Ini-lah pěti těmpat měnyimpan chamchah teh.

8. Jangan takut měngaku salah.

9. Dia pěrgi měnchari umpan.

10. Dia yang měněbang pohon kayu ru itu.

11. Orang pěngail itu lambat měngěrti (or měnghěrti).

12. Mudah měmotong roti děngan měmakai pisau yang tajam. (lit. " with using ". In conversation such a sentence would be more likely to take the following shape : "Ada pisau yang tajam, mudah měmotong roti ".)

Keys for Chapter XIII

Exercise 28.

(a) When the buffalo heard this, he came and slid his horns under the tree trunk, and lifted it. The crocodile was freed, and suddenly, without a moment's warning, he seized the leg of the buffalo who had done him this service.

(Then) the buffalo said sorrowfully, " Oh, how could you have the heart to do such a thing, Sir Lasher! I do you a good turn, and you pay me back with evil. A fine nature, yours is!

Now all this had been seen by Sir Mousedeer (or, leave it as "Sang Kanchil"). At once he leapt on the trunk, exclaiming: " Hi! Sir Buffalo, you foolish creature, your enormous body (lit. the size of your body) is not much use if you yourself have no wits. Haven't you heard that all creatures in this world, men and beasts, repay acts of courtesy and kindliness by evil and cruel deeds ?

(b) 1. di–děngar . The passive form, as is usual in the written language (for the 3rd person) when there is no stress on the subject. The point is, that the crocodile's words were heard.

2. datang . one of the intransitive verbs that never take " mě- " (see par. 114(b))

3. měnyusupkan from " susup ". The " mě- " derivative used participially, ". . . came and ".

4. lalu . used to join two verbs having the same subject, when one action follows immediately after the other.

5. lěpas–lah . simple verb, passive.

6. langsong . used because the second action followed immediately on the first.

7. měnangkap . a finite verb : connecting the action with the agent. The crocodile deliberately caught the buffalo.

8. běrkata . verbal use of *běr–*.

9. měmbuat . stressing the agent. " *I* do a good action ".

10. balas . . not stressing the agent. " and this is the return ". *Měmbalas* might have been expected here.

11. sěraya . . used to join two actions that are almost simultaneous (par. 97 (d))

12. těrsangat . " *těr–* " intensive.

Exercise 29.

1. Ada orang měnaroh rakit di–kampong ini ?—Ada, Che 'Ngah baharu lagi měmbuat.—Barang kali dia boleh měnggalahkan saya ka–hilir jěram itu ?—Agak saya těntu dia boleh. Biar saya tanya.

2. Awak jangan lewat esok. Patut kita sampai di–Kuala Sěrau sa–bělum mula bichara itu. Sa–lewat–lewat–nya sa–bělum saksi itu di–panggil. Harap saya bichara itu di–putuskan děngan sěgěra.

Keys for Chapter XIV
Exercise 30.

When the host (lit. "master of the house") caught sight of Pa Kadok coming, he said " Well ! I am sorry indeed to see you arriving so tired. (lit. There is pity in my heart from seeing you arrive utterly weary.) There's not a scrap left. (Lit. not even any one thing more which is.) Everything is finished. You *are* an unlucky creature, Pa Kadok ! " " Well ! " said Pa Kadok when he heard this, " That's that. It can't be helped." (Lit. " What can be done ?) It's just my luck ".

Then he paddled downstream again, in order to get back to the house where they were killing a buffalo, but the incoming tide was flowing strongly. Pa Kadok paddled with all his might, pushing against the rising tide, in the full heat of the day, and hungry and thirsty, but because of his stupidity he would not call at his own house, but went straight on, down–stream, meaning to make a dive for any of the buffalo that was left. Not until the tide was almost on the turn did he reach the house, in the late afternoon, and all the guests were just on the point of going down to the river to make their way (lit. " paddle their way ") home, because the feast was at an end.

Notes

1. těrlihat . . *těr*– for " accidental accomplishment ".

2. akan . . . itu . Note that the *itu* qualifies the whole phrase.

3. Pa Kadok ini . There have been several instances of this idiomatic use of *ini* in the conversations, often with the feeling of " You're a fine one, you are ! "

4. sahajakan . Usually means " to do a thing purposely ", but here the word retains its adverbial force. Cf. the *–kan* suffix with a few conjunctions, e.g. *asalkan*— provided that ".

5. hasrat, etc. . Lit. " the desire of him, he intended to reach ". *Měndapatkan* nearly always, as here, in the sense of " going to get " or " going to meet ". *Di-*

dapati usually in the sense of "finding something to be . . ." e.g. *Di–dapati–nya pĕti itu tĕrkunchi*. "He found that the box was locked".

6. ayer . . . surut . Note the exact repetition of phrasing.

7. asar rĕndah . "Late afternoon"; See par. 199c. *Rĕndah* (low) refers to the sun.

Exercise 31.

1. Ĕnche' orang Kuala Lumpor ?—Tidak. Saya lahir (*or* dzahir) di–Kuala Lipis.—Kuala Lipis itu di–Pahang, bukan ?—Di–Pahang. Mak bapa saya pindah bila saya kĕchil lagi, lĕbeh kurang tiga tahun umor saya masa itu. Kaum saya banyak tinggal di–Pahang. Sĕlalu saya pĕrgi chuti ka–sana.

2. Elok bĕnar pagi ini. Untong kita bangun pagi–pagi. Tengok gunong itu baharu nampak kĕmonchak–nya di–saput awan. Bĕrapa tinggi tĕmpat ini agak–nya ? Dĕngar pula bunyi wak-wak itu, bukan main hingar–nya.

Keys for Chapter XV

Exercise 32.

Then Sang Si–Perba saw a very wide estuary, and he asked the navigating officer, "What is the name of this river ?" The officer answered, "This is Kuala Kuantan; many people live here". The king said, "Let us go upstream to the head–waters of this river". And all the people were without (drinking) water. There was no place from which they could get water. (Note the *kĕ . . . an* derivative, used here as the equivalent of an English finite verb : "They lacked". Note also the *mĕ–* derivative used to show purpose : "a place for getting water ".) Then Sang Si–Perba ordered (them to make) a circle of rattan as big as a large shield, and it was placed on the sea. Then the king got into a small boat in order to dip his feet into the salt water within the rattan circle. By the decree of God Most High, because of the blessing that rested on the king, being the descendant of Alexander the Great, the salt water became fresh. The people filled all their water vessels. And even to this day (note the phrase : *datang sĕkarang ini*) that water is fresher than the salt water opposite Muara Sapat.

Exercise 33.

1. Pakai pĕrcha kain ini buat chuchi kĕreta. Lĕpas itu basoh, kĕmudian sidai jemor.

2. Mat bĕrduit pula sĕkarang. Sudah di–tĕbus butang mas–nya. 'Tapi bĕlum habis bulan ini tĕntu masok pajak lagi. Mat itu boros. Dalam itu pun baik juga budak–nya. (Note the phrase *dalam itu pun*— even so.)

Keys for Chapter XVI

Exercise 34.

Chief Batin Alam returned, and he saw that there was a man, asleep, at the end of the verandah. Then he asked the princess Dayang Nuramah : " Who is that man, sleeping there ? " and she answered : " Brother Sulong, he came back just now ". Then Awang Sulong started up from his sleep and Chief Batin Alam asked him, " Have you finished making the boat ? " Awang Sulong answered : " Yes, it is finished, in accordance with my lord's command ". Then in wrath said Batim Alam, " You ought to have shown me your workmanship ".

Then the Lord Chieftain Batin Alam ran and seized an axe, and went to the river–side to cut to bits the boat that Awang Sulong had made. He dealt one blow and

the smiling figureheads, of which there were several,
so far from being spoilt, became even more beautiful.
The axe broke in his hand and he ran back to the palace.
got a long adze in its place, and raced back to the boat.
Again he dealt a blow at the smiling figureheads. He
wore himself out, his hatchet snapped—but the boat, so
far from being ruined, grew ever more fine to look upon.

Exercise 35.

1. Suroh dia bělikan saya lampu pichit. Chari yang
   běsar. Saya 'nak pakai bila kita dudok di-bukit.

2. Chat ta' běrapa banyak yang tinggal. Agak-nya
   ta' chukup. Panjang pagar itu. Barang kali
   chukup-chukup juga. Agak saya chat itu boleh
   kita chayerkan. Ambil minyak tarbantin. Ada
   dalam botol chuka di-pěnjuru almari, těmpat pasu
   bunga itu.

Key for Chapter XVII

Exercise 36.

Then Khalis said: "First there was God and then his
Prophet! It is I who will find the antidote for the poison
of that snake. Said the prince to Khalis, "Friend, if
that is so, let us go to the king and make certain that his
promise holds good". So the three of them went to
present themselves before the king. Khalis made
obeisance and said "Is it true, oh King, even as your
illustrious Highness has said, that you promise to give
your royal daughter to anybody who will cure her?"
The king answered, "It is true, even as I said. I shall
not break my promise". Then Khalis made obeisance
and withdrew to re-join the prince, and he told him what
the king had said. When the prince heard this he went
into the king's presence together with Khalis. And the
prince took Khalis into the room where the princess was.
Then Khalis told them to let down the curtain round

the princess' couch. Khalis and the prince went inside
the curtain, and Khalis told them to wrap a quilt round
the body of the princess, leaving only her big toe
uncovered. After that he bade all the watchers go
outside the golden curtain. Only Khalis and the prince
remained inside. Then Khalis turned himself into a
snake. He sucked the princess' big toe three times, and
the poison came out. Then he vomited three times in
succession, and the princess, with a start, sat up.

Exercise 37.

Bĕrapa lama bĕlayar baharu sampai ka–tanah Mĕlayu ?
—Ta'tĕntu. Kalau kita singgah tiga ĕmpat pĕlabohan,
sa–bulan baharu sampai. Kalau pĕrgi tĕrus, ĕnam tujoh-
bĕlas hari sahaja. Tĕtapi agak–nya ta'ada kapal yang
bĕlayar tĕrus sahaja, kĕrana walau macham mana pun
sĕmua kapal singgah di–Port Said, sĕbab ta'boleh masok
di–tĕrusan Suez itu mĕlainkan dĕngan izin.

Keys for Chapter XVIII

Exercise 38.

At that time Hang Tuah and his four friends were
playing in the shop. When he saw the Batin coming, he
greeted him, respectfully, and invited him to enter. The
Chief entered, saying, as he took Hang Tuah's hand,
" Is this where you live, my friend ? " Hang Tuah
answered, " This is my home ". The Batin sat down
in the booth and Hang Mahmud came out, bringing the
betel–nut set, and said, " Take sireh, Batin. For your
kindness towards my son, I can never repay you ". The
Batin made himself a quid of sireh and said, " My father,
do not say such a thing. As for Hang Tuah and the
other four they have become my friends ". For a time he
sat and chatted, then took his leave and returned to his
boat.

Notes

1. Batin . . An ancient title, equivalent to " headman ", or lesser chief.

2. Makan–lah sireh . Note exactly the same words of welcome in the 16th century and the 20th century. See conversation 13.

3. tiada těrbalas . A good example of " těr- " used for inability to complete.

Exercise 39.

Baik kita ukor dahulu běrapa jauh dari bangsal kěreta ka–parit itu. Lěpas itu baharu kita měnggali tanah. Agak–nya boleh di–tanam anak pokok ěmpat banjar kalau tidak jarang sangat. Mana tali kita pakai tadi? Ini dia. Saya pěgang hujong. Daud pěgang hujong yang sa–bělah sana itu, bawa tali hala ka–parit. Sudah těgang tali itu buat tanda. Jangan serong. Lalu ikut pagar itu bětul.

Keys for Chapter XIX

Exercise 40.

A crowd of boats followed the Sultan's boat. All the instruments of music were beaten, and that reach of the river resounded from end to end with the clamour from the royal boats. When they had gone some distance, the Sultan came to Sungai Budiman, where they were to fish. When evening came, the king halted there. During the night all the *pawang* set the traps. By the next morning, all the traps had been let down into position. Then the *tuba* was pounded. When it had all been pounded, the war drums were beaten, and three signal shots were fired. After that the *tuba*

was let down into the river. Before long the fish came
floating up in great numbers, and crowds of young nobles
joined the Sultan in spearing them. And all the royal
ladies, a multitude of them, and all the people of quality
fished with scoops. All the court damsels, and the
Sultan's slaves and the ordinary people were there fishing,
large numbers of them, both men and women, some
using landing nets and some using spears. There
was a joyous uproar all along the river. All the Sultan's
slaves and the ordinary folk were shouting and cheering
and the women too were shrieking and squealing with
delight as they gathered the fish. Some of them tumbled
headlong and tore their clothes, others fell into the water.
Many of them struggled and grabbed each other's fish.
By this time, evening had fallen, and many fish had been
killed. Then they gave up spearing and netting the fish.

Exercise 41.

London Restaurants

Ever since I moved from Cambridge and came to live
in London, I have been in the habit of dining at home,
but I sometimes go out for a meal if I have an invitation
from a friend, or if I myself wish to entertain friends.
There are numbers of restaurants in London, with a great
variety of dishes to offer, and very tasty food. When I
am alone, I usually go to a restaurant in Regent Street
where one can get meat and fish dishes and appetising
salads. All their cakes are good, and their coffee, too.
Moreover, the place is clean, and the crockery is clean,
the lighting is good, and the waitresses are all courteous
and smiling. (lit. with a pleasant expression.)

There is one district in London which is famous for
its restaurants, the district called Soho. Most of the
restaurants are kept by foreigners. There are French
shops and Spanish shops, Chinese shops and Indian shops.

When I first began to visit Soho, I used to go to a

French shop in Old Compton Street, a small shop with only twelve tables. There is another place, too, that I like to visit, a Spanish shop. The owner always welcomes his guests with great courtesy. Often he will shake hands with you when you arrive, and again when you leave, and have a little chat with you. In that shop you can get food cooked in Spanish fashion, rice cooked with chicken, or with lobster, and various sorts of vegetables.

Whoever wants to taste foreign dishes, if he has the time, and the money, let him go wandering about in Soho.

Exercise 42.

1. Jumlah ini ta' bĕtul. Ta' sama dĕngan rasit ini. Kurang $2.50. Ada kĕtinggalan agak–nya. Biar saya bacha sa–mula. Tolong ĕnche' buboh tanda pada tiap–tiap satu pĕrkara di–daftar ini.

2. 'Man balek karang bawa pahat itu, ia? Kĕmudian pun boleh. Habiskan kĕrja dahulu. Sa–kurang–kurang–nya lima minit baharu habis kĕtam papan pĕnudong ini. Ada engsel lagi? Chari dalam pĕti pĕrkakas itu. Barang kali tĕrtinggal di–luar pintu dapor.

Keys for Chapter XX

Exercise 43.

He knew well how to greet people with the respect that was due to them, and with a pleasant expression. He was courteous in his manner of addressing people, using correctly the words *enche'* and *tuan*. Moreover, he was sympathetic to distress, and his hand was always open for the poor. Whenever he talked, it was with a smile. He was very successful in probing into all that concerned the past ; moreover, if anything came to his ears he was not content to leave it until he had got to the bottom of it. He liked to be alone, and was constantly writing and reading. When he was engaged in study or in conversation, no matter who called, he refused to see him until he had finished. Moreover, I noticed that he carried out all his tasks according to time-table, never letting one thing interfere with another.

Exercise 44.

My well-remembered friend, Mr. Smith, with good wishes.

I rejoiced, and so did my friends, when I received from Mr. James the news that you were safe.

Thank you for your very welcome letter. Just as you have remembered all of us here, so have we not forgotten all our friends in England.

I wrote you a letter last week but I was not able to send it by 'plane because there is no longer an air mail service from this state. But with luck there may be planes picking up mail at some place or other in Malaya. If not, it will have to go by the ordinary steam-ship route . . . War is like *kudis*. As soon as you have cured it (in one place), it breaks out somewhere else. If we could find a cure that would destroy the seeds of the disease then at last the world would be freed from fear. But it seems to me that as long as man remains cruel by nature and aggressive in mien, there is not much chance of recovery for us . . . In England people suffered because of the constant air-raids; in Malaya people suffered because they had lost the freedom which they once knew . . . But I am rambling on. I must give you news of all your friends. Salim, 'Man, Minah all send their greetings, and ask for news of you. Che Osman, Che Timah and Che Arifin all send their greetings with affectionate remembrances.

(I apologise for this shabby scrap of paper. I had to buy it because there was nothing else to be had. We reached a very low ebb when the war was on. We had scarcely more than we stood up in.   But what does it matter, as long as we still live ?)

Written 2.11.45.

Exercise 45.

> In the swamp the monkeys play,
> Swinging down from leafy tree.
> Plain, uncomely, others say ;
> Sweet and fair she seems to me.

KEYS FOR PASSAGES FOR TRANSLATION

1. Masa Hang Tuah Kĕchil

Ada pun akan Hang Mahmud itu, kĕrja–nya mĕngambil kayu api, di–jual–nya. Maka Hang Tuah, apabila sudah ada kayu itu di–bawa bapa–nya, Hang Tuah pun sĕgĕra mĕngambil kapak mĕmbĕlah kayu itu. Maka dudok–lah ia mĕmbĕlah kayu itu di–hadapan kĕdai ayah–nya, dĕmikian–lah kĕrja–nya.

2. Chĕrita Empat Orang Anak Raja

Ada pun anak raja kĕĕmpat, tĕlah di–lihat–nya nakhoda itu sudah kĕmbali ka–pĕrahu–nya, maka ia pun kĕluar–lah dari chĕlah batu itu, lalu kĕmbali ka–Bukit Sĕguntang. Maka bĕginda pun bĕrtanya ka–pada anakanda* kĕĕmpat itu, kata–nya, " Ka–mana pĕrgi tuan kĕĕmpat, maka tiada ayahanda* lihat ? " Maka Sang Maniaka pun bĕrkhabar tatkala ia pĕrgi ka–pada pulau itu, bĕrtĕmu dĕngan sa–buah pĕrahu mĕmgambil ayer, maka tiada ia sĕmpat lari, lalu ia bĕrsĕmbunyi pada satu tĕmpat : " Sa–tĕlah nakhoda itu kĕmbali, maka patek kĕĕmpat pun kĕluar–lah."

* See Exercise 36, Note 5.

3. Chĕrdek-nya Awi Dichu

Tĕlah sudah mustaed, maka Awi Dichu pun bĕlayar-lah ka-nĕgĕri Sĕmudra, pura-pura bĕrniaga, hingga habis-lah pĕrahu itu bĕlayar; tĕlah sampai sakalian-nya mĕngatakan diri-nya utusan dari-pada Raja Shahru'n-nuwi.

Sa-tĕlah sampai ka-darat, maka oleh Awi Dichu di-isi-nya pĕti ĕmpat buah ĕmpat orang hulubalang yang gagah. Maka kata Awi Dichu pada hulubalang ĕmpat itu, " Apabila kamu datang kĕlak ka-hadapan raja Sĕmudra, kamu buka-lah pĕti ini dari dalam, kĕluar kamu tangkap raja Sĕmudra itu ". Maka pĕti itu pun di-kunchi-nya dari dalam, maka di-arak-lah pĕti itu, di-katakan-nya bingkis dari-pada Raja Shahru'n-nuwi. Tĕlah datang-lah ka-hadapan raja Sĕmudra, maka surat itu pun di-bacha orang-lah tĕrlalu baik sa-kali bunyi-nya. Sa-tĕlah itu maka pĕti itu pun di-hantarkan orang ka-hadapan raja Sĕmudra. Maka hulubalang ĕmpat yang di-dalam pĕti itu pun masing-masing mĕmbuka pĕti itu lalu ia kĕluar, di-tangkap-nya-lah raja Sĕmudra itu.

4. Di-mana Che' Hamid?

Mr. White : Nampak Che' Hamid, 'tak ? 'Dah janji bĕrjumpa di-sini bĕtul-bĕtul pukul ĕmpat. Mana dia agak-nya ?

Che' Daud : Nampak dia sa-tĕngah jam tadi. Dia bĕrsandar di-pagar itu. Bĕrbual dĕngan Tĕngku Ismail.

Mr. White : Ka-mana agak-nya dia bĕrdua itu ? Saya hĕndak bĕrjumpa juga dĕngan Tĕngku Ismail. Dia bĕrjanji 'nak bagi saya tĕlor pĕnyu.

Che' Daud : Tuan suka makan tĕlor pĕnyu ?

Mr. White : Bĕlum tahu lagi.   Ta'pĕrnah makan.
Tengok pun 'dak lagi.   Itu–lah sĕbab–nya
saya minta dia bawa tunjokkan saya.
Kata–nya adek pĕrĕmpuan–nya hĕndak
pĕrgi mĕmungut tĕlor pĕnyu malam sa–
malam.   Tĕlor itu bĕsar dari pada tĕlor
ayam, agak–nya ?

Che' Daud : Lĕbeh bĕsar.   Lagi pun kulit–nya lĕmbut,
boleh di–pichit.

Mr. White : Ini dia, dua orang itu.   Tengok, bĕrlari
macham orang gila.

Che' Daud : Dia baharu tengok orang main sepak raga
di–padang, agak–nya.

5. Lĕpas Chuti

Wan Chik : 'Dah balek pula.   Macham mana chuti ?
Bagus ?

Mr. Black : Bagus–lah.

Wan Chik : Macham mana rupa Cameron Highlands ?

Mr. Black : Tĕmpat makan angin bĕtul–bĕtul.   Luas
juga, boleh kita bĕrjalan ka–sana sini.

Wan Chik : Tĕntu–lah tuan sĕgar badan lĕpas chuti
itu.   Dahulu bĕrupa lĕmah.

Mr. Black : Bĕtul.   Dahulu sĕlalu badan rasa ta'sĕdap.
Sĕkarang sĕgar rasa–nya, boleh kĕrja balek.
Hairan, lĕpas sa–minggu tidor di–tĕmpat
hawa yang sĕjuk, 'dah puleh rasa badan.

Wan Chik : Dua tiga bulan ini bukan main panas
di–sini.   'Tapi ta' lama lagi tĕntu–lah sĕjuk
sa–dikit sĕbab musim hujan 'dah sampai.

Mr. Black : Saya harap ĕnche' ta'bĕkĕrja sampai hilang
nyawa sa–pĕninggalan saya.   Kata saya
kalmarin mana–mana kĕrja yang ta' wajib,
tinggalkan–lah dahulu.

Wan Chik : Ta'apa. Che Hashim patut di–puji, kěrja-
nya běrlěbeh–lěbeh. Kěrani lain pun bagitu
juga. Tapi bakul surat tuan pun pěnoh
jua lagi.

Mr. Black : Těntu. Baik–lah saya habiskan kěrja itu
sěmua, jangan běrtanggoh lagi.

6. Měnanam Běneh

Mrs. Brown : Saya baharu dapat běneh–běneh yang
di–pěsan minggu lěpas itu.

Tukang Kěbun : Běneh yang maju tumboh di–něgěri ini,
mem ?   Sa–paroh poko' ta' boleh tum-
boh di–sini. Hawa těrlampau panas.

Mrs. Brown : Běneh ini dari Ipoh, bukan–nya dari
něgěri Inggěris. Běneh ini yang baik
sa–kali.   Omar jaga–lah bětul-betul.

Tukang kěbun : Baik, mem.   Di–mana 'nak tanam
běneh ini ?

Mrs. Brown : Agak–nya chantek kalau kita tanam
bunga merah sa–bělah–měnyabělah
jalan masok ka–rumah itu. Sudah
lama sangat bunga zinia di–situ, baik
kita tukar.

Tukang kěbum : Dalam bungkus yang mana, bunga
merah itu ?

Mrs. Brown : Dalam bungkus hijau ini. Biar saya
tuliskan nama–nya. Omar pandai
bachi Rumi ? Tidak ?   Biar saya
choba tulis Jawi. Saya ta' běrapa
pandai měnulis, baharu bělajar . . .
Boleh Omar bacha, 'tak ?

Tukang kěbun : " Bunga merah di–těpi jalan ". Boleh
saya bacha, mem. Apa yang di-
dalam bungkus kuning itu ?

Mrs. Brown :	Bunga pětiunia.
Tukang kĕbun :	Kita 'dah ada banyak bunga itu, mem.
Mrs. Brown :	Bĕtul, 'tapi jĕnis ini yang baik sa–kali. Yang ini 'nak di–tanam di–bawah anjong.
Tukang kĕbun :	Mem 'nak tanam di–dalam pasu ?
Mrs. Brown :	Tidak. Omar buat kotak panjang sapĕrti yang Omar buat dahulu itu. Ingat–kah ?
Tukang kĕbun :	Yang bĕrkaki itu ?
Mrs. Brown :	Itu dia. Tiga kaki tinggi lĕbeh kurang. Jadi boleh bunga–nya bĕrumbai–umbai.
Tukang kĕbun :	Mem boleh bagi duit bĕli papan ?
Mrs. Brown :	Omar buat pondok bunga kalmarin. Tiada tinggal lagi kayu–nya ?
Tukang kĕbun :	Ada juga, mem, 'tapi ta'chukup, agak–nya.
Mrs. Brown :	Ta'apa. Baik bĕli lagi juga. Saya hĕndak suroh Omar buat pagar jala–jala dĕpan jĕndela, tĕmpat mĕrayap bunga puteh yang bĕsar itu, di–panggil orang " bunga bulan ". Wangi bau–nya pada malam hari.
Tukang kĕbun :	Baik mem. Saya siap tanah dahulu, kĕmudian tanam bĕneh–bĕneh ini di–dalam kotak.

7. Bĕlajar Mĕlayu

Mr. McNeil :	Sila ĕnche' masok. Apa khabar ĕnche' ?

Che' Abdul Rahman : Khabar baik, tuan. Minta maaf lewat sikit saya sampai. Tĕngah jalan hujan lĕbat.

Mr. McNeil : Baju ĕnche' ta' basah nampak-nya. Dapat bĕrtĕdoh di-tĕpi jalan ?

Che' Abdul Rahman : Tuan. Mujor ada pokok rendang suku batu dari sini. Kalau tidak, tĕntu-lah basah kuyup. Bila hujan rĕda sa-dikit, kawan lalu, saya tumpang payong-nya.

Mr. McNeil : Sila ĕnche' dudok. Saya minta maaf juga. Kĕrja mĕnyalin karangan masok bahasa Mĕlayu itu ta' sĕmpat di-buat.

Che' Abdul Rahman : Khabar-nya ada bichara bĕsar di-mahkamah ? Tĕntu-lah tuan sibok.

Mr. McNeil : Sibok juga di-mahkamah. Di-rumah pun ada kĕrja. Tukang P.W.D. 'nak mĕngganti papan lantai di-bilek tidor. Tadi saya kĕna aleh sĕmua buku yang tĕratur di-tĕpi dinding itu.

Che' Abdul Rahman : Papan   di-makan   anai-anai barang kali ?

Mr. McNeil : Tidak. Di-makan api. Ĕnche' ta' dĕngar ? Minggu lalu sa-kĕrat rumah tĕrbakar. Puntong rokok tĕrtinggal di-meja chĕrmin agak-nya.

Che' Abdul Rahman : Saya ta' dĕngar. Hari apa ?

Mr McNeil : Malam khamis, pukul sa-puloh.

Che' Abdul Rahman : Sĕbab itu–lah saya ta'dĕngar. Pada masa itu saya dĕmam. Sakit tĕrok sĕndi tulang.

Mr. McNeil : 'Dah baik, sĕkarang ?

Che' Abdul Rahman : Lĕga sa–dikit.   'Tapi sampai sĕkarang pun bĕrasa lĕngoh.

Mr. McNeil : Kalau bagitu, jangan–lah saya bĕlajar lama.

Che' Abdul Rahman : Ta' usah–lah.   Mari kita bacha buku sa–dikit. Yang mana tuan tĕngah bacha ?   Chĕrita " Hang Tuah " ?

8. Mĕnembak Buaya

Che' Saleh : Kalau tuan ta'ada kĕrja hari jumaat ini, mari kita mudek mĕnembak buaya.

Mr. Smith : Ai ! Ingat–ingat sa–dikit, ĕnche' !   Kata orang Mĕlayu siapa jadi pawang buaya, lambat laun–nya masok ka–mulut buaya juga.

Che' Saleh : Itu masa dahulu, orang mengalir buaya. Sĕkarang kita pakai sĕnapang. Saya 'dah bĕrsatuju dĕngan Wan Mahmud hĕndak mudek pada hari jumaat ini. Khabar–nya ada buaya ganas dĕkat Tanjong Ru.

Mr. Smith : Baik–lah. 'Tapi yang sa–bĕnar–nya saya 'dah bĕrjanji dĕngan mem saya hĕndak ka–Singapura. Saya ta' tahu apa hĕndak di–buat–nya di–situ. Baik ĕnche' tanya, pujok dia pĕrgi. Sĕlalu dia bĕrchakap hĕndak tengok orang mĕnembak buaya. Ini–lah pĕluang–nya.

Che' Saleh : Ta'apa. 'Tapi kalau mem hěndak sama, harus kita sewa motor Haji Ibrahim. Pěrahu Wan Mahmud kita boleh tunda. Buaya ganas chělaka itu khabar–nya sělalu běrjěmor děkat Tanjong Ru. Kalau nasib baik, dapat kita měnembak dia těngah běrjěmor. Kalau tembak bila dia timbul di–sungai, walau kěna bětul pun, ěmpat lima hari baharu bangkai–nya timbul, kita tahu dia mati.

Mr. Smith : Běsar buaya itu ?

Che' Saleh : Běsar. Lagi pun běrani běnar, khabar–nya. Kadang–kadang dia timbul děkat perahu orang. Jangan takut ! Motor Haji Ibrahim itu pun běsar juga. Kalau kěna sěbat ekor buaya itu pun, ta'těrbalek.

Mr. Smith : Baik–lah, Saleh. Esok kita běrjumpa.

9. Pekerja Che' Mat sělalu lambat kěluar běkěrja. Sěbab apa? Barang kali Che' Mat sěndiri tidak kěluar ambil nama–nya sa–bělum dia běkěrja. Che' Mat mahu hadzir sělalu pagi–pagi, kěmudian běri saya tahu siapa–siapa pekerja lambat kěluar, boleh di–ganti orang lain. Dalam daftar nama ada tiga ěmpat orang yang kěrap tidak kěluar karna sakit, patut di–rěntikan dia. Bělum habis tahun, mahu di–sělěsai kěrja ini. Sěkarang nampak–nya lagi ěnam bulan baharu habis.

10. Sapěrti pěngaduan orang itu sa–paroh sahaja benar. Kira–kira sa–puloh tahun dahulu tanah itu di–běri akan měnanam padi sahaja : nyata–lah sharat itu di–dalam surat gěran (*i.e. grant*). Bukan–nya tuan tanah itu tidak měngětahui ; bukan–nya dia bodoh. Tětapi sa–panjang jalan, dua tiga rantai lebar–nya, tanah itu di–tanam děngan poko' nyior dan lain buah–

buahan ; ada juga tĕmpat di–dirikan rumah di–tĕngah bĕndang. Dato' sendiri boleh tengok. Jikalau dia orang tidak bĕrtanam padi tĕntu kĕrajaan mĕngambil balek tanah–nya itu. Tolong dato' bĕri tahu.

11. Kĕnyataan bĕrkĕnaan barang makan–makanan

Ada–lah di–dapati khabar oleh pĕgawai daerah ia–itu banyak orang sĕdang mĕnyimpan barang–barang makanan di–dalam rumah–nya tĕrlĕbeh sangat dari pada yang di–kĕhĕndaki. Oleh sĕbab kĕkurangan barang–barang makanan itu, harus di–kĕluarkan pĕraturan yang tĕrsĕbut di–bawah ini supaya sĕmua orang boleh mĕndapat makan–makanan akan mĕnyĕgarkan badan–nya.

Dĕmikian–lah di–bĕri tahu :

1. Tidak di–bĕnarkan siapa–siapa pun simpan di–rumah bĕras (gula, tĕpong, d.s.b.) lĕbeh dari pada yang lazim di–makan dalam tempoh tiga hari.

2. Bĕrapa yang chukup tiga hari itu, ada–lah tĕrsĕbut di–dalam jadual yang di–bawah ini.

3. Jika siapa–siapa mĕnaroh lĕbeh dari pada yang tĕrsurat itu, dĕngan sĕgĕra–nya hĕndak di–bĕri tahu kapada pĕgawai yang bĕrkuasa, ia–itu Wan Suleiman bin Wan Harun.

4. Bĕrkuasa–lah pĕgawai itu masok mĕmĕreksa mana–mana rumah supaya mĕnghasilkan maksud pĕraturan ini.

5. Bĕrkuasa–lah juga pĕgawai itu mĕngambil apa–apa barang yang di–dapati tĕrlĕbeh dari pada yang di–bĕnarkan itu.

Hukuman.

Barang siapa yang tidak mĕnurut sharat–sharat

pĕraturan yang di–atas ini atau yang 'mĕnggalang pĕgawai itu dari pada mĕnjalankan dia, boleh–lah ia di–tangkap dĕngan tiada warant, sĕrta di–daawa di–dalam mahkamah.

Di–kĕchualikan dari pada sharat–sharat pĕraturan yang di–atas ini sĕgala orang yang di–daftarkan di–bawah, ia itu :

1. Mĕreka yang memang mĕngumpulkan barang–barang makanan karna pĕrniagaan, ia–itu saudagar dan tuan–tuan kelang bĕras.

2. Mĕreka yang bĕrtanam padi sĕrta mĕnyimpan bĕras–nya di–jĕlapang.

12. Dari pada sĕgala mĕreka yang bĕrjalan dĕngan kami, pada sangka saya orang Mĕlayu yang tĕrbaik sa–kali. Sĕbab apa ? Mĕreka itu tidak bĕrgaji hanya–lah mĕngikut kĕhĕndak saya, di–tinggalkan–nya anak bini sĕrta rumah dan barang apa yang tĕrlĕkat pada hati orang Melayu. Sunggoh pun bagitu, tiada pĕrnah dia bĕrsungut atau mĕmbantahi pĕrentah mĕlainkan sakalian–nya orang bĕsar dan orang rayat lĕbeh lagi dia buat dari pada yang di–pinta. Kĕring basah, panas sĕjuk, mata–nya mĕngantok karna jaga, badan–nya lĕteh lĕsu karna tĕrok bĕkĕrja, makin di–suroh makin dia bĕrgĕlut. Barang siapa bĕrfikir orang Melayu malas chulas, nĕschaya dia hairan mĕlihat usaha mĕreka itu.

APPENDIX

GLOSSARY OF GRAMMATICAL TERMS USED

PARTS OF SPEECH.

Noun . a naming word. e.g.
gate, Mary.

Pronoun . a word that replaces a noun. e.g.
he, that, which.

Adjective . a word that belongs to a noun

(a) as an epithet (attributive) e.g.
a *red* book ; *that* box; *which* club ?

(b) as a statement (predicative) e.g.
The book is *red*.

Verb . a " doing " word or a " being " word. e.g.
He *plays* squash.
She *is reading*.
The jungle *was* thick.

Subject and Predicate.

The subject of a sentence is the person or thing, about whom or which, the verb makes a statement. e.g.

The grey car is new.
All mosquitoes bite.

The predicate is the whole of the rest of the sentence. e.g.

429

The man in the Rolls Royce *owns several houses along the sea shore.*

Object.

The object of a verb is the person or thing which is affected by the action performed by the subject. e.g.

I bought *a putter.*
He killed *the snake.*

Copula.

A copula is a verb which is merely a link between a subject-word and its description e.g.

He *is* an engineer.
She *looks* happy (i.e. she is, by appearance, happy.)

Complement.

The complement is the description that is so linked to the subject. e.g.

He is *a clerk in a shipping firm.*

Transitive and Intransitive.

A verb is transitive when it has an object. e.g.

She *drives* a two–seater.

They *have* a refrigerator.

A verb is intransitive when it has no object. e.g.

He *comes* here frequently.
She *swims* well.

Active and Passive.

A verb is active when the subject performs the action.   e.g.

> The carpenter *made* the shelves.

A verb is passive when the subject has the action performed upon it.   e.g.

The shelves *were made* by the carpenter.

Tense.

Tense shows time.   e.g.

> I *wrote* or *was writing* — past tense.
> I *write* or *am writing* — present tense.
> I *shall write*   — future tense.

Mood.

The indicative mood makes a statement.   e.g.

> Buffaloes *wallow*.

The imperative mood gives an order.   e.g.

> *Come* in !

The subjunctive mood expresses a wish, or a condition.   e.g.

> God *save* the King !
> If I *were* you . . .

The infinitive mood expresses the verbal idea, with no subject to bound it. It usually has " to " in front of it.   e.g.

> *To err* is human.
> He likes *to get up* early.
> I dare *say*.

Person and Number.

First person :

Singular   Plural

I am   . We are   . (i.e. the speaker refers to himself or to himself and others.)

Second person :

Singular   Plural

You are   . You are   . (i.e. the speaker refers to the listener or listeners.)

Third person :

Singular   Plural

He, she   . They are   . (i.e. the speaker
it is   refers to somebody
                        else.)

Adverb   . (a) a word attached to a verb, to indicate time, place or manner. **e.g.**

He came *immediately*.
Park the car *here*.
She dances *well*.

(b) a word attached to an adjective or to another adverb, to indicate degree. e.g.

It is *very* hot.
He was driving *rather* fast.

Preposition. a word that shows the relationship (usually time or place relationship) between some word (usually a verb or an adjective) and a noun. e.g.

He was sitting *on* the sea–wall.
Wait *until* to–morrow.
She is clever *with* her hands.

Conjunction . a joining word.

> (a) joining words of equal weight, i.e. a co–ordinating conjunction. e.g.
>
> cups *and* saucers.
> foolish *but* kind.
> black *or* white.
>
> (b) attaching an explanatory statement (expressing condition, time, reason, etc.) to a main statement, or an object clause to its verb, i.e. a subordinating conjunction. e.g.
>
> I will ring up *if* I can't come.
> They finished the match *when* the rain cleared.
> He skidded *because* his tyres were worn.
> She said (*that*) she was tired.

MISCELLANEOUS TERMS

Enclitic . . a short word that is always attached to the preceding word by a hyphen.

Proclitic . a short word that is always attached to the following word by a hyphen.

Substantive . any word that is used to do the work of a noun.

Verbal noun . a noun (ending in " –ing ") formed from a verb and retaining its verbal function. e.g.

> *Weeding* the garden is a tiring pastime.

Antithesis . balancing one word or statement against another word or statement, for the sake of contrast.